The Lady and the Virgin

Women in Culture and Society

A Series Edited by
Catharine R. Stimpson

The Lady
·&·
the Virgin

Image, Attitude, and
Experience in Twelfth-Century France

Penny Schine Gold

The University of Chicago Press
Chicago & London

The author gratefully acknowledges permission to reprint "Male/Female Cooperation: The Example of Fontevrault," from vol. 1 of *Distant Echoes: Medieval Religious Women*, pp. 151–68, ed. John A. Nichols and Lillian Thomas Shank (Kalamazoo, Mich.: Cistercian Publications, 1984) (with minor changes now part of chap. 3 of this volume).

The University of Chicago Press, Chicago 60637
The University of Chicago Press, Ltd., London

Library of Congress Cataloging in Publication Data

Gold, Penny Schine.
   The lady and the Virgin.

   (Women in culture and society)
   Substantial and thorough revision of author's
dissertation.
   Bibliography: p.
   Includes index.
   1. Women—France—History—Middle ages, 500–1500.
2. Social history—Medieval, 500–1500. 3. Mary,
Blessed Virgin, Saint—Symbolism. I. Title.
II. Series.
HQ1147.F7G65 1985   305.4'0944   84-23701
ISBN 0-226-30087-0 (cloth) ISBN 0-226-30088-9 (paper)

To
Joseph Gold
and
Helen Schine Gold

Contents

Illustrations

Tables

xi

Foreword

by Catharine R. Stimpson

The Lady and the Virgin turns to twelfth-century France, a time
and place that haunt the Western historical imagination, to ask im-
mense, returning questions. How did women think, feel, act? How
did the sacred and secular arts treat them? What is the relationship
between material reality and representation, especially when women
live out the material realities, but men represent them?

The answers of *The Lady and the Virgin* are incisive. Penny Schine
Gold begins with a series of premises about writing women's history.
Like all careful historians, she wants to interpret the *pastness* of the
past, its complex specificities, even if its values are not ours. While
acknowledging her debt to a feminist critique of society, Professor
Gold also rejects assumptions that in some cases seem to have con-
stricted analysis: a tendency to believe that images simply mirror
"reality"; to label images of women as "good" or "bad"; and to reify
the concept of the "status of women" and then to seek it across
cultures. Her revisionary measures help to prove the self-refining ca-
pacities of the new scholarship about women.

Professor Gold then moves toward the justification of her premises.
Like reflecting panels, four chapters explore the image of women in
secular literature; in sacred art; in the convent, those women's communities in sacred space; in the secular world of family and property.
In her conclusions, Professor Gold stresses the ambiguity and ambivalence that women experienced and that men projected into their
representations of women. Frequently, one element of an ambiguous
compound might dominate the others, but ambiguity never col-

lapsed into the transparencies of a single thought or of a pure social structure.

As *The Lady and the Virgin* clearly explores the self-contradictory, its readers must confront a sobering mystery of the history of women: why that ambiguity, that ambivalence, are so persistent, and so present.

Preface

This study began as a response to the familiar commonplace about medieval women found in both textbooks and scholarly works about the Middle Ages and about the history of women. We have been told repeatedly, with a uniformity that comes from uncritical acceptance, that the twelfth-century creation of the images of the lady in love literature and of the Virgin Mary indicates a dramatic improvement in attitudes toward women or in the actual position of women in society. Yet few works have actually explored in detail the cultural interrelationships implied in this judgment.[1] The long, unexamined life of this cliché can be partially attributed to its appeal within modern culture. To nineteenth-century romantics, and their twentieth-century heirs, the elevated ideals of women they found in medieval culture could be viewed nostalgically as precursors of their own "cult of true womanhood."

I started this research, then, with the intention of investigating more thoroughly the nature of the images of the lady and the Virgin Mary, and of the relationship between these images and the actual experience of women. Strongly influenced by the contemporary feminist critique of the twentieth-century version of chivalric attitudes toward women, my original hypothesis was that these twelfth-century idealizations of women, rather than indicating a positive

1. Henry Adams, *Mont-Saint-Michel and Chartres* (Boston: Houghton Mifflin, 1904), is the major exception. This book is also probably the source, direct or indirect, of many twentieth-century historians' notions of twelfth-century women.

trend in attitude and experience, could be seen instead as expressing a negative view of women contemporary with increasing strictures on women's experience.[2]

I persisted with this hypothesis for a long time, and it can be seen in the dissertation that was the first fruit of my labors.[3] But in the process of revising the dissertation for publication, I was struck by the ways in which I had sometimes forced an interpretation of the evidence for the sake of simplicity, particularly when trying to come to a unified general conclusion, linking together the several parts of my study. Historians, like other social scientists concerned with the study of society as a whole and the interconnection of its parts, have sometimes succumbed to the temptation to draw simple, specific causal connections between a cultural phenomenon and its social setting. An image, ritual, or institution is thus pinned to a particular economic, political, or social change. The two heuristic pitfalls of this approach are: (1) an oversimplification of the meaning of the specific cultural phenomenon, and (2) an oversimplification of the complex relationship between culture and society.[4] In this book, which is

2. I was helped early on by the important work of John F. Benton, which challenges both the notion that medieval concepts of love implied a positive attitude toward women, and the notion that love literature reflects actual behavior: "Clio and Venus: An Historical View of Medieval Love," in *The Meaning of Courtly Love*, ed. F. X. Newman (Albany: State University of New York Press, 1968), pp. 19–42; "The Court of Champagne as a Literary Center," *Speculum* 36 (1961): 551–91. For examples of recent critiques of the mainstream cliché, see Jo Ann McNamara and Suzanne Wemple, "The Power of Women through the Family in Medieval Europe: 500-1100," *Feminist Studies* 1 (1973): 126–41; R. W. Southern, *Western Society and the Church in the Middle Ages* (Baltimore: Penguin Books, 1970), pp. 311–12. There are other contemporary feminists (usually not medievalists) who have given credence to the cliché, probably because of too easy an acceptance of the assertion that twelfth-century literature was supported by female patronage and written according to female taste. See below, pp. 2–3. Most influential among such scholars has been Joan Kelly-Gadol, "Did Women Have a Renaissance?" in *Becoming Visible: Women in European History*, ed. Renate Bridenthal and Claudia Koonz (Boston: Houghton Mifflin, 1977), pp. 137–64. Another example is Carolyn G. Heilbrun, *Toward a Recognition of Androgyny* (New York: Knopf, 1973), pp. 21–23.

3. Penny S. Gold, "Image and Reality: Women in Twelfth-Century France" (Ph.D. diss., Stanford University, 1977).

4. My understanding of this analytical problem has been clarified by the comments of Sherry B. Ortner and Harriet Whitehead in their introduction to *Sexual Meanings: The Cultural Construction of Gender and Sexuality* (Cambridge: Cambridge University Press, 1981), pp. 3–4.

a thorough and substantial reworking of my dissertation, I have yielded to the data's demand for sensitivity to complexity and ambiguity. The result incorporates a recognition that the images express not one attitude but many, that the experience of women, even of the women of the noble elite, was diverse and sometimes contradictory, and that the relationship between image, attitude, and experience is not always direct or causal.

The method I have employed has been to break apart the traditional assertion into its component parts, beginning with the two key images, one secular—the *dame* of love literature—and one religious—the Virgin Mary. Each is put within its immediate imagistic context, so that the romance is viewed together with the *chanson de geste*, and the Gothic iconography of the Virgin together with the Romanesque. The particular lived experience with which to compare female imagery was more difficult to choose, but rather than focus on the lives of prominent individuals like Eleanor of Aquitaine, I have selected two areas of life, one religious and one secular, that affected large numbers of women and that illuminate the experience of real-life virgins and "ladies"—monasticism and property relations. As with the images, the phenomena of experience are described and analyzed within their immediate contexts—female monasticism within the context of contemporary reform movements, and women's participation in the transfer of property within the context of family control of property. Also, while the heuristic focus is on female imagery and women's experience, these phenomena only make sense in a context of comparison to the images and experience of men. My analysis, in fact, centers on the interaction of men and women, whether they be two lovers in a romance, the Virgin and her son, the monks and nuns of the reform movements, or husband and wife in a property transfer.

Each chapter contains an element of general overview, but I have chosen to explore the issues and questions raised by such an overview through the close analysis of carefully circumscribed phenomena. The chapter on secular image thus focuses on a few texts of vernacular literature, the chapter on religious image on a specific iconographical development, the chapter on monastic experience on one religious order, and the chapter on control of property on one particular region. I have thus sacrificed breadth for depth, with the conviction that these detailed analyses will illuminate the many other examples that will come to the minds of scholars in the disparate fields touched upon in this book. My goal is to be suggestive and provocative rather than exhaustive.

Within each analysis my purpose is to penetrate to the attitude or emotional content expressed in both image and experience, to the central concerns that are embedded in forms of thought and action. Created for the most part by men, the images tell us of male attitudes toward women. The experience of twelfth-century women shows us the actuality of women's lives, but this too must be seen within the context of institutional structures shaped largely by men and reflecting male concerns. The mediation between image and experience consists of the attitudes of men toward women, embodied both in images and in the structures of religious and social life. Indeed, part of the experience of women consists of a living with and accommodation to society's dominant notions of the nature and proper role of women.

In such an analysis, we must discard certain premises implicit in the commonplace understanding of the relationship of female imagery to attitude and actuality. The following assumptions have clouded the phenomena they purport to explain:

1. That the relationship between images of women and actual women is a simple, unambiguous one of direct reflection or representation.

2. That images of women can be read as either positive or negative, and the presence of "good" images of women indicates a "positive" attitude toward actual women.

3. That the procession of "good" and "bad" images of women can be used as a key to the progress or decline in the status of actual women.

4. That there is a unitary status of women in every society that can be measured over time and compared cross-culturally (for example, "Women had a lower status in the Middle Ages than they do in the contemporary United States").

These assumptions must all be modified to allow for both the diversity and the ambiguity of human culture:

1. The relationship of an image to the reality external to it is more complex than simple reflection; images can also embody fears, fantasies, and wishes. An image is an *interpretation* of reality, an interpretation achieved through a selective emphasis on particular aspects of lived experience; through such reshaping and exaggerating images

may not only report but also distort reality. The nature of an image can be clarified by locating it within its artistic context—seeing the image in relationship to the overall purpose and impact of the work in which it appears—and by placing that work, when possible, within its larger social context.

2. Images (and action) are too complex to be summarized as either positive or negative. Rather, an image can be a funnel for more than one attitude, and can even embrace conflicting attitudes. A characterization as "positive" or "negative" is not only too simple, it is also inappropriate as an imposed value judgment; a commitment to seeing complexity can help us avoid such anachronism and ethnocentricity.[5]

3. The drawing of moral judgments about particular images or actions contributes to the tendency to perceive linear progress or decline in history, a tendency long ago challenged by Herbert Butterfield, and one to which many historians of women have succumbed. Just as "Whig" historians have been prone to see every affirmation of democratic institutions as a step forward into the glory of the present, some women's historians, writing within the context of the twentieth-century surge of feminism, have tended to see the modern age as the culmination of a progressive achievement of equality between men and women. The author of one essay on women in medieval history shows particular sensitivity to the diversity and complexity of women's experience in the Middle Ages, and yet he concludes his essay with a "progress" report: "The balance of change was in [women's] favor."[6] Other historians, while rejecting the notion of progress, still hold to the notion of a linear development but see the line as going down instead of up, or zigzagging instead of proceeding in a uniform direction. Thus one recent work on medieval women calls for the charting "of womankind's progress and reversals during the formative period of European history."[7] Some historians of women, in fact, seem driven to find decline rather than progress, as

5. The historian's tendency to make moral judgments is sometimes linked with the temptation to exaggerate the conclusiveness or coherence of one's findings. See Herbert Butterfield, *The Whig Interpretation of History* (London: G. Bell & Sons, 1931), especially pp. 1–6, 15–22, 74.

6. David Herlihy, "Women in Medieval History," Smith History Lecture, 1971 (Houston: University of St. Thomas, 1971), p. 14. Essay reprinted in David Herlihy, *The Social History of Italy and Western Europe, 700–1500: Collected Studies* (London: Variorum Reprints, 1978).

7. Suzanne Fonay Wemple, *Women in Frankish Society: Marriage and the Cloister, 500–900* (Philadelphia: University of Pennsylvania Press, 1981), p. 197.

though an answer to modern problems would be found if we could ascertain when all the problems began.[8] In sum, images themselves are too complex to be labeled and ranked as "good" or "bad" and thus cannot be made to line up on a graph of linear development. More generally, the notion of progress or decline in history obfuscates the complexity, variety, and ambivalence of historical reality.[9]

4. Central to the discussion of women's progress and decline is the concept of the "status" of women, the notion that the many aspects of women's lives can be combined in one unitary construct, which can then be compared cross-culturally. Investigators in all social science disciplines have relied heavily on this construct in the shaping of scholarship on women, much of which is devoted either to the assessment of women's status in one society relative to others, or to the assignment of one aspect of women's lives (economic roles, political participation, etc.) as the key element that determines women's overall status. The concept of "status" is coming under increasing fire, particularly from anthropologists.[10] These scholars argue that investigators should move their attention away from the general status of women (an artificial construct) toward more particular aspects of women's situations, so that the complexity of the interrelationship of these parts can be recognized.[11] We should study property relations, for example, for the sake of learning about property relations, and not because we can assume that women's ability to possess and alienate property is necessarily linked to participation in other realms or to some general attitude toward women.[12]

This emphasis on the particular, without the presumption of a

8. See, for example, Joan Kelly-Gadol, "Did Women Have a Renaissance?" which characterizes the Renaissance as a period of decline from the Middle Ages.

9. A similar point is made with reference to women in colonial New England by Laurel Thatcher Ulrich, *Good Wives: Image and Reality in the Lives of Women in Northern New England, 1650–1750* (New York: Knopf, 1982), pp. 240–41.

10. A thoroughgoing attack can be found in Martin King Whyte, *The Status of Women in Preindustrial Societies* (Princeton: Princeton University Press, 1978). (The title of the work is misleading, as one of Whyte's conclusions is that there is no such thing as a general status of women; see especially pp. 116–17.) See also Michelle Zimbalist Rosaldo, "The Use and Abuse of Anthropology: Reflections on Feminism and Cross-cultural Understanding," *Signs: Journal of Women in Culture and Society* 5 (1980): 401; Naomi Quinn, "Anthropological Studies on Women's Status," *Annual Review of Anthropology* 6 (1977): 181–83.

11. Rosaldo, p. 396, n. 10; Quinn, p. 183.

12. Whyte, pp. 107, 170.

fixed causal relationship, frees us from the impulse to make a final pronouncement of the general condition of medieval women as "good" or "bad." Connections still appear, but they are the connections of a common attitude or a common structure of thought and action. We will see that when we examine the complexity of the interactions between men and women as expressed in both image and experience, the common bond is a pattern of ambivalence and contradiction: ambivalence in the attitudes of men toward women and contradiction within the actuality of women's experience. This ambivalence is not only the simple intellectual opposition of Eve and Mary—or of the pit and the pedestal, in Eileen Power's famous formulation [13]—but a complex of oppositions: women seen as helpful and harmful, as central and peripheral, as powerful and submissive. The contradiction within the actuality of women's experience encompasses women included and excluded, in control and controlled, autonomous and dependent. These are more complicated oppositions than "good" and "bad," but they help us to bypass the temptation of judgment, and they are more true, for in their diversity they force us to grapple with the complex texture of the lives of medieval women and men.

13. Eileen Power, "The Position of Women," in *The Legacy of the Middle Ages*, ed. C. G. Crump and E. F. Jacob (Oxford: Clarendon, 1926), pp. 401–33.

Note—This study is limited to northern France, a region generally seen as the cultural vanguard for Europe of the High Middle Ages. Even the conventions of love poetry, first formulated in the south of France, were picked up, adapted, and disseminated through the north. Although I concentrate on the twelfth century—the period in which the key images originated—developments are followed, when appropriate, into the first half of the thirteenth century. The people studied are the social and religious elites who dominated the creation and consumption of images of women, and who dominated the institutional and economic structures.

Acknowledgments

The production of scholarship is a solitary activity that deprives me of time with family, friends, and students. Yet research and writing have also brought me into the social network of the scholarly world, and here my intellectual efforts have beeen sustained by the encouragement, support, criticism, and advice of teachers, colleagues, and friends. Karl Joachim Weintraub initiated my interest in history and shaped my vision of historical studies. My graduate training was guided by the gifted teaching of Alan E. Bernstein, William C. Calin, and Suzanne Lewis. Their interest in and criticism of my dissertation research made possible the interdisciplinary nature of this book. I am particularly grateful to Alan Bernstein as my advisor; both the shape and substance of my work owe much to his careful guidance and detailed criticism.

Many people have helped me by reading the manuscript in part or whole. Marcia Colish, Caroline Walker Bynum, and Elizabeth A. R. Brown generously read the work of a young scholar then unknown to them. Comments from the readers for the Press helped improve the manuscript significantly; I am especially grateful for Robert W. Hanning's suggestions for Chapter 1. Others have given advice and encouragement, sharing their ideas and reacting to mine. Thanks in particular to John F. Benton, Sharon Elkins, Mary Martin McLaughlin, Jane Tibbetts Schulenburg, Emily Zack Tabuteau, and Stephen D. White, all of whom also shared with me unpublished material of their own; Jean-Marc Bienvenu, Georges Duby, Mikiso Hane, David Herlihy, Gavin Langmuir, Jacques Le Goff, Carolyn

Chappell Lougee, Douglas Wilson, Charles T. Wood, and Ellen Rose
Woods. Thanks also to the nuns and monks of Our Lady of the Mis-
sissippi and New Melleray Abbeys, and particularly to Sisters Lillian
Thomas Shank and Mary Ann Sullivan and to Father James Kerndt.
My observation of monastic life and conversations with contemporary religious have, I hope, deepened my understanding of Christian
monasticism.

For aid and consideration I am indebted to the staff of the depart-
mental archives of Maine-et-Loire and to its director, Mlle. Poirier-
Coutansais. Thanks, too, to those at Knox College who made available word processing equipment for the editing of the manuscript,
especially William Ripperger and Charles Gibbs, whose patience,
help, creativity, and willingness to accommodate my deadlines were
essential to the timely completion of the book. Much of the work
of revision was done while in residence at the Newberry Library.
Providing the wealth of its collections, the solitude of a carrel, and
the collegiality of staff and Fellows, the Newberry fostered many
happy months of work. Conversations with other members of the
community, especially Alice Kasakoff, Clark Hulse, Paul Gehl, and
Mary Beth Rose, yielded many fruitful suggestions.

Support from several sources made possible initiation and completion of this project: the Trustees of the Mabelle McLeod Lewis Me-
morial Fund, the Charitable and Educational Trust under the Will of
Georges Lurcy, the Monticello College Foundation for its fellowship
at the Newberry Library, and Knox College for the funding of on-
going research expenses.

Finally, I would like to give special thanks to David Amor, who
has read the entire book, most of it two or three times. He has been
the audience and interlocutor in the initial working out of my ideas,
many of which were reshaped through our discussion; his skill as a
historian and as an editor marks every page. Through periods of
frustration and fatigue, his confidence in the merit of my work
helped keep me going.

This book is dedicated to my parents, Helen Schine Gold and
Joseph Gold, in gratitude for all they have contributed to my emotional and intellectual life. I can give back only a small portion of the
love, attention, and confidence they have placed in me, all of which
have made possible my sustained efforts, whether on this book, in
my job, or in my personal relationships.

· I ·

Secular Image

Women in *Chanson de Geste* and Romance

Literature and History: Some Methodological Concerns

Works of imaginative literature written in the vernacular provide vivid portrayals of the interactions between men and women in the secular sphere. Without diaries, personal letters, or autobiographies from nonecclesiastical sources, narrative fiction is one of the few sources available for the reconstruction of the sentiments and concerns of the medieval laity. Yet the richness of medieval literature also has been a trap for historians, who have sometimes too readily assumed that the world portrayed in literature is a direct reflection of the actual experience of medieval people. All literature reshapes, reorders, and distorts the reality of lived experience, creating a pattern, and hence a meaning, out of the chaos of everyday life. Rather than searching through literature for particular vignettes showing details of daily life, the historian needs to take each text as a whole, discern the major concerns that are embedded in it, and analyze the values and attitudes that are implicit in these concerns. In particular, when using literature as a source for understanding medieval attitudes toward women, we must not simply pluck out the female characters, using literary images as portraits of women, but must view the female characters in the context of the work as a whole, analyzing the structures shaping the interactions of men and women and the relationship of both men and women to the central values expressed in the text.[1]

1. Most scholarship on women in medieval literature has focused on description of the types of women portrayed. Some examples of this approach are: W. W. Comfort,

I

To understand fully the values and attitudes conveyed in literature, it is helpful to know the context of the work's production. Who was the author? What was his or her background? For whom was the work written? Who was the audience? These are vexing questions for the two genres that are the subject of this chapter, *chanson de geste* and romance. Virtually all *chansons de geste* and many romances were written anonymously, and when we know the name of an author, that is usually all we know. With regard to audience, many scholars have asserted that *chanson de geste*, an epic form, was a "popular" genre, addressed to the general populace, whereas romances were intended for a more restricted audience of clerics and knights.[2] Another common assertion about audience, which bears also on the matter of patronage, is that *chansons de geste* were written for a male audience, to male taste, whereas romances were written for women

---

"The Character Types in the Old French *Chansons de Geste*," *PMLA* 21 (1906): 279–434; Myrrha Borodine, *La femme et l'amour au XIIe siècle d'après les poèmes de Chrétien de Troyes* (Paris: A. Picard, 1909); Bertha L. de Kok, *Guibourc et quelques autres figures de femmes dans les plus anciennes chansons de geste* (Paris: Presses Universitaires de France, 1926); Margaret W. Henderson, "Woman in the Medieval French Epic" (Ph.D. diss., New York University, 1965); Jean-Charles Payen, "Figures féminines dans le roman médiéval français," in *Entretiens sur la renaissance du douzième siècle, le 21 au 30 juillet 1965* (Paris: Mouton, 1968), pp. 407–28; Marie-Noëlle Lefay-Toury, "Roman breton et mythes courtois. L'évolution du personnage féminin dans les romans de Chrétien de Troyes," *Cahiers de civilisation médiévale* 15 (1972): 193–204, 283–93; Rita Lejeune, "La femme dans les littératures française et occitane du XIe au XIIIe siècle," *Cahiers de civilisation médiévale* 20 (1977): 201–17. Micheline de Combarieu du Gres divides women into two types (*jeunes filles* and married women), and then pursues each type thematically: *L'idéal humain et l'expérience morale chez les héros des chansons de geste, des origines à 1250*, 2 vols. (Aix-en-Provence: Université de Provence, 1979), pp. 351–450. One work that goes beyond a typological analysis is Joan M. Ferrante, *Woman as Image in Medieval Literature from the Twelfth Century to Dante* (New York: Columbia University Press, 1975).

2. For example, Erich Köhler, "Quelques observations d'ordre historico-sociologique sur les rapports entre la chanson de geste et le roman courtois," in *Chanson de geste und höfischer Roman* (Heidelberger Kolloquium, 30. Januar 1961) (Heidelberg: C. Winter, 1963), pp. 22–23. For this position he relies, as do others, on a passage from the prologue of the *Roman de Thèbes* [ed. Constans, S.A.T.F. (Paris, 1890)]:

> Or s'en voisent de tot mestier
> Se ne sont clerc o chevalier
> Car aussi puent escouter
> Comme li asnes al harper
> Ne parlerai de peletiers,
> Ne de vilains, ne de berchiers . . .
> [13–18]

and at their behest. Unfortunately, little evidence exists to support these assertions about audience and patronage, whether popular or aristocratic, male or female.[3] What evidence can be found is usually internal to the literature itself, thus presenting us with a "fact" itself part of the literary fiction, and so not easily interpreted.[4] Rather than looking for such isolated "facts" about audience, we are better off examining the values and attitudes expressed in the literature and then, considering the contemporary social-political setting, judging for ourselves the audience likely to have been served by this literature. We will see that the pervasive concerns expressed in both *chanson de geste* and romance can best be understood as expressive of the situation of the French nobility, particularly the male members of that class.

These two genres, different as they are in technique, subject matter and worldview, both voice the concerns of the nobility at a time of particular trauma for that class, when political, social, and economic roles previously dominated by them were being taken over by either royalty or the bourgeoisie. Scholars commonly speak of romance as a genre developing later than, and replacing, *chanson de geste*. It is true that the earliest *chanson de geste* was written about 1100, the earliest romance about 1150. Yet the most productive period for both genres was the period from 1150 to 1225.[5] The difference in the expressed attitude toward women between the two genres does not primarily arise from change over time; rather, *chanson de geste* and romance embody two contrasting models or paradigms employed by or for the male nobility of twelfth-century France to resolve in the imagination the conflicts arising from their troublesome social circumstances. Both models made a place for women, but the roles assigned them reveal a

3. John F. Benton is one of the few historians to have studied carefully the actual historical context of medieval literary production: "Clio and Venus. An Historical View of Medieval Love," in *The Meaning of Courtly Love*, ed. F. X. Newman (Albany: State University of New York Press, 1968), pp. 19–42; idem, "The Court of Champagne as a Literary Center," *Speculum* 36 (1961): 551–91; idem, "The Evidence for Andreas Capellanus Reexamined Again," *Studies in Philology* 59 (1962): 471–78.

4. For a brief discussion of the limitations on our knowledge of the social context of medieval literature, see R. Howard Bloch, *Medieval French Literature and Law* (Berkeley and Los Angeles: University of California Press, 1977), pp. 6–7.

5. Köhler, "Quelques observations," p. 22; Paul Zumthor, *Histoire littéraire de la France médiévale (VIe-XIVe siècles)* (Paris: Presses Universitaires de France, 1954), pp. 206–54. According to Zumthor, epic themes were exhausted after about 1220 and romance themes by about 1230 (pp. 231, 250).

deep-seated ambivalence, not only because the contrasting epic and romance roles develop at the same time, but because within each genre an ambivalent attitude toward women is expressed, with women both helping and hindering men in the resolution of the problems they face.

Chanson de Geste

The close analysis of male/female interaction in these genres must rest on a detailed exposition of a small number of works; the reader is encouraged to test the results of this analysis on works other than those chosen here. No text can be entirely "typical," but I have selected works that include structures, themes, and character types prevalent in many texts. I have also chosen works dating from different points in the life span of each genre, for the *chanson de geste*, the *Song of William*, one of the oldest French epics, and *Raoul de Cambrai*, written about 1180–1185.[6] Why not the *Song of Roland*, the early epic we all know and love? Unfortunately, *Roland* is one of the least typical of the hundred or so surviving works of the genre.[7] Although its singularity is usually noted in terms of its style and seriousness, its treatment of women is also unusual. A woman like Aude, who appears only to die immediately of grief, can be found in other *chansons de geste*, but most include other female characters who serve more important functions in the stories.[8] The reader must therefore put

6. The four oldest surviving French epics are the *Song of William*, the *Song of Roland*, *Gormond et Isembard*, and the *Pélerinage de Charlemagne* (William C. Calin, *The Old French Epic of Revolt: "Raoul de Cambrai," "Renaud de Montauban," "Gormond et Isembard"* [Geneva: Droz, 1962], p. 199). The early dating of *William* has been subject to debate. (Indeed, the dates assigned to many medieval texts are very provisional.) A summary and analysis of the various opinions about *William* can be found in Jean Frappier, *Les chansons de geste du cycle de Guillaume d'Orange* (Paris: Société d'Edition d'Enseignement Supérieur, 1955), 1: 38, 149–56. Opinions range from about 1080 to the last third of the twelfth century. I have accepted Frappier's judgment that the poem was probably written close to the time that *Roland* was, and that it cannot be viewed as later than mid-century (p. 156).

7. Calin, *Revolt*, p. 223; idem, *The Epic Quest: Studies in Four Old French Chansons de Geste* (Baltimore: Johns Hopkins University Press, 1960), pp. 237–38; Howard Robertson, *La Chanson de Willame: A Critical Study*, University of North Carolina Studies in the Romance Languages and Literatures, no. 65 (Chapel Hill: University of North Carolina Press, 1966), pp. 14, 52.

8. Henderson's dissertation demonstrates the variety and importance of these female characters; see also de Kok.

aside notions of the insignificance of epic women that may have been formed from an overreliance on the *Song of Roland*.

The *Song of William* opens with a Saracen attack on seven hundred French knights, including Vivien, a nephew of William.[9] While one group retreats in cowardice, Vivien, his cousin Girard, and the remaining men stay to fight. Vivien sends Girard to Barcelona to get help from William and his wife Guiburc. William, just returned from a battle at Bordeaux, seems reluctant to leave for another battle, but Guiburc presses him to agree to fight, and entrusts him with her recently knighted nephew, Guischard. That night, William leaves with thirty thousand men, but this help is to no avail, and in the ensuing battle all the French die except William. Meanwhile, Guiburc has gathered together thirty thousand more men. William returns to Barcelona and presents Guiburc with the body of her dead nephew. Undaunted, Guiburc rallies the gathered men to go back to the battle with William by lying to them, telling them that William has won the battle, but at great cost, and that he needs reinforcement to finish off the Saracens. Before leaving, William, who is childless, arranges for the disposal of his land and his wife in the event that he dies; his nephew Gui will inherit the land and the responsibility for protecting Guiburc. That night, William returns to the battlefield, having ordered Gui to stay at home with Guiburc because of his tender age. Once William is gone, however, Gui persuades Guiburc to let him join William, and Gui turns out to be the hero of the day, saving William and delivering the final blow to the Saracen king.

The spatial structure of this epic provides us with a framework for an analysis of the role of women, here represented by Guiburc. The long first section of the poem takes place on the battlefield, where no women are present. The action then shifts to the home of William and Guiburc, where Guiburc is the dominant participant in the story. Then there is another battle, after which the scene shifts back to the home and Guiburc. The final section of the poem is another battle, making a clear structure of battle/home/battle/home/battle. The male sphere of action and the female sphere of action are clearly separated geographically (with the men, but not the women, present in both spheres), and the male sphere is clearly the predominant in-

---

9. *La chanson de Guillaume*, ed. Duncan McMillan, 2 vols. (Paris: Picard, 1949–50). The translations given are from Lynette Muir, *The Song of William*, in *William, Count of Orange: Four Old French Epics*, ed. Glanville Price (Totowa, N.J.: Rowman and Littlefield, 1975).

terest—more than three-quarters of the action takes place on the battlefield. Awareness of this separation and contrast is expressed by Vivien when he is encouraging his men to fight the Saracens: "But Vivien said: 'I know your views, you are thinking of the vineyards and fields, castles and cities, and your wives at home. A man who is thinking so will never fight boldly.'" [10] A man who is thinking of home, the locus of women and civilization (vines, fields, castles, cities), will not be able to participate valiantly in battle. We can find a similar contrast made later: when William leaves Barcelona, the men go to battle while the woman, Guiburc, is left alone in the city: "Dunc remist sule Guiburc en la bone cité" (1509). Later, when young Gui becomes hungry in the middle of the battle, he first complains of the gentle upbringing he received from Guiburc, and then wishes he were back with her so he could be fed: "'I rue the time when Guibourg brought me up so kindly and gave me food so early in the day. Now is the hour when she used to serve me and I am so hungry I shall die of it. . . . I am so ravenous it is driving me mad. I would like to be in my lady's service now!'" [11] In this case, Gui's youth has kept him overly reliant on the care he would receive at home—he is not quite ready for the separation of home and battlefield.

Equally important as the separation of the two spheres of home and battle is the interdependence, or integration, of the two. This integration can be seen in Guiburc's role as provider of two things needed by the men: nourishment and advice. On two occasions Guiburc is shown taking care of the men by providing them with food and drink and by putting them to sleep. After Girard has arrived at Barcelona, and the decision to send aid has been made, Guiburc serves food and drink to Girard: "Guibourg herself brought water to

10.   Dist Vivien: "C'est plaid soi jo assez.
                        Ore vus remenbre des vignes et des prez,
                        E des chastels e des larges citez,
                        E des moillers que a voz maisuns avez.
                        Que de ço menbre ne frad ja barné."
                              [580–584]
11.   "Mar vi Guiburc qui suef me norist,
                        Qui me soleit faire disner si matin!
                        Ore est le terme qu'ele le me soleit offrir;
                        Ore ai tel faim ja me verras morir. . . .
                        Car tele faim ai, ja m'enragerai vif;
                        Ore voldreie estre a ma dame servir!"
                        [1737–1740, 1746–1747]

Gerard and afterwards offered him a towel. Then [she] sat him down
at the top table and brought him a shoulder of boar. The count took
it and ate it quickly, she brought him a great bread-cake made of fine
flour and after that a great mazer of wine."[12] When he has finished
eating, he goes to bed, and Guiburc sits by him until he falls asleep:
"Gerard stood up and rose from the table. The bed was ready and he
went to lie down. The noble Guibourg willingly attended on him
and stayed at his side until he was sleeping, then commended him to
the care of almighty God."[13] After the second battle, William returns
home, and his revival by food and rest, administered by Guiburc, is
described in lines closely parallel to those used for Girard (1401–
1411). Similarly, after he is through eating, he goes to sleep, watched
over by Guiburc. In this telling, the poet includes high praise for
Guiburc's capabilities:

> Count William got up from the table and went to rest, for the
> bed was ready. The noble Guibourg gently caressed him. In all
> Christendom there was no wife fitter to serve and honour her
> lord, nor exalt holy Christianity nor uphold and maintain the
> rule of law. She stayed by his side till he was sleeping quietly and
> commended him to God the most high. Then she went back to
> the hall to talk to the warriors.[14]

12.   Guiburc meismes servi Girard de l'eve,
        E en aprés le servit de tuaille;
        Puis l'ad assis a une halte table,
        Si lui aportat d'un sengler un espalle.
        Li quons la prist, si la mangat a haste.
        Ele li aportat un grant pain a tamis,
        E dunc en aprés sun grant mazelin de vin.
                    [1042–1048]

13.   Girard se dresce e levad del manger,
        Prest fu li liz, si s'est alé colcher,
        Guiburc la franche le servi volenters,
        Tant fud od lui qu'il endormi fu.
        Puis le comande al cors altisme Deu.
                    [1065–1069]

14.   Li quons Willame est del manger levé,
        Prest fu li liz, s'i est culcher alé.
        Guiburc la franche l'i tastunad suef;
        Il n'i out tele femme en la crestienté
        Pur sun seignur servir e honorer,
        Ne pur eschalcer sainte crestienté,
        Ne pur lei maintenir e garder.
        Tant fu od lui qu'il s'endormi suef;

Vivien, too, was nourished by Guiburc. When he is instructing
Girard on how to ask for help from William and Guiburc, he instructs him to remind William of the numerous battles in which
Girard helped William out. He also instructs him to remind Guiburc
of the nurture she provided him for more than fifteen years; it is on
this basis that she should now send William: "'Do you know what to
say to my dear lady Guibourg? Remind her of the care with which
she nurtured me for fifteen years and more. Let not that care for
God's sake be wasted. Let her send me her lord to help me, for if she
does not send the count there is no-one I want.'" [15] Gui also acknowledges his debt to Guiburc's nurturing in a more positive way than his
hungry complaint on the battlefield. When William is deciding on an
heir, Gui asserts that he would serve Guiburc well because of the nurture she provided him: "'If you should die I would defend your lands
and faithfully serve my lady Guibourg. She would never suffer anything I could prevent, for she has brought me up most kindly.'" [16]
Guiburc's role as nurturer, the provider of the food and rest necessary to any knight, is emphasized by the frequent use of the various
forms of the word *nurir*. [17]

Guiburc's other role, that of adviser, is illustrated by three decisions that she makes or influences, decisions crucial to the action of

---

      Puis comandad sun cors a l'altisme Deu,
      Dunc vait en la sale as chevalers parler.
          [1484–1493]
15.   "Sez que dirras dame Guiburc, ma drue?
      Si li remenbre de la grant nurreture,
      Plus de quinze anz qu'ele ad vers mei eue.
      Ore gardez, pur Deu, qu'ele ne seit perdue,
      Qu'ele m'enveit sun siegneur en aïe.
      S'ele ne m'enveit le cunte, d'altre n'ai jo cure."
         [683–688]
These lines are repeated virtually verbatim when Girard makes his request to William
and Guiburc (993–998).
16.   "Si tu murreies jo tendreie tun païs;
      Guiburc ma dame voldreie ben servir;
      Ja n'averad mal dunt la puisse garir,
      Pur ço qu'ele m'ad tant suef nurri."
         [1447–1450]
17. See the etymological glossary prepared by Guérard Piffard and included in the
edition of the poem by Nancy V. Iseley, *La chançun de Willame*, University of North
Carolina Studies in the Romance Languages and Literatures, no. 35 (1961; reprint ed.,
New York: Garrett Publishing Co., 1966).

the story. The first instance is the decision to send help to Vivien. After Girard has presented his plea for aid, William's response is one of despair rather than commitment: "'O God,' said William, 'shall I find him alive?'" Guiburc interprets this plaint as hesitation, for which she rebukes him: "But Guibourg replied: 'Such talk is useless. Go to his help, my lord, without asking questions. If you lose him, you will have no friend left but God.'"[18] On hearing her words, William shakes his head and weeps, presumably a sign of his reluctance to do battle for Vivien. But this reluctance is apparently feigned, as we are told that William wants to test his wife's love for him and his family: "He spoke to Guibourg, pretending to remonstrate with her for the baron wanted to test her feeling and see how much she loved him and his kin."[19] His speech repeats his hesitation to go to battle, and he asserts that Vivien can handle the fighting himself. At this, Guiburc herself weeps and pleads with him to aid Vivien. Whether or not William's hesitation was feigned, Guiburc's commitment to William's family and to the need for battle is clear, and her active participation in this decision is significant. The male and female spheres may be delimited geographically, but Guiburc is included in decisions that affect action to be carried out on the battlefield.

Guiburc's decisiveness is most important when William comes home from the first battle, bringing only the corpse of Guischard, nephew of Guiburc. Guiburc meets William alone at the gate, and after his presentation of the corpse of her nephew,[20] William bemoans his loss of honor. On hearing William's complaint, Guiburc forgets her own grief at the death of her nephew and implores William to

18.   "A, Deus," dist Willame, "purrai le vif trover?"
       Respunt Guiburc: "Pur nient en parlez.
       Secor le, sire, ne te chalt a demander.
       Se tu l'i perz, n'avras ami fors Deu."
                        [1003–1006]
On the advice-giving role of wives in *chansons de geste*, see Combarieu du Gres, pp. 396–99.
19.   Guiburc apele, si li prist a mustrer
       De son corage li volt li bers espermenter.
       De si cum ele aime lui e sun parenté.
                        [1011–1013]
20. William lays the corpse in her arms, but Guiburc is unable to hold the weight of the body. In this context the poet makes the only reference in the poem to the weakness of women:

live up to the reputation of his family (*parenté*). William responds with despair of being too old (three hundred and fifty!) to ever regain his honor. He concludes: "'Whatever others may suffer, I am left alone, never again in this life to have honour.'"[21] Guiburc, however, presents a plan for recovering from his losses; she asks William for permission to lie, so that she can supply him with thirty thousand more men. William begs her to tell him where these men might be. Her reply that they are in the palace makes him laugh instead of weep, and he gives her permission to lie. Guiburc then addresses a long speech to the men, falsifying William's situation and promising them land and women if they go to help William finish off the last of the Saracens. So once again, Guiburc has forcefully encouraged her reluctant husband to fight for the honor of his family and, in this latter instance, manipulated thirty thousand men to join him.

Guiburc's third sending-off-a-man-into-battle is done against William's wishes but saves his life. Guiburc goes against William's specific instructions to keep the young Gui at home with her.[22] She allows Gui to leave after he persuades her that William will not return alive without his help. Gui's prediction is true; he saves William's life, and Guiburc has again influenced the outcome of action on the battlefield, even though she never leaves the sphere of the home, the *chimené*.

Although the main focus of the *Song of William* is the battlefield and the three battles against the Saracens, Guiburc, separated spatially in the female sphere of the home, appears as an important actor, providing the nurture and advice necessary to sustain the fighting. Guiburc knows and accepts the value-system of the warrior class, and her actions are designed to support and promote that system. Indeed, as quoted above, the poet himself praises Guiburc as

La franche femme li tendi ses braz,
E il li colchat desus le mort vassal;
Peise le cors, si li faillerent les braz;
Ele fu femme, si out fieble la char.
Contre tere en prist le cors un quas,
Tote la langue li turnad une part.
[1290–1295]

21. "Ki qu'en peise, jo sui tout sul remés;
Ja mais en terre n'avrai honur mortel!"
[1348–1349]

22. "Pren le Guiburc, meine le en ta chimené."
[1481]

the woman most fit to "serve and honour her lord," "exalt holy Christianity," and "uphold and maintain the rule of law." In addition to the defense of Christianity and the maintenance of law, another value underlies this integration of the male and female spheres, and that is the importance of the family (*parenté, lignage*). P. Matarasso has described the fundamentality of the bond of family to the whole genre of *chanson de geste*:

> Does not the term "chanson de geste" signify "chanson du lignage"? The poems of the king aside, the body of epic poetry celebrates the glory of one or another feudal family, real or imaginary. The hero, who is not always the head of the family, appears surrounded by his relatives, who support and counsel him, sometimes leading him into trying situations of which he shares the responsibility. Everywhere and always the *lignage* stands behind him.[23]

The kinship-bond is what compels William to battle—his motivation is not so much to oppose the Saracens as to aid Vivien, his nephew. It is also concern for the preservation of the honor of the *parenté* that compels William to act, a concern that Guiburc emphasizes in her counsel to William. All the major characters—Vivien, William, Guiburc, Gui, Girard, Guischard—are closely related to each other, a relationship stressed by the common first letter of all the names except Vivien ("Willame" being the equivalent of "Guillaume"). The two cowards Tedbalt and Esturmi are related to each other (uncle and nephew) but not to the other, more valiant, characters of the story. Not only is the family one of the primary values in the *chansons de geste*, it is also the organizing principle of the many cycles of epics created concerning the epic heroes. These cycles explore the early and later life of the heroes as well as the lives of their ancestors and descendants.[24]

Given the family as a value and as a motivating force, the function of women in the *chanson de geste* becomes apparent. It is not simply a matter of providing the heirs necessary to the continuation of the lineage; William must arrange for the inheritance of his responsibilities

23. P. Matarasso, *Recherches historiques et littéraires sur "Raoul de Cambrai"* (Paris: Nizet, 1962), p. 127. On the shared value-system of men and women in *chansons de geste*, see Combarieu du Gres, pp. 411–12.

24. R. Howard Bloch, *Etymologies and Genealogies: A Literary Anthropology of the French Middle Ages* (Chicago: University of Chicago Press, 1983), pp. 93–96.

when he dies, but Guiburc is not the one who provides him with an heir as the couple is childless. The correspondence of the importance of the family and the constructive role of women is, rather, a result of the fact that if both public life (war) and private life (home) are organized on the same basis (the family), the two spheres necessarily interact. Since women are an essential component of a family, they can be expected to be integrated into the male sphere of action if that sphere, too, is oriented toward the family, as it is in *chansons de geste*. In *William* we see the integration through the female roles of nurture and advice.[25]

This epic female presence is, however, not without ambivalence. The loyal, wise, nurturing Guiburc remains at the periphery of the story, encouraging, aiding, and advising the men who are the central characters. Both men and women subscribe to the same values, but only the men can actively defend those values through battle, which remains the primary focus of epic literature. Furthermore, Guiburc's strength as advisor to her husband is undercut by a mocking, humorous tone. Although I would not go so far as one critic, who sees in Guiburc a parody of the adviser role,[26] Guiburc's successful craftiness and her ready defense of her husband's lineage serves to highlight the fatigue, uncertainty, and failure of her husband. Guiburc, in this perspective, bears some resemblance to the manipulative, chiding wife of the *fabliaux*.

Other *chansons de geste* show a similar integration of women through the family, while maintaining women on the periphery and with a subtle undercurrent of hostility. *Raoul de Cambrai*, written toward the end of the twelfth century, is one of the most famous and

---

25. The connection of the importance of the family in *William* and the importance of Guiburc is noted by Reto R. Bezzola, *Les origines et la formation de la littérature courtoise en Occident (500-1200)*, 3 vols. in 5 (Paris: H. Champion, 1944–63), 2, pt. 2: 503–4.

I have not included in my discussion the continuation of the poem, which virtually all critics agree was appended at a much later date. The continuation is different in tone and style and focuses on the mock-hero Rainouart. Yet, Guiburc retains her advisory role in the continuation, and at one point William, once again accepting her advice, refers to how important her advice has been to him on many occasions:

> E dit Willame: "Jol ferai mult iree,
> Mais tun conseil en dei jo creire ben;
> En plusurs lius m'ad eu mult grant mester."
> [2432–2434]

26. Robertson, p. 33.

most masterful of the many "epics of revolt," poems whose central
concern was the struggle of a feudal baron and his family against the
king or another family.[27]

Raoul de Cambrai centers on the family of Raoul Taillefer, a man
whose service to King Louis had been rewarded with the fief of
Cambrai and a wife Aalais, Louis's sister. Aalais is soon widowed but
bears her husband's son, also named Raoul. The fief of Cambrai is
given by King Louis to Gibouin of Mans, and Louis commands
Aalais to marry him. Raoul Taillefer's brother Guerri urges Aalais to
marry Gibouin; he is angry that Louis has disinherited his own
nephew but sees the marriage as being necessary to make peace.
Aalais refuses to marry, and Guerri promises to support her in this
decision. He also discusses the matter with three-year-old Raoul,
who promises vengeance. Fifteen years later, Raoul goes to Louis's
court to be knighted, accompanied by his friend and squire Bernier
(a bastard). Raoul, successful in his service at court, asks the king for
his father's land, his rightful inheritance. Louis instead upholds
Gibouin's claim to Cambrai but promises Raoul the land of the next
count to die. One year later Herbert of Vermandois dies, but to give
Raoul this land would mean disinheriting Herbert's four sons, one of
whom is Ybert, Bernier's father. Nonetheless, Louis gives Raoul the
land. Raoul goes back to Cambrai, where Aalais urges him to fight
for his father's fief rather than for the Vermandois, against the family
of Herbert, who had always been a friend to Raoul Taillefer. When
Raoul angrily insults her and rejects her advice, Aalais curses him.
She soon regrets her curse and tries to give Raoul advice about the
reliability of some of the men he has chosen. Raoul again rejects her
advice, again insults her, and leaves with his men for Vermandois.
They pitch their tents outside the church of Origny, where
Bernier's mother Marsent, who is abbess, tries to reason with Raoul.
Marsent also talks with Bernier and advises that between Ybert, his
father, and Raoul, his lord, his primary allegiance should be to
Raoul. But Raoul orders the town burned, and all the nuns die, although Raoul had pledged to Marsent that he would not harm the
nuns. Bernier quarrels bitterly with Raoul and joins Ybert. A recon-

27. Calin, *Revolt*, p. 9. *Raoul de Cambrai*, ed. P. Meyer and A. Longnon (1882; re-
print ed., Paris: Johnson Reprint Corporation, 1965). The translations given are from
Jessie Crosland, *Raoul de Cambrai: An Old French Feudal Epic* (New York: Cooper
Square Publishers, 1966).

ciliation is unsuccessfully attempted; a long battle ensues, in the course of which Bernier kills Raoul. His body is brought back to Cambrai, where Raoul's death is mourned by his mother and his fiancée, Heluïs. Gautier, Raoul's nephew and the only surviving heir, swears vengeance. After five years of peace, Gautier and Guerri provoke another battle. A duel between Gautier and Bernier is to determine the outcome, but neither wins. King Louis summons his vassals to Paris and arranges for another duel between the two, during which they are both severely wounded. The king puts them in beds close together. Aalais enters the city, berates the king, and in her presence Gautier and Bernier make peace with each other. Guerri proclaims that it is the king who has caused the war, and they should all unite against Louis; Bernier and Ybert agree. The king announces that when Ybert dies, he will give Vermandois to one of his nobles. Bernier, who would be disinherited by such action, orders the pillaging of the city, and Paris burns. The families return to Vermandois and Cambrai.

The spatial structure underlying this action is similar to that of the *Song of William*, although more complex. The later poem, more than twice as long as *William*, switches scenes more frequently, and the battles, once begun, range over a large territory rather than beginning and ending at one place. The action begins at Louis's court at Paris, moves to Cambrai (the childhood of Raoul), goes back to court (Raoul's service to the king), to Cambrai again (confrontation of Raoul and his mother). Here the war between the families of the Cambresis and Vermandois begin; this long section takes up almost half the poem. Then we go back to Cambrai (mourning for the death of Raoul, the childhood of Gautier). When Gautier is grown, the war begins again; in its course, the battle includes Cambrai itself. The final dénouement brings us full cycle back to the court in Paris. This gives us the pattern of court/Cambrai/court/Cambrai/war/Cambrai/war(including Cambrai)/court. The sections of war, as in *William*, make up the bulk of the poem. Aalais's major actions take place at home (Cambrai), but the division of male and female spheres is not as absolute as in *William*. Since the second war takes place around Cambrai, Aalais occasionally appears during battle interludes, although she does nothing significant in this section. The most important break in the separation of male and female spheres occurs at court; Aalais's wedding takes place at court, and the final reconciliation, with Aalais present, occurs at court.

Even though the physical separation is not as rigid, a self-conscious expression of the necessity of separation is strongly stated. When Aalais advises Raoul not to fight the sons of Herbert, Raoul answers that Aalais should stay in her own chamber and limit herself to household affairs: "'Let that knight be accursed and held for a coward, who takes counsel of a woman before going into battle! Go to your apartments, lady, and take your ease; drink pleasant draughts to fatten your body. Think out for your household what they shall eat and drink, and meddle not with other things.'"[28] Aalais's later advice to Raoul is also rewarded with an insult (1212). As in the *Song of William*, a woman gives advice concerning matters of war to the men who alone carry out the battle. Aalais's advice is not taken, but this is a sign of Raoul's *desmesure*, his tragic flaw of immoderacy, rather than a flaw in Aalais's advice, which, if followed, would have saved many lives, including Raoul's. Marsent also participates in the counsel of war, first when she convinces Raoul not to attack the nunnery, and then when she advises her son Bernier regarding his feudal duty.

The other supportive role of women, that of nurturer, is frequently referred to in the poem but not shown. That is, Aalais and Marsent are often referred to, or refer to themselves as, nurturers, but they are not shown performing this role, unlike Guiburc, whom we saw feeding her men and putting them to rest. For example, Aalais prefaces her advice to Raoul with a reminder of her role: "'Fair son,' said she, 'I have watched over thee many a year [longement t'ai norri]'" (986). When he rejects her advice, she again begins her remarks with reference to her nurture of him: "'Dear son Raoul,' said the fair Aalais, 'I nourished thee with the milk of my own breast, and why doest thou give me such a pain now beneath my heart?'"[29] In the *Song of Wil-*

---

28.   "Maldehait ait, je le taing por lanier,
             Le gentil homme, qant il doit tornoier,
             A gentil dame qant se va consellier!
             Dedens vos chambres vos alez aasier:
             Beveiz puison por vo pance encraissier,
             E si pensez de boivre et de mengier;
             Car d'autre chose ne devez mais plaidier."
                          [1100–1106]
29.   "—Biax fix Raoul," dist Aalais la bele,
             "Je te norri del lait de ma mamele;
             Por quoi me fais dolor soz ma forcele?"
                          [1001–1003]
Other examples of the use of the word *norrir*: Aalais, enraged at Louis's command of

liam, Guiburc's advice was taken, and her nurture appreciated; in
Raoul de Cambrai, Raoul rejects Aalais's advice, a rejection she interprets as ingratitude for her nurture of him. Bernier, on the other
hand, a character with more *mesure* than Raoul, follows his mother's
advice, at least until he is driven to another course by grief over the
death of his mother, the person who had nourished him. Although
we do not find the same cooperative integration of functions of men
and women that we saw in *William*, we still find men and women
sharing the same values. Both men and women are concerned with
the duties of vassalage and of loyalty to lineage. Again, the value
of the family supports, or contributes to, the importance of women
in the story. The action of the first half of the poem (until Raoul's
death) is motivated by the desire to procure or defend the land seen
as rightfully belonging to one's lineage; the second half by the desire
for vengeance for slain kin. It is only at the very end of the poem that
these motivations are overcome by the newly perceived need to unite
against the king. The value of one's lineage is expressed throughout
the poem. There is the familiar web of kin relationships; virtually
everyone in the poem is related to either Raoul or to Herbert. The
need for family solidarity is clearly recognized. Aalais sends Raoul to
be baptized by her cousin, bishop Guion of Beauvais, since she does
not want to remove him from his family: "'Qe del lignaje ne le vieut
eslongier'" (72). Guerri and Aalais both bitterly rebuke Louis for his
lack of concern for his nephew (305, 5232); Ernaut fights Raoul in a
quest for vengeance for the death of his children (2848). In their final
resolution to unite against the king, Guerri says to Ybert and Bernier that they all will now be like close kin: "'Dès or serons comme
prochain parent'" (5383). Marsent advises Bernier to put his loyalty to
his lord before his family, but we would not expect the mother of a
bastard, now a nun, to have the same sense of lineage as a landed
feudal family. Aalais, on the other hand, is the poem's strongest sup-

---

marriage, swears to *norrir* her child until he is old enough to bear arms (334); when
Raoul announces his plans to fight against Herbert's sons, Aalais asks what will become of Bernier, whom she brought up (*norri*) (1078); at another point in her advice
to Raoul, Aalais refers to the fact that she nurtured him until he became a knight
(1114); Aalais regrets that she has cursed the child that she nurtured (1147); Marsent
asks Raoul where Bernier is—she has not seen him since she nurtured him as a boy
(1313); Bernier, who was present at the burning of Origny, tells Guerri that he has seen
the breasts from which he was nursed burn (1527); when Bernier pleads for peace, he
calls on Aalais as the one who nurtured him, who gave him food and drink (5252).

porter of the value of lineage. Although Raoul argues with his mother that his heirs will be disgraced unless he fights against Herbert's sons, Aalais more justifiably identifies the concern of the lineage to be the preservation of the family's own rightful land from the usurper Gibouin. As Raoul has previously complained to the king, the fief of the father should by right be passed on to the child.[30]

As in the *Song of William*, however, Aalais's devotion to the family has another side, this time not of affectionate mockery but of excess and violence. Aalais's actions can be seen as one of the sources of strife: her refusal to marry Gibouin, her curse of her son, her frequent reminders to the men of the need for vengeance. Raoul himself, of course, is not without fault, but his mother contributes to his defensive response to her by insulting him in public:

> Then the lady spoke to him in the hearing of many barons: "Fair son," said she, "you are tall and well-grown; you are seneschal of France, thanks be to God. But I am much amazed at King Louis; you have served him [a] long time now and he has not recompensed your service in any way. He ought to give you now of his own free will all the land of Taillefer the bold, thine own father and my husband. The knight of Mans has had possession of it too long, and I am amazed that thou hast consented to it for so long, and hast neither killed him nor brought dishonour upon him."[31]

Aalais also reminds Gautier of his duty, accusing him of having forgotten his uncle (3752–3754). And finally, when Guerri comes to join

30.   "L'onnor del pere, ce sevent li auquant,
                    Doit tot par droit revenir a l'effant."
                    [700–701]

31.   Ele l'apele, maint baron l'ont oï:
                    "Biax fix," dist ele, "grant vos voi et forni;
                    Seneschax estes de France, Dieu merci.
                    Molt m'esmervel del fort roi Loeys;
                    Molt longuement l'avez ore servi,
                    Ne ton service ne t'a de rien meri.
                    Toute la terre Taillefer le hardi,
                    Le tien chier pere qe je pris a mari,
                    Te rendist ore, par la soie merci,
                    Car trop en a Mancel esté servi.
                    Je me mervelg qe tant l'as consenti,
                    Qe grant piece a ne l'as mort ou honni."
                    [968–979]

Gautier to fight Bernier and his family, Aalais rebukes him for his long absence (3778–3779). These reminders and rebukes by Aalais feed the tragic violence of the story. Other epic literature stresses this function of women as the ones who encourage, and sometimes provoke, the pursuit of blood-revenge. The Loherain cycle of *chansons de geste* stands out in this regard, as do some of the epics of Germany and Iceland—the *Nibelungenlied, Njal's Saga, Laxdaela Saga.*[32] In the end, Aalais must give up her desire for vengeance. Although she rejoices to God when Gautier tells her he has cut off Bernier's ear (5241–5242), she gives in to Bernier's plea for mercy when he prostrates himself at her feet and recalls the nurture she gave him as a child (5252–5253). It is, in any case, time to give up family partisanship in recognition of a larger common threat, the king (both in the time of the poem, and in actual historical time).

In both the *Song of William* and *Raoul de Cambrai* the female roles of nurturer and advisor are related to the male role of warrior through their joint foundation in the maintenance of the family and its heritage. Both poems, and *chansons de geste* in general, center on a collective struggle to pursue or maintain some social value, often the honor of one's family. Women are enmeshed in the action because of the goals that they share with men and that they encourage men to pursue, yet women remain physically on the sidelines (Guiburc at Barcelona, Aalais at Cambrai), and their encouragement of men is portrayed with ambivalence, to the extent that it shows up a male hero's failings or provokes violence that may be unnecessary.

Romance

The romance introduces us to a different world. Both in form and in content, twelfth-century romances differ markedly from the contemporary *chansons de geste*. The accompanying differences in the image of women will be viewed through an analysis centering on the romance *Yvain*, written by Chrétien de Troyes, and roughly contemporary with *Raoul de Cambrai.*[33] Chrétien de Troyes was one of the most influential and popular writers of the generation that created the romance, making his work especially suited for this study. Com-

32. See Henderson for a thorough discussion of the Loherain cycle.
33. Jean Frappier dates *Yvain* between 1176 and 1181 (*Etude sur "Yvain" ou le "Chevalier au lion" de Chrétien de Troyes* [Paris: Société d'édition d'enseignement supérieur, 1969; first published in 1952], p. 16). I have used the edition of *Yvain* by Mario

parison will be made to other romances, including Chrétien's *Erec and Enide*, the *Roman d'Eneas*, *Partonopeu de Blois*, and *The Death of King Arthur*.

Chrétien's story opens with the mission of Yvain, a knight at King Arthur's court, to avenge the shame of his cousin, who had been defeated seven years before by a knight guarding a magic fountain. Yvain leaves the court in secret, to insure that he alone engages the knight. He succeeds in killing the knight, and with the help of Lunete, a serving lady, he also succeeds in marrying Laudine, the knight's wife, with whom he has fallen in love. Gawain, who arrives with Arthur and other knights, convinces Yvain that he must leave his new domestic tranquillity, since his knightly reputation will degenerate if he stays at home with his wife. Having agreed to leave with Gawain for the tournament circuit, Yvain asks Laudine for permission to leave. She gives him permission to do so, but makes him promise to be back in one year. Yvain is so successful in the tournaments that he forgets to return at the end of the year. Rejected by Laudine, Yvain goes mad. After a time spent living like an animal in the forest, Yvain is brought back to his senses by the application of a magic ointment. He then proceeds to do six good deeds. In one of these deeds, Yvain helps a lion, who in turn befriends him and helps him in battle. The other good deeds are all performed to save women who are in some kind of danger. In his final battle, Yvain is pitted against his friend Gawain, though both are in disguise. Fighting this time without the lion, Yvain and Gawain fight to a draw. They end in revealing their real identities, and Yvain also identifies himself as the mysterious Knight of the Lion. Having reestablished himself at Arthur's court, Yvain goes back to the magic fountain to repair his relationship with Laudine. Yvain is reconciled with his wife through the artful intercession of Lunete, and the story ends happily.

The spatial analysis used to map the participation of men and women in the *chansons de geste* cannot be applied to *Yvain*. In the *Song of William*, the action of the story could be divided into segments at home and segments at battle, with battle exclusively the man's sphere and home predominantly the woman's. The division was still present, though less sharp, in *Raoul de Cambrai*; the battle

---

Roques, *Le chevalier au lion (Yvain)* (Les classiques français du moyen âge, 89) (Paris: H. Champion, 1960). The translations given are from W. W. Comfort, *Arthurian Romances* (London: Dent, 1914).

was extended to Cambrai, and the court was the scene of action for women as well as men. In *Yvain*, the geographical separation of men and women disappears almost entirely. This is partially due to the different narrative style of the romance; continuity of narration is more evident in romance, in contrast to *chanson de geste* in which there can be abrupt changes in scene. The court world, with its mixture of men and women, also has become a more significant locus of action. A major change, however, is that women are no longer excluded from the scenes of battle. Women are attendants at tournaments and at the various duels that Yvain fights. Fighting has been domesticated; it now takes place in the vicinity of court or castle rather than on a distant battlefield. If we were to draw an outline of the plot of *Yvain*, the main dividing line would not be the external or spatial one of geography (home versus battlefield), but rather would be found in the *internal* or psychological development of the main character; the division is signaled by Yvain's madness, which occurs halfway through the poem. By reviewing the circumstances and causes of Yvain's madness, we will see, however, that the geographical integration of men and women in the romance has not led to increased cooperation between the sexes but that, instead, there is a conflict between men and women caused by conflicting desires within the male hero. Furthermore, there is a stress on individual achievement and identity as opposed to the group solidarity, and in particular the family solidarity, that is so important in *chansons de geste*. The absence of the family as a common value binding men and women together helps explain the tension between the hero and the heroine.

The cause of Yvain's madness illuminates the nature of this tension. Yvain had been convinced by Gawain to leave Laudine only one week after his marriage. Gawain insisted that Yvain's knightly prowess would decline if he stayed at home with his wife:

> "What? Will you be one of those," said my lord Gawain to him, "who are valued less because of their wives? Cursed be he by Saint Mary who degenerates because he marries! Whoever has a fair lady as his mistress or his wife should be the better for it, and it is not right that her affection should be bestowed on him after his worth and reputation are gone. Surely you, too, would have cause to regret her love if you grew soft, for a woman quickly withdraws her love, and rightly so, and despises him who degenerates in any way when he has become lord of the realm. Now

ought your fame to be increased! Slip off the bridle and halter and come to the tournament with me, that no one may say that you are jealous."[34]

Gawain presents a conflict between marriage and preservation of a knight's fame (*pris*); if Yvain stays with Laudine, he will degenerate, lose value (*anpirier, valoir mains*). Gawain suggests that the woman herself will lose respect for her husband if he becomes worse (*devenir de li pire*) when he becomes lord of the realm. Accordingly, when Yvain asks for permission to leave, he says his action will increase her honor as well as his (2555). But when Yvain leaves, he forgets all about his wife. His madness is the sign of his realization that in avoiding the trap of which Gawain had warned him, he went too far in the other direction: he has sacrificed his love to seek adventure— the company of woman for that of man.[35]

34.   "Comant! seroiz vos or de çax,
        ce disoit mes sire Gauvains,
        qui por leur fames valent mains?
        Honiz soit de sainte Marie
        qui por anpirier se marie!
        Amander doit de bele dame
        qui l'a a amie ou a fame,
        que n'est puis droiz que ele l'aint
        que ses los et ses pris remaint.
        Certes, ancor seroiz iriez
        de s'amor, se vos anpiriez;
        que fame a tost s'enor reprise,
        ne n'a pas tort, s'ele despise
        celui qui devient de li pire
        el rëaume dom il est sire.
        Or primes doit vostre pris croistre.
        Ronpez le frain et le chevoistre,
        s'irons tornoier moi et vos,
        que l'en ne vos apiaut jalos."
                                                [2486–2504]
(I have slightly altered Comfort's translation of verses 2486–2490.) Similar advice is given by Gawain to the hero of another twelfth-century romance, *Fergus* (Marie-José Southworth, *Etude comparée de quatre romans médiévaux: "Jaufre," "Fergus," "Durmart," "Blancandin"* [Paris: Nizet, 1973], p. 75).

35. Yvain's madness on forgetting his wife makes a striking contrast with a similar episode from *Le couronnement de Louis*, a *chanson de geste* about William of Orange. The wedding ceremony between William and the daughter of King Guaifier (not the same person as Guiburc) is about to begin when William is called away to help King Louis. Many battles later, messengers come to remind him that the woman he left at the altar still loves him and is waiting his return. But the messengers are more troubled

In his earliest romance, *Erec and Enide*, Chrétien had played out the conflict between marriage and knightly reputation in the opposite direction.[36] Erec, rather than forgetting his wife, becomes so thoroughly immersed in the pleasures of married life that he forgets about his reputation. In both works, the second half of the story entails a working out of this conflict of allegiances. For Yvain, the resolution is accomplished by fighting in order to help women rather than fighting a tournament—a battle whose only purpose is to increase the reputation of the knight. Yvain is still very much concerned with his reputation, but it is now specifically that of one who helps women: "qui met sa poinne a conseillier / celes qui d'aïe ont mestier" (4811–4812).

There is a conflict, then, within Yvain between the call of love (identified with a woman) and the call of adventure (identified with men). This conflict is widely recognized by critics as the major theme of this poem, as it is of other romances, and has been characterized variously as a conflict between love and adventure, honor, prowess, loyalty, duty, or *chevalerie*.[37] Yvain, like Erec, Lancelot, and Tristan, must deal with a conflict of loyalty to his female lover, and loyalty to

---

by another matter—the city of Rome has been captured by Guy of Germany. William hurries to Rome to save the city, and there is no further mention in the poem of his waiting betrothed. For an epic hero like William, great military deeds are clearly of more importance than a lover. (*Le couronnement de Louis*, ed. E. Langlois [Société des anciens textes français, 27] [Paris: Didot, 1888], trans. David Hoggan, *The Crowning of Louis*, in *William, Count of Orange: Four Old French Epics*.)

36. *Erec et Enide*, ed. Mario Roques (Les classiques français du moyen âge, 80) (Paris: H. Champion, 1953); trans. W. W. Comfort in *Arthurian Romances*.

37. The best treatment of this theme is in Robert W. Hanning, "The Social Significance of Twelfth-Century Chivalric Romance," *Medievalia et Humanistica* 3 (1972): 3–29; his analysis is extended further in *The Individual in Twelfth-Century Romance* (New Haven: Yale University Press, 1977). Some of the other critics discussing this theme are: Reto Bezzola, *Le sens de l'aventure et de l'amour (Chrétien de Troyes)* (Paris: La Jeune Parque, 1947); Joan M. Ferrante, *The Conflict of Love and Honor: The Medieval Tristan Legend in France, Germany and Italy* (The Hague: Mouton, 1973); Alfred Adler, "*Militia et Amor* in the *Roman de Troie*," *Romanische Forschungen* 72 (1960): 14–29; Eugene Vance, "Signs of the City: Medieval Poetry as Detour," *New Literary History* 4 (1973): 557–74; Eugène Vinaver, *The Rise of Romance* (Oxford: Clarendon, 1971); Southworth; Emilie Kostoroski, "Quest in Query and the *Chastelaine de Vergi*," *Medievalia et Humanistica* 3 (1972): 179–98. For the view that there is *no* conflict between love and adventure in *Yvain*, see A. H. Diverres, "Chivalry and *fin'amor* in *Le Chevalier au lion*," in *Studies in Medieval Literature and Languages in Memory of Frederick Whitehead*, ed. W. Rothwell et al. (Manchester: Manchester University Press; New York: Barnes and Noble, 1973), pp. 91–116.

a male warrior ethic.[38] For Yvain and Erec the loyalty to men is defined by their male companions at the king's court; for Lancelot and Tristan the loyalty is feudal obligation to a specific male, King Arthur and King Mark, respectively. That Arthur and Mark are the husbands of the heroes' female lovers adds a further complication to a conflict that is essentially the same, though less intense, for Erec and Yvain. Adultery, a common theme in romance, is thus part of a larger scheme of conflict of allegiance.

Although many critics have discussed the conflict between love and adventure, very few have examined the ambivalent view of women that this conflict involves. Central as women are to the action of the romance, there is a distancing between the sexes not found in *chanson de geste*. In romances, women do not provide the supporting functions to men that pervade the *chansons de geste*; we see only traces of woman's nurturing and advisory roles. The word *norrir* is unused, and Laudine on no occasion provides the sustaining functions of Guiburc. Laudine's involvement with Yvain's fighting life is limited to the gift of a magic ring which is to protect him from harm; she provides none of the practical, strategic advice of Guiburc, Aalais, or Marsent. The only female character to carry on this advisory function is Lunete. Besides giving Yvain a ring that makes him invisible, she also gives him practical advice on how to win, and win back, Laudine; she is the crucial go-between for the two. Urraque plays a similar, but even more extensive, role in *Partonopeu de Blois*.[39] There are two important differences, however, between Lunete or Urraque and Guiburc or Aalais. Lunete is only the companion to the lady, Urraque is her sister; neither is the *dame* herself. The female nurturer/advisor is here an intermediary between the knight and his lady; she is not a woman acting in conjunction with her son or husband for the attainment of shared goals, as was Guiburc or Aalais. Furthermore, the advice and help that Lunete and Urraque give, even when they include aid in preparation for fighting, as in the case

38. In an earlier version of this chapter, I had described the basic conflict in *Yvain* as being between male desires (Gawain's urging Yvain to go on the tournament circuit) and female desires (Laudine's wanting Yvain to be back with her). I am grateful to both Alan Bernstein and Marcia Colish for pointing out to me that the conflict is not one of male versus female desires, but is rather an internal struggle within the male hero between allegiance to women and allegiance to men.

39. *Partonopeu de Blois: A French Romance of the Twelfth Century*, ed. Joseph Gildea, O.S.A., 2 vols. (Villanova, Pa.: Villanova University Press, 1967–70). This romance is judged to have been written in the 1180s, shortly after Chrétien's *Yvain*.

of Urraque, have as their primary aim the personal goal of the reunion of the estranged lovers rather than a social goal of defense of
Christendom, king, or family.

Reinforcing the contraction of women's role as a provider of aid
and support to men is the presentation of women as helpless beings
who must be protected or rescued by men. Laudine's gender renders
her incapable of defending her estates. Unlike Aalais, who could
choose to remain unmarried after the death of her husband, Laudine
must marry again immediately in order to have someone who can
defend the fountain. Lunete tells Laudine that all her knights are
not worth a chambermaid, and she needs someone to defend her
land when Arthur arrives at the fountain (1618–1622, 1630–1634).
Laudine's seneschal, in asking her knights to approve a new husband,
remarks on Laudine's inability, as a woman, to defend herself, and
her consequent need to marry (2083–2101). This theme of a woman
needing the protection of a man (and the desire to formalize that
need in the long-term protection of marriage) is reiterated throughout the rest of the story in the several instances of Yvain's services to
women in need.

The distancing between men and women is further emphasized by
Yvain's relationship with Gawain. Gawain, who in Arthurian romances serves as "the quintessential upholder of court values,"[40] "the
criterion against which others are to be measured,"[41] urges Yvain not
to let their male comradeship suffer because of his new relationship
with a woman, his marriage to Laudine. After pleading with Yvain
to slip off the bridle and halter and to go with him to the tournaments, he urges Yvain to take care to maintain their comradeship;
Gawain himself pledges to uphold his share: "But really, you must
come, for I shall be in your company. Have a care that our comradeship shall not fail through any fault of yours, fair companion; for
my part, you may count on me."[42] Gawain not only encourages
Yvain to leave his wife, but also is responsible for Yvain's prolonging

---

40. Hanning, *Individual*, p. 220.
41. W. T. H. Jackson, "The Nature of Romance," *Yale French Studies* 51 (1974): 20.
42.   "Certes, venir vos an estuet
                       que ja n'i avra autre essoine;
                       gardez que en vos ne remoingne,
                       biax conpainz, nostre conpaignie,
                       que en moi ne faura ele mie . . ."
                                      [2510–2514]

his separation from her. When the poet describes Yvain's distress on leaving Laudine, he adds:

> Yet I think he will overstay the term, for my lord Gawain will not allow him to part from him, as together they go to joust wherever tournaments are held. And as the year passes by my lord Yvain had such success that my lord Gawain strove to honour him, and caused him to delay so long that all the first year slipped by, and it came to the middle of August of the ensuing year . . . [43]

Gawain cannot absorb all the blame for Yvain's breach of promise; certainly Yvain blames only himself (2792–2797). But Gawain's influence continues through the rest of the story. Although the good deeds that Yvain performs can be seen as expiation for his sin against Laudine, he must also still prove himself to Gawain. It is to Gawain that Yvain's giant-slaying is to be reported, in order to build up the reputation of the Knight of the Lion (4263–4290). Yvain's final test, the one which must be accomplished without the help of the lion, is against Gawain; he must prove himself the equal of the man, the *compainz*, who first set him astray with the taunt that marriage would result in a loss of prowess. This last test results in a joyous reunion of the two men (6302–6307).

And what of Yvain's reunion with Laudine? It can hardly be described as joyous—on Laudine's part, that is—yet the poet assures us that the story has come to a good end, and the love between Yvain and Laudine is mutual (6793–6795). Are we to believe that this couple will actually live happily ever after? Yvain has promised to Laudine that he shall never do wrong by her again (6779). Yet, I do

43.   Et je cuit qu'il le passera,
             que departir ne le leira
             mes sire Gauvains d'avoec lui.
             Aus tornoiemanz vont andui
             par toz les leus ou l'en tornoie;
             et li anz passe tote voie,
             sel fist tot l'an mes sire Yvains
             si bien que mes sire Gauvains
             se penoit de lui enorer,
             et si le fist tant demorer
             que toz li anz fu trespassez
             et de tot l'autre encor assez,
             tant que a la mi aost vint . . .
             [2669–2681]

not believe that in this story the conflict has been resolved in its essence; the tragedies of Lancelot and Guinevere, Tristan and Isolt, perhaps carry the conflict through to its only final resolution. Joan Ferrante has stated that when the problem posed by love, that is, the conflict between the hero's love and his larger social commitment, "is squarely faced . . . , the ending must be tragic. There is no other solution."[44]

The story of Lancelot, as it culminates in the thirteenth-century prose romance *The Death of King Arthur*, is a good example of a narrative that emphasizes the tragic consequences of love.[45] Lancelot's dilemma is similar to Yvain's, but unresolvable: his love for Guinevere is fundamentally incompatible with his loyalty to Arthur, her husband. The story witnesses the failure of the three major romance values. (1) There is a failure of love: although Lancelot carries off Guinevere after her repudiation by Arthur, he sends her back once Arthur will accept her, as keeping her with him would have demonstrated his disloyalty to Arthur. This is reminiscent of Tristan and Isolt who, though happy in their "love grotto," feel obliged to return to the court of King Mark. Lancelot and Guinevere never see each other again, and both die in monasteries. (2) There is a failure of loyalty: not only does Lancelot commit treason by his love of the queen, he also ends up opposing Arthur in battle. (3) There is a failure of knightly friendship: although Lancelot and Gawain are the closest of friends, this friendship is ruptured because of Lancelot's defense of Guinevere, and Lancelot becomes the cause of Gawain's death.

Although the work is called "the death of King Arthur," the tragic figure is Lancelot, torn by his conflicting allegiances to Guinevere and Arthur. As in *Yvain*, the conflict between love and prowess, the company of women versus the companionship of men, is the dynamic force which sets the story in motion and dictates its development. This conflict is one experienced by men only. *Yvain*, and other

44. Joan Ferrante, "The Conflict of Lyric Conventions and Romance Form," in *In Pursuit of Perfection: Courtly Love in Medieval Literature*, ed. Joan M. Ferrante and George D. Economou (Port Washington, N.Y.: Kennikat Press, 1975), p. 173. Ferrante remarks on the unsatisfactory nature of the ending of *Yvain* (p. 157); see also L. T. Topsfield, *Chrétien de Troyes: A Study of the Arthurian Romances* (Cambridge: Cambridge University Press, 1981), pp. 205–6.

45. *La mort le roi Artu*, ed. Jean Frappier, 3rd ed. (Geneva: Droz, 1964); trans. James Cable, *The Death of King Arthur* (Baltimore: Penguin Books, 1971). The work dates from ca. 1230.

romances, are stories built around a central male figure, one of whose goals is the attainment of a woman through love. The love felt by the woman is unimportant; rather, the woman serves as the inspiration for the passion of the man.[46] *Erec and Enide* is one of the few cases in which any development of a female character is shown, yet even Enide's development is a negative one: she must learn not to assert herself so inappropriately as she did in telling Erec that his reputation was suffering (2540–2571). In this and other assertions, Enide shows her lack of confidence in Erec's knightly abilities, and it is this lack of confidence that is her major flaw (2996–2997, 3100–3112, 3553–3554). In the course of their joint adventures, Erec recovers his reputation and Enide learns to control herself in the better service of her husband.[47] "This is the story of Erec, the son of Lac," Chrétien announces at the opening of the story (19), and Erec remains the central figure in spite of Enide's prominence.[48] For although the journey can be understood as a joint trial of Erec and Enide, the test of Enide is closely linked with a second development for Erec: not only must he prove his military daring and skill, but he must also attain a more proper relationship with his wife. Tellingly, Erec's final adventure (the Joy of the Court episode) is against Mabonagrain, who has been forced by his lady (Enide's cousin) to stay shut up with her, killing any knight who entered the garden where they were (6023–6047).[49]

46. On *Yvain*, see Jackson, *Literature*, p. 109. The lack of any interest in Laudine's feelings is particularly marked. The centrality of the male hero in the Middle English metrical romances is emphasized by Nanette McNiff Roberts, "Making the Mold: The Roles of Women in the Middle English Metrical Romance, 1225–1500" (Ph.D. diss., New York University, 1976), p. 405.

47. For a summary of the scholarly controversy on the motivation of the journey of Erec and Enide, see Z. P. Zaddy, "Pourquoi Erec se decide-t-il à partir en voyage avec Enide?" *Cahiers de civilisation médiévale* 7 (1964): 179, 182. Zaddy's own position is that while Erec is indeed testing Enide's devotion to him, it is her love and devotion that concerns him, not her submission, and that, in any case, the main purpose of the journey is to prove his daring to Enide. I would argue that Enide's love and devotion are proved through her submission. For a guide to recent literature discussing the relationship between Erec and Enide, see Barbara Nelson Sargent-Baur, "Erec's Enide: 'sa fame ou s'amie'?" *Romance Philology* 33 (1980): 373, n. 1.

48. William Albert Nitze, "Erec's Treatment of Enide," *Romanic Review* 10 (1919): 27–28; Bezzola, *Sens*, p. 142. For a contrasting view, emphasizing a positive development in Enide, see Sally Mussetter, "The Education of Chrétien's Enide," *Romanic Review* 73 (1982): 147–66.

49. William Albert Nitze, "The Romance of Erec, Son of Lac," *Modern Philology* 11 (1914): 459–60; idem, "Erec's Treatment of Enide," pp. 26–27.

In the development of the male hero, attainment of a woman is a
key factor, and more attention is thus focused on women in romance
than in epic literature. As important as Guiburc and Aalais are in
their *chansons de geste*, they are secondary figures, and one can imagine the stories without them; those epics without notable women,
the *Song of Roland* among others, can develop major epic themes without the representation of women.[50] Yet the actions of the women who
do appear in epic literature are integrated with those of men by the
fact that women and men are working toward the same goals. In contrast, romances would not exist without women, yet the female characters are attendants to the central drama of the stories rather than
participants. In the romance, we do not see men and women working together toward a common goal but, rather, we see a goal pur-
sued by men alone, with woman as one object of that pursuit. The
hero must, through his own efforts, balance his conflicting allegiances to a martial life with men and an amorous life with women.

The goal of the romance hero may also be described as a quest of
an individual man for identity, an identity that includes love for a
woman as well as loyalty to men. "Identity" does not, in this context,
have the modern connotation of a consciousness of one's unique individual personality.[51] Yvain's search for identity is perhaps better described as a search for internal balance, "for the perfection and harmony of the self's desires."[52] In *chansons de geste* the characters do

50. At least one *chanson de geste* has an indispensable, central female character: *Aye
d'Avignon*, a poem, however, that is in many ways a combination of *chanson de geste*
and romance. See Ellen Rose Woods, *Aye d'Avignon: A Study of Genre and Society* (Geneva: Droz, 1978). Woods discusses at length the genre problem in this work and the
unusual role of Aye as part of this question of genre.

51. Caroline Walker Bynum, "Did the Twelfth Century Discover the Individual?" in
Jesus as Mother: Studies in the Spirituality of the High Middle Ages (Berkeley and Los
Angeles: University of California Press, 1982), pp. 82–109. Bynum's argument, stated
for religious texts of the twelfth century, can readily be adapted to secular literature.

52. Hanning, "Social Significance," p. 12. Hanning also describes the search as one
for "self-fulfillment" (ibid., p. 4). Colin Morris speaks of the "hero's search for his true
self" (*The Discovery of the Individual, 1050–1200* [New York: Harper Torchbooks, 1972],
p. 137). John Stevens speaks of the hero's need "to realize his potential" (*Medieval Romance: Themes and Approaches* [London: Hutchinson, 1973], p. 170). Hanning's book,
The Individual in Twelfth-Century Romance, is the key work on this topic. The classic
statement of the romance concern with the individual, introspection, and growth of
self-consciousness is found in Marc Bloch, *Feudal Society*, trans. L. A. Manyon (Chicago: University of Chicago Press, Phoenix Books, 1964; first published in English
in 1961), 1: 106. Another recent essay on the growth of "self-awareness" in twelfth-

not need to search for their identity; they are given a group identity of family and polity by their situation in a family (*parenté, lignage*) and by their close affiliation with their king or lord. In a romance, on the other hand, the hero must forge his own identity, through his own efforts. ("His" is the correct adjective here, the identity of the woman not being a concern of the romance.)[53] The immediate symbol of this process in *Yvain* is the loss and retrieval of the central character's name.[54] Yvain loses his name when he goes mad, giving himself the anonymous identification of the knight with the lion; he finally names himself again when he sustains himself solely by his own efforts in his fight against Gawain, thus proving himself the equal of the man who had first challenged his identity by accusing him of an excessive commitment to his wife. Yvain had to build his new reputation under a pseudonym, devoid of any reference to past associations or actions. The adventures and the testing undergone by the knight are lonely, individual affairs in comparison to the group battles of the epic. Such individual heroism in the *chanson de geste* bordered dangerously close on personal pride, *desmesure*, the tragic flaw of Raoul as well as Roland. In *chansons de geste* one should be a hero for the sake of one's family, and in turn, the reputation of one's family enhances that of the individual members.

In *Yvain*, family relationships are of a vestigial nature. Yvain's journey to the fountain begins in his desire to avenge the shame of his cousin Calogrenant, but Yvain's eagerness to get to the fountain before any other of Arthur's knights, and his subsequent preoccupation with obtaining proof of his kill, indicates that Yvain is more concerned with proving his own ability and, in particular, with refuting Kay's mockery of him (590–611). In any case, the motivation of

century culture is John F. Benton, "Conceptions of Self and Perceptions of Individuality," in *Renaissance and Renewal in the Twelfth Century*, ed. Robert L. Benson and Giles Constable (Cambridge: Harvard University Press, 1982), pp. 263–95.

53. It is curious that Hanning at times alternates between referring to "the hero" or "his identity" and "personhood" or "he or she" (*Individual*, pp. 1, 4, 15–16, 202). His discussion of the twelfth-century biography of Christina of Markyate would indicate that Hanning is not mechanically using gender-free language but, rather, that he sees a concern for individual fulfillment to be equally the concern of men and women in the twelfth century. I do not think the romances support this position, and the use of gender-free language, rather than clarifying, in this case confuses the issue.

54. For the importance of this technique, used by Chrétien in other stories as well, see Bezzola, *Sens*, p. 33.

kin vengeance is soon forgotten. The word *lignage* is used only once in the poem, when Laudine asks Lunete for a recommendation of Yvain's character. There is, on a much reduced scale, a kin-web between the characters, but it no longer unites people functionally. A man besieged by a giant is Gawain's brother-in-law, but since Gawain is away looking for the queen, he is not available to help this man in his time of need. Another failure of kin solidarity is portrayed in an inheritance dispute between the two daughters of the lord of Noire Espine. Just as the characters within the romance are not bound together by family, the stories themselves do not interrelate on this basis—romances are not susceptible to grouping in family cycles, as is common with *chansons de geste*.[55]

Laudine too is an isolated individual. Aalais shared Laudine's inability to defend herself, but she had other members of the family who could help her protect her land. Laudine's isolation forces her to go so far as to marry the man who killed her husband. She convinces herself that this is all right in an imagined discussion with Yvain; she argues that he meant, after all, no harm to *her*:

> "Canst thou deny that my lord was killed by thee?" "That," says he, "I cannot deny. Indeed, I fully admit it." "Tell me then, the reason of thy deed. Didst thou do it to injure me, prompted by hatred or by spite?" "May death not spare me now, if I did it to injure you." "In that case, thou hast done me no wrong, nor art thou guilty of aught toward him. For he would have killed thee, if he could. So it seems to me that I have decided well and righteously."[56]

---

55. Zumthor, *Histoire littéraire*, p. 251.
56.   "Viax tu donc, fet ele, noier
                        que par toi ne soit morz mes sire?
                        —Ce, fet il, ne puis je desdire,
                        einz l'otroi bien.—Di donc por coi
                        feïs le tu? Por mal de moi,
                        por haïne, ne por despit?
                        —Ja n'aie je de mort respit
                        s'onques por mal de vos le fis.
                        —Donc n'as tu rien vers moi mespris
                        ne vers lui n'eüs tu nul tort,
                        car s'il poïst, il t'eüst mort;
                        por ce, mien esciant, cuit gié
                        que j'ai bien et a droit jugié."
                                  [1762–1774]

The only vengeance enacted for the death of her husband is the ironic vengeance of Laudine's love for Yvain—a love, says Chrétien, which makes a more lasting wound than any made by a sword (1366–1381). Whereas Yvain's identity is shaped through his own efforts (his good deeds), Laudine's identity comes through her marriage, as evident in her naming: Chrétien delays naming Laudine until the moment of her marriage with Yvain (2153).[57] Similarly, Enide's name is only made known at the time of her marriage to Erec (1979).

Without the thematic and structural importance of the family, the woman, like the man, has lost her source of identity, which for her can now only be achieved through marriage. Even more significant, the woman has lost her former sphere of action, her role as provider of nourishment and advice. Instead of relying on the shelter and support of the family (including women), a man must now forge his own individual identity, a process in which his lover, wife, and/or mother do not participate actively. One of the most poignant examples of this opposition of the male and female spheres is in Chrétien's *Conte du Graal.*[58] Perceval's mother attempts to shelter her son from any knowledge of knights and war, which had been the cause of her husband's death. Perceval finally meets some knights and leaves home for Arthur's court, much against his mother's wishes. As he leaves, he looks back and sees his mother faint, perhaps dead, but he continues on. This maternal opposition to martial pursuits is a strong contrast to Guiburc sending Gui off to battle, or Aalais preparing Raoul for knighthood and Gautier for revenge.

The conflict Yvain experiences between love and adventure can also be described as a struggle between the personal, private world of love, in which woman is the object to be attained, and the public community of Arthur's court and Gawain's standards, in which Yvain's reputation as a knight is at stake. This opposition between personal and social concerns, between individual and community, between private and public realms, is a characteristic of romance

---

57. In the manuscript used by Roques for his edition, she is even there given only a family name, not a personal name—dame of Landuc, daughter of duke Laududez; in Foerster's edition she is named as Laudine.

58. *Der Percevalroman (Li Contes del Graal)*, ed. Alfons Hilka (Christian von Troyes sämtliche erhaltene Werke, ed. Wendelin Foerster, vol. 5) (Halle [Saale]: Max Niemeyer Verlag, 1932).

widely recognized and described by critics.[59] Epic heroes experience
a similar conflict between individual desires and social duties:

> *Chansons de geste*, at least the finest ones, place the individual up
> against society, the individual who, by a pride often synonymous
> with egoism, refuses to occupy the place that falls to him, to
> faithfully acquit himself of his responsibilities and his duties. This
> is the case with almost all the great epic heroes (with the excep-
> tion of William of Orange)—they place their own interest above
> that of the community.[60]

Yet there is a crucial difference in the individual/community or per-
sonal/social opposition in romance and epic. Although both are concerned with the same fundamental issue, epic stresses the importance
of the community over the individual, whereas romance focuses
on the individual himself. According to Georg Lukács, the epic is
concerned with the "destiny of a community" rather than of an individual;[61] according to Larry Crist, "Epic deals with insertion of persons (actors) in societal conflicts, not with personal conflicts with
society (this latter being part of the structural characterization of romance)."[62] In *chanson de geste*, the individualism of the hero is
"pride" or "egoism," and individualistic actions bring disaster. In romance, the hero faces the world alone and must build up his personal
identity through individual actions. Although fighting and military
skill are central to both genres, romance focuses on individual adventures, epic on collective action.[63] Both genres have a central male
hero who must accomplish a goal, but in *chanson de geste* the hero has
a concrete goal that is tied up with defense of his community. This

59. Most important is Erich Köhler, *L'aventure chevaleresque: Idéal et réalité dans le
roman courtois. Etudes sur la forme des plus anciens poèmes d'Arthur et du Graal*, trans.
E. Kaufholz (Paris: Gallimard, 1974; first published in German in 1956: *Ideal und
Wirklichkeit in der höfischen Epik*). See also Hanning, *Individual*, pp. 4, 21, 82; Z. P.
Zaddy, *Chrétien Studies: Problems of Form and Meaning in "Erec," "Yvain," "Cliges," and
the "Charrete"* (Glasgow: University of Glasgow Press, 1973), pp. 47–48; Calin, *Epic
Quest*, p. 239; R. Howard Bloch, *Literature and Law*, pp. 141–43, 233–34; idem, *Etymologies*, p. 226.
    60. Matarasso, p. 161.
    61. Georg Lukács, *The Theory of the Novel: A Historico-Philosophical Essay on the Forms
of Great Epic Literature*, trans. Anna Bostock (Cambridge: MIT Press, 1971; originally
published in German in 1920), p. 66.
    62. Larry Crist, "Deep Structures in the *chansons de geste*: Hypotheses for a Tax-
onomy," *Olifant* 3 (1975): 6.
    63. Zumthor, *Essai*, p. 346; R. Howard Bloch, *Literature and Law*, p. 143.

community may be based on family, nation, religion, or a combination of these, and the goal usually involves a military defense or extension of that community to another city or territory. This territory is a concrete entity that can either be won or lost. In romance, however, the hero's goal is internal rather than external, and it is abstract in comparison to the concrete epic goal of territory; it involves attainment of personal fulfillment or happiness, a personal goal which yet must be achieved without loss of public reputation or honor.[64] This is a goal that cannot simply be won once, for all time, like an epic battle, but rather must be a life-long struggle within the individual.

Two romances illustrate especially well the personal nature of romance as opposed to the social nature of epic: *Eneas*, generally considered one of the earliest romances (ca. 1165), and *Partonopeu de Blois* (written shortly after Chrétien's *Yvain*).[65] The special fascination of *Eneas* is that while staying, for the most part, close to Virgil's epic poem, of which it is a translation/adaptation, it manages to transform the Latin epic into a romance. The most drastic change the poet made to achieve this end was to add a 3,000-line section at the end of the poem in which Lavinia, the Italian woman whom Aeneas is to marry, but who is barely mentioned by Virgil, falls in love with Eneas, and he with her. Eneas's final battle with Turnus becomes as much a duel for the beloved Lavine as a battle for the homeland of Italy. Most critics judge this lengthy addition and the attempted transformation from epic to romance as awkward and unsuccessful.[66] The conversion to romance may not be entirely convincing, but the poet has done more than add a long love episode at the end; he has also deleted crucial social and religious elements of Virgil's poem. These deletions are more subtle than the 3,000-line Lavine addition

64. For another statement of the concrete nature of epic goals versus the abstract goals of romance, see R. Howard Bloch, *Literature and Law*, pp. 141, 189–91. Bloch puts this in the context of a common concern with violent conflict.

65. *Eneas, roman du XIIe siècle*, ed. J. J. Salverda de Grave (Classiques français du moyen âge, vols. 44, 62) (Paris: Champion, 1925–29); trans. John A. Yunck, *Eneas: A Twelfth-Century French Romance* (New York: Columbia University Press, 1974). For bibliography, see Yunck, and the study of the poem by Raymond J. Cormier, *One Heart One Mind: The Rebirth of Virgil's Hero in Medieval French Romance* (University, Miss.: Romance Monographs, 1973). Also useful is the section on the *Eneas* in Rosemarie Jones, *The Theme of Love in the "Romans d'Antiquité"* (London: Modern Humanities Research Association, 1972).

66. For example, Hanning, *Individual*, pp. 58–59.

but are nonetheless important to the poet's effort to transform epic into romance.

Easily noticed is the poet's minimization of the role of the gods. In the Old French version, Venus and Juno are virtually the only deities present, and even their role has been extremely limited. There is none of the complex interaction between divine and human action that is so central to Virgil's poem. In Virgil, the omnipresence of the gods highlights a basic human dilemma: how much are we ourselves responsible for our actions, and how much is the course of human events beyond our control? And if beyond our control, are events accidental, or do they conform to some higher purpose? This is an issue that is a common concern in epic literature, including twelfth-century *chansons de geste*. But the romance is in its essence a story of an individual on his own, a story on a personal level of a man's development as he comes to understand goals and attain them. Thus in the *Eneas*, as in all medieval romances, the gods—whether pagan or Christian—have no place. We witness only an individual's struggle to attain his personal goals.

This emphasis on the individual devoid of social, political, and religious context is apparent in another major adaptation of the *Eneas* poet: he has severely restricted the role of duty in the poem. The key adjective used by Virgil for his hero was *pius*, a word which in its Roman context referred to a man who understood his duty, who knew to put other considerations (country, gods, family) before his own. The major lesson of Virgil's *Aeneid* is that Aeneas must learn to put aside personal desires (Dido) and to accept and act on his duty, which is to make a new city for the Trojan people in Italy, the home of their ancestors. Virgil emphasized the theme of duty from the very beginning of his poem with many references, both short and extended, to Aeneas's mission. Virtually all of these references are omitted in the Old French version. Some brief mentions of his mission remain—the story would make little sense unless he had some reason for going to Italy—and he still leaves Dido when reminded of this mission, but many exhortations and symbolic events are left out or transformed. For example, in Virgil's poem, when Aeneas prepares to fight Turnus, his mother Venus has Vulcan make armor for him. On the armor, Vulcan puts the story of the destiny of Rome (the history of Rome, from the audience's point of view). The accounting of the story of Rome serves as an important reminder of the significance of the fighting to come, and Aeneas's picking up of the shield is a symbol of his acceptance of his duty:

Aeneas marvels at his mother's gift,
the scenes on Vulcan's shield; and he is glad
for all these images, though he does not
know what they mean. Upon his shoulder he
lifts up the fame and fate of his sons' sons.[67]

This crucial scene is altered fundamentally in the Old French. The armor is described at length, but the description focuses upon the excellence of its workmanship, and there is no mention of images of Roman history. And instead of Aeneas's shouldering of Roman destiny, we find: "Eneas took the arms his mother had sent him: it is no wonder if he loved them [referring to their beautiful workmanship]."[68]

The *Eneas* poet has thus eliminated the standard epic themes of the role of the gods, destiny, and duty, as well as added the new theme of Eneas's love for Lavine. Whereas Virgil's poem typifies the epic concern for the relationship between individual and community, between personal desires and larger forces (both societal and divine), this early French romance shifts away from communal concerns to personal motivations. Considering the poet's effort to stay, for the most part, within the constraints of Virgil's story, the differences between the *Aeneid* and *Eneas* provide an especially remarkable illumination of the individual, personal concerns of romance, and of how the introduction of woman as love-object (3,000 lines worth) is a part of larger romance goals.

In *Partonopeu de Blois* the division between personal desire and community obligations is underscored by the geographic separation of Mélior's realm of Chef d'Oirc and Partonopeu's home territory of

---

67.   Talia per clipeum Volcani, dona parentis,
           miratur rerumque ignarus imagine gaudet
           attollens umero famamque et fata nepotum
           [*Opera*, ed. R. A. B. Mynors (Oxford: Clar-
           endon, 1969), *Aeneidos* 8: 729–31]
English translation by Allen Mandelbaum (New York: Bantam, 1972), 8: 951–55.
68.   Eneas a les armes prises
           que sa mere li ot tramises,
           n'est mervoille s'il les ama.
           [4559–4561]

Blois and France. In Chef d'Oire, the magical powers of his *amie* Mélior insure that Partonopeu has all his individual, personal needs taken care of: he is given wonderful clothing, horses, food, and wine; he can hunt every day, and every night he enjoys the embraces of Mélior (1453–1466). But Mélior requires that he forego all social connections: he will have the companionship of no men, and no women besides her, for two-and-a-half years.[69] Partonopeu enjoys his charmed existence for a year, forgetting his country (*païs*), his family (*parens*), and his male friends (*amis*), and thinking only of his *amie* Mélior, and of his hunting dogs and birds.[70] But then he remembers Clovis, his king, and asks Mélior for leave to go back to France. Mélior allows him to leave, and while at home he does great deeds of prowess in battle, giving crucial aid to his king. But while in France, Partonopeu comes under the influence of family and country, mother and king, and he betrays Mélior by entering into a betrothal with the king's niece. Realizing his error, Partonopeu returns to Chef d'Oire and Mélior, and he is forgiven by her, but six months later he again asks leave to return to France. His second betrayal of Mélior, urged on him by mother, king, and bishop (thus adding the community of church to that of family and country), is not forgiven by Mélior, and Partonopeu's resulting madness, much like Yvain's, occurs about halfway through the poem. But for Partonopeu the reunion with Mélior is the only goal of the second half of the poem, and the dominance of this love goal and the hero's apparent lack of concern for the world of men contrast with the delicate balance Yvain must achieve between the worlds of prowess and love. Yet despite Partonopeu's abandonment of France for Mélior, some integration of the two realms is at-

69.   "Mais n'avrés home en compagnie
              Ne feme fors moi, vostre amie;
              Home ne feme n'i verrés,
              Ne a nului n'i parlerés
              Desci que li jors iert venus
              Que li conciles iert tenus."
                              [1467–1472]
70.   Ne li menbroit de son païs,
              De ses parens, de ses amis,
              Ne de rien nule ne pensoit
              Fors de s'amie qu'il amoit,
              De ses chiens et de ses oisiax,
              Car trop avoit de ses aviax.
                              [1895–1900]

tained by the end of the poem. Although Partonopeu does not make
a final return to France, the king of France (now Lohier) comes to the
tournament at Chef d'Oire, the winner of which will be selected by
Mélior and her advisers as her husband. (Lohier comes not to fight
on his own behalf but to avenge the loss of his cousin Partonopeu
[7255–7259].) In addition, the military prowess that Partonopeu first
exercised in the defense of France is now used in the tournament,
with the companionship and aid of his new friend Gaudin; this male
partnership contributes to the insertion of the world of men into
Mélior's domain, and it is important to Partonopeu's development
that he attains the friendship of a man as well as the love of a woman.
Yet despite the great prowess demonstrated by Partonopeu during
the tournament, the author puts a final emphasis on a personal rather
than social virtue by having Mélior insist that the winner of the tournament be he who, when disarmed, is the most beautiful (10313–
10320, 10385–10404). In this attribute, Partonopeu clearly surpasses
his opponent Margaris (10463–10466).[71] Thus in *Partonopeu de Blois*,
the personal realm of love triumphs over the social world of family,
church, and king.

The different concerns of epic and romance contribute to the different roles of women in the two genres. In medieval French epics,
the hero needs to promote or act within the concerns of his society,
and female characters, themselves devoted to the epic values of family
and community, can, through their nurture and advice, enhance (or
try to enhance) the hero's achievement of these social concerns. But
in romance, individual and community, private and public, are split,
and women are identified, through love, with the personal realm
only. The primary female character cannot help the hero resolve his
conflict between love and adventure because she, identified with love,
is herself part of the problem. Thus a woman also cannot be at the
center of romance; the central experience of the romance is a conflict
between personal and social concerns in which love for a woman is
part of the personal aspect of the inner development of the man.

In an essay written in the early years of this century, W. W. Comfort gave an apt characterization of women in *chanson de geste* and
romance. He noted that *chansons de geste* represent woman "as the
companion of man, as his spouse, as his constant helper and adviser

71. This emphasis on Partonopeu's beauty recalls the lengthy description early in
the poem of his physical beauty (551–582).

even in military and political matters," whereas romances show women as "a romantic object."[72] As "romantic object," the lady of the romance is a key figure in the development of the hero, and she has a structural prominence not found in the *chanson de geste*. The attainment of the woman is a difficult, sometimes impossible, task, through which the hero's identity is forged. The task is so difficult because allegiance to one's female love and allegiance to one's male world of battles and prowess are in opposition to each other. The tension provoked by this conflict is sometimes resolved through much effort (*Yvain, Partonopeu*), but sometimes is irresolvable and ends in tragedy (*Tristan, The Death of King Arthur*, and most thirteenth-century romances).[73] The romance image of woman is thus an ambivalent one, bounded by both desire and anxiety.[74] Beyond the ambivalence of the image of woman in both *chanson de geste* and romance is the duality of the contemporary development of these two images, Aalais contemporary with Laudine. The presentation of such different images itself expresses a deep ambivalence toward women, rendered both as forceful, if sometimes bothersome, helpmates, or as distressed and desirable objects. Many critics and historians have stressed a development from epic to romance and have assessed the change from epic to romance mentality,[75] but it makes equal, if not greater, sense to recognize the contemporary nature of the development of the two genres in France, and to see them as complementary rather than contradictory, and to understand them in the light of their common sociopolitical source: the French nobility of the second half of the twelfth century.[76] A main feature of the situation of

72. "Character Types," pp. 375–76.

73. Hanning, "Social Signficance," p. 24. The *Roman d'Eneas* is unusual in its easy amalgamation of love (Lavine) and prowess (defeat of Turnus, conquest of Italy).

74. Some recent critics stress a negative aspect to the portrayal of women in romance literature: on German romance see Andrée Kahn Blumstein, *Misogyny and Idealization in the Courtly Romance* (Bonn: Bouvier, 1977); on the Middle English metrical romances, see Shirley Marchalonis, "Above Rubies: Popular Views of Medieval Women," *Journal of Popular Culture* 14 (1980): 87–93.

75. Particularly influential are W. P. Ker, *Epic and Romance: Essays on Medieval Literature*, 2nd edition (New York: Dover Publications, 1957; first published 1908); and R. W. Southern, *The Making of the Middle Ages* (New Haven: Yale University Press, 1953), chap. 5: "From Epic to Romance."

76. Authors stressing the similar sociopolitical background of *chanson de geste* and romance include: Calin, *Revolt*, p. 128; Köhler, "Observations," p. 27; R. Howard Bloch, *Literature and Law*, pp. 8–10, 257–58, and passim.

the nobility in this period was the threat to its political and economic dominance. This threat came from two sources: the growing centralization of political authority in the hands of the Capetian monarchs with a corresponding diminution of the administrative, judicial, and military importance of the nobility, and growth of a money economy and a bourgeois class, both of which undermined the economic superiority of the nobility, many of whose members suffered a financial crisis because of lack of monetary revenues.[77] *Chanson de geste* and romance are two different imaginative responses to the same situation. The complementarity of the two genres is perhaps most readily seen in the example of attitudes toward the king. *Chansons de geste*, while set in a distant past, deal directly with the problematic relations between king and feudal lords, with many poems expressing a clear antipathy toward the encroachment of the king.[78] Even Count William, the loyal defender of King Louis, is in one poem subject to royal games of fief-giving similar to those undergone by Raoul de Cambrai.[79] In romances, the king is usually a benevolent figure, but Erich Köhler argues convincingly that romance, "in representing an ideal of feudal royalty, opposes itself more or less consciously against the [actual] French monarchy."[80] That is, both genres can be seen to express noble anxiety about the growth of royal power, but the *chanson de geste* expresses this directly as negative sentiment (or occasionally positive, as in the *Song of Roland*), whereas the romance expresses it in an escapist fashion, creating a fantasy of

77. In addition to the references cited in the previous note, the following works discuss the sociopolitical context of romance: Köhler, *L'aventure chevaleresque* (the basic work); Pierre Galais, "Littérature et mediatisation. Réflexions sur la genèse du genre romanesque," *Etudes littéraires* 4 (1971): 44–45; Southworth, p. 25; Woods, pp. 99–100; Vance, pp. 558–66. The Vance article is a particularly lucid study. Also important are Georges Duby, "Dans la France du Nord-Ouest. Au XIIe siècle: les 'jeunes' dans la société aristocratique," *Annales: Economies, sociétés, civilisations* 19 (1964): 835–46 (essay also in Georges Duby, *The Chivalrous Society*, trans. Cynthia Postan [Berkeley and Los Angeles: University of California Press, 1980], pp. 112–22); and idem, *Medieval Marriage: Two Models from Twelfth-Century France*, trans. Elborg Forster (Baltimore: Johns Hopkins University Press, 1978), esp. pp. 108–9.

78. For a different view, see Dominique Boutet, "Les chansons de geste et l'affermissement du pouvoir royal (1100–1250)," *Annales: Economies, sociétés, civilisations* 37 (1982): 3–14.

79. *Le charroi de Nîmes*, ed. Duncan McMillan (Paris: Klincksieck, 1972); trans. Glanville Price in *William, Count of Orange*.

80. Köhler, *L'aventure chevaleresque*, p. 44 and chap. 1.

an ideal world in which the king is sometimes generous and gentle, sometimes weak and indecisive.[81]

A similar explanation of *chanson de geste* and romance as complementary reactions to a similar situation can be applied to the portrayal of women. The two genres share a concern with the relationship between individual and community, between private and public worlds, a concern that makes sense in the context of the actual encroachment of royal and bourgeois power on the power and prestige of the feudal nobility. Just as *chansons de geste* give a realistic, if exaggerated, portrayal of noble/royal competition for power, these epics also provide a portrayal of women reflective of the actual political situation: women played a peripheral role, although individual women could on occasion be influential. What influence women had was exercised through family-level politics, in a fashion that must have been quite similar to that we see in characters like Guiburc and Aalais. In *chanson de geste*, the private (home) sphere of women is integrated with the public (battle) sphere of men through the common base structure of the family. In the world of these epics men do not experience a strict dichotomy between public and private, symbolized in *chanson de geste* by the fact that men belong both at home and in battle. Because of this integration, through the family, of public and private spheres, women, though still on the periphery of power, can sometimes be influential. When, in reality, the public sphere began to be more defined, and public functions previously exercised privately by the male nobility were taken over by royalty, the epics express directly the anxiety and anger of the nobility, while retaining as the valued world to be portrayed one in which the nobility itself is, or should be, in control. The epics are in this sense a kind of escape to an imagined world of a past time in which traditional values were maintained. This literary posture is possible through the mid-thirteenth century; after that the sociopolitical trend toward centralization is no longer new, and this direct mode of response has become irrelevant. The epic dies out as a form of literary expression, not to be renewed until the sixteenth century.

On the other hand, romance reacts to the difficult situation of the nobility by an escape to a fantasy world in which none of the con-

---

81. The classic analysis of the differing interpretations of reality in medieval epic and romance is Erich Auerbach, *Mimesis: The Representation of Reality in Western Literature*, trans. Willard Trask (Garden City, N.Y.: Doubleday, Anchor Books, 1957; first published in German in 1946), chaps. 5 and 6.

crete problems of reality exist. In romance the problems are made more abstract, or symbolic. Problems treated on a social level in epic are treated on a psychological level in romance. The historical context of the genre is the same, but the romance provides a different kind of mediation between audience and reality. Romance, rather than portraying realistically the separate but coordinate roles of men and women as does *chanson de geste*, focuses instead on the psychology of the individual male. This individual, portrayed outside of a meaningful social context, has the task of building up a personal identity, and in his quest woman is symbolically associated with this private, emotional goal.[82] But, as we have seen, attainment of this private goal is in conflict with the search for public renown in the world of men, and this conflict is at the center of romance. Women, though important to romance, cannot be at its center, as they act only in the private, personal realm—they cannot themselves experience a conflict between public and private. If they do experience conflict, it is within the personal realm only, and has to do with competing relationships to individual men: Laudine's conflict is between her dead husband and Yvain, Guinevere's is between Arthur and Lancelot. The woman's dilemma is thus different in kind from the central concern of the romance: the conflict within the male between personal and social involvements, the one involving commitment to a woman, the other to men. The public/private dichotomy is one that has continued to be important in Western history, and the romance portrayal of the conflictual nature of love has remained a key theme in Western literature, even after the decline of the genre of romance itself.[83]

What attitudes toward women are embedded in and expressed through these images? What attitudes can we infer on the part of the authors, and what attitudes toward women might such images en-

82. According to Ferrante, the union of man and woman in the romance is symbolic of "the harmony and integration of the man's being" (*Woman as Image*, p. 99).

83. The shift to a stricter separation of public and private is also central to the argument of Jo Ann McNamara and Suzanne Wemple, though they perceive a change at a much earlier period: "The Power of Women through the Family in Medieval Europe: 500-1100," *Feminist Studies* 1 (1973): 126–41. An excellent and suggestive anthropological study of the public/private split in a modern rural community in southern France is Rayna R. Reiter, "Men and Women in the South of France: Public and Private Domains," in *Toward an Anthropology of Women*, ed. Rayna Reiter (New York: Monthly Review Press, 1975), pp. 252–82.

gender or reinforce in a contemporary audience? The commonplace assertion that the image of women in romance literature indicates a great improvement in attitudes toward women or in their actual status may now be seen as woefully inadequate.[84] Not only do French epic and romance develop contemporaneously rather than in succession, but one cannot say, in any case, that the romance image is "better" than that found in epic. The images, different as they are, are joined by a common ambivalence toward women, as underscored by the contemporary development of the two genres. The genres also share a common center: the struggle of a man for success and fulfillment, and in both genres the portrayal of women is in service to that goal. In *chanson de geste*, a genre that embraced and idealized the past, women were accepted into the values and the world of action that were dominated by men. In romance, a genre that created a fantasy world, women were separated from the world of men and became a goal to be attained by men through love. "Better" and "worse" make no sense here: in both genres it is the concerns of men that are worked out, a working out that involves some kind of interaction with women. The attitude that unites the two genres is the attitude that women's importance rests in their relationship to men, whether as active helpmate or passive object.[85]

84. For a critique of this cliché based on evidence from Middle English metrical romances, see Roberts's dissertation, pp. 403–36.

85. On the general cultural tendency to define men in terms of status and role categories, and to define women in terms relational to men, see Sherry B. Ortner and Harriet Whitehead, eds., *Sexual Meanings: The Cultural Construction of Gender and Sexuality* (Cambridge: Cambridge University Press, 1981), Introduction by Ortner and Whitehead, pp. 8, 19. On the specific case of women in *chansons de geste*, see Combarieu du Gres, p. 351. Appearing after this book was in press is the important article by Joan M. Ferrante, "Male Fantasy and Female Reality in Courtly Literature," *Women's Studies* 11 (1984): 67–97.

·2·

Religious Image

The Iconography of the Virgin Mary

Beginning in the second half of the eleventh century, a new interest in the Virgin Mary became manifest in many areas of religious thought and practice. Evidence of this increased interest can be found in the growing numbers of treatises written about her and churches dedicated to her, in the creation of collections of stories of her miracles, and in liturgical innovations.[1] Although Mary had been the subject of theological debate and religious art since at least the fifth century, the surge of interest in her that began at this time and that continued to grow throughout the twelfth and thirteenth centuries brought her to a new position of prominence, one that has been sustained into the modern era. This prominence of a female religious figure has frequently been cited as evidence for a new rever-

1. The most useful general work on the cult of the Virgin in France is not readily accessible: Marie Louise Chatel, "Le culte de la Vierge en France du Ve au XIIe siècle" (Thèse Lettres, Paris, 1945). A recent popular work is well worth consulting: Marina Warner, *Alone of All Her Sex: The Myth and the Cult of the Virgin Mary* (New York: Knopf, 1976); a useful chronology of the cult of the Virgin is provided in an appendix. Still useful is Stephan Beissel, *Geschichte der Verehrung Marias in Deutschland während des Mittelalters. Ein Beitrag zur Religionwissenschaft und Kunstgeschichte* (Freiburg im Breisgau: Herder, 1909). Helpful for information about artistic monuments and devotional objects is Charles Rohault de Fleury, *La Sainte Vierge: Etudes archéologiques et iconographiques*, 2 vols. (Paris, 1878); an excellent survey of prayers to Mary is provided by Henri Barré, *Prières anciennes de l'occident à la mère du Sauveur: Des origines à saint Anselme* (Paris: P. Lethielleux, 1963). An article by E. Sabbé provides a useful analysis of the signs of increased interest in the Virgin Mary in the second half of the eleventh century: "Le culte marial et la genèse de la sculpture médiévale," *Revue belge d'archéologie et d'histoire de l'art* 20 (1951): 101–25.

ence for women in general, and has been linked with the contemporary development of secular love literature with its central role for women. We have seen in Chapter 1, however, that the female imagery in secular literature was varied, complex, and ambivalent rather than univocal. To understand religious ideology in its complexity, we must look beyond the simple fact of increased attention to the Virgin Mary to identify the particular aspects of her life and character that were emphasized and how this emphasis changed over time. Only when the images and their emotional contents have been clearly identified can the question of the relationship between these images and attitudes toward actual women be addressed.

Religious art is a convenient and useful focus for the analysis of changes in the image of Mary in the twelfth and early thirteenth centuries. Changes in iconography are readily visible when a traditional image is treated in a new way or when a new event is portrayed. Medieval art relied so strongly upon the repetition of traditional representations that we are assured of finding multiple representations of important images. Furthermore, when a change in a common image does occur, the fact that the weight of tradition has been overcome indicates a significant impetus to change. I have chosen to focus in particular on the monumental sculpture erected at church entrances, which was intended as a public expression of belief addressed to both laity and clergy, and which was designed to instruct and impress all who entered. The limitations on available space compelled the planners of portals to select images that embodied the most important doctrines of the church. Major changes in sculptural images thus reflect major developments in religious ideology.

The interpretation of artistic representations of the Virgin, however, is not without its difficulties. A primary difficulty is the non-verbal nature of art. Artistic images provide tangible testimony of changes in ideas; indeed, because of the concrete nature of artistic images, changes here may be more readily identifiable than in the subtleties of theological exposition. However, because medieval art is rarely accompanied by detailed literary explanation, it can be difficult to penetrate beneath the concreteness of the image to its deeper meaning, to the attitudes, concerns, and values contained in the images. Additionally, the point in time at which a change in artistic image occurs does not necessarily coincide with the corresponding moment of change in other areas of thought—for example, in theological opinion. In fact, it is possible that different artistic media will themselves respond at different rates to changes in the intellectual milieu. This problem will be discussed below with reference to manuscript illumination and sculpture.

A major innovation in the iconography of the Virgin Mary occurred in late twelfth-century architectural sculpture. Just as the literary depiction of female characters was an aspect of the broader differences in genre between epic and romance, this artistic innovation was part of a more general stylistic shift in the art of the twelfth century, the change from Romanesque to Gothic. The fundamental differences in these two styles must be a part of any explanation of the differences between the earlier and later images of the Virgin.

The stylistic shift of Romanesque to Gothic itself incorporates a geographical shift from southern to northern France. Until approximately 1140 there was little figure sculpture in the region of Paris.[2] From the time of Louis VII (1137–1180), however, the growing political self-consciousness of the monarchy was matched by the rapid growth of a new artistic style, centered in the Ile-de-France. The initial distinction between Romanesque and Gothic art was not chronological, but geographical, with a subsidiary center of artistic production becoming the major center.[3] Of course, a chronological differentiation ensued, as this new major center began to dominate the artistic production of France, and the previous Romanesque styles tended to die out. There was, however, a substantial period of stylistic and iconographic overlap, an overlap exactly contemporary with that of *chanson de geste* and romance.

The present analysis of the development of sculptural representations of the Virgin will begin with the Romanesque iconography, in which the seated Virgin and Child is the central image; it will then take up the early Gothic image—the Triumph of the Virgin—which shows Mary and the adult Christ seated next to each other in heaven. In elucidating this image, manuscript and sculptural sources and the theological context of its development will be discussed. I will also

---

2. Arthur Kingsley Porter, *Romanesque Sculpture of the Pilgrimage Roads*, 10 vols. (Boston: Marshall Jones, 1923), 1: 13. And likewise, Gothic sculpture was unsuccessful in the south of France (Willibald Sauerländer, *Gothic Sculpture in France 1140–1270*, trans. Janet Sondheimer [New York: Harry Abrams, 1972], p. 62).

3. Henri Focillon, *The Art of the West in the Middle Ages*, ed. Jean Bony, trans. Donald King, 2 vols. (London: Phaidon, 1963), 1: 133.

describe the transformation of the Triumph of the Virgin image into the Coronation of the Virgin in the first half of the thirteenth century, and the introduction of another new image of the Virgin, that of the standing Virgin and Child. Finally, the question of the possible connection between attitudes toward the Virgin and attitudes toward women will be taken up once the concrete analysis of the sculptural images has been concluded.

The Romanesque Image: The Virgin and Child

In Romanesque architectural sculpture, images of the Virgin were subordinated to the central theme of the vision of the Apocalypse. The main image of church portals was usually the figure of Christ, surrounded by attributes of his majesty or accompanied by images depicting his awesome power: Christ in Majesty (Christ surrounded by the four beasts of the Apocalypse, the symbols of the four Evangelists), the Ascension of Christ, the Pentecost, Christ in Limbo. It was common for these images to be accompanied by a lintel portraying several smaller scenes, concerned frequently with the childhood of Christ—the Infancy Cycle. This sequence might include: the Annunciation to Mary, the Visitation of Mary and Elizabeth, the Nativity of Christ, the Annunciation to the Shepherds, the Adoration of the Magi (sometimes with the waking of the Magi as well), the Presentation of Jesus in the Temple. Mary is present in these scenes, but the primary focus of the narrative is the life and destiny of Christ. The story of his birth is a complement to the portrayal of his heavenly end. Not infrequently, the Adoration of the Magi is isolated as the major subject of a tympanum or relief. At Vézelay (plate 1) the right portal of the west facade shows the Adoration of the Magi with the Annunciation, Visitation, Annunciation to the Shepherds, and the Nativity, while the central and left portals are devoted to the Pentecost, the mission of the Apostles, and Christ's appearances after his resurrection. The image of Mary and Child is a statement of the Incarnation of Christ, in the context of a larger sculptural cycle devoted to Christ.[4]

4. Although two of these scenes, the Annunciation and Visitation, occur before Christ's birth, and might be considered as scenes of the life of the Virgin rather than the life of Christ, the context makes it clear that it is the Incarnation of Christ that is being stressed. Narrative series of scenes from the life of the Virgin do not become

The images of the seated Virgin and Child and of the Adoration of the Magi were not Romanesque creations; they go back to early Christian times.[5] The twelfth century simply transferred these images to the tympana of church portals, giving them a large place in Romanesque iconographic programs. I know of only two major Romanesque sculptural representations of Mary other than as the Virgin and Child. One is an image of Mary received into heaven by Christ at La Charité-sur-Loire, and the other is a representation of the miracle of Theophilus at Souillac.[6] It is significant that the assumption scene at La Charité is accompanied by scenes from the Incarnation Cycle (the Annunciation, Visitation, Nativity, Annunciation to the Shepherds), as this emphasis indicates that it is as the mother of Christ that Mary's assumption is justified.[7] Other Romanesque images include the Virgin, but as a subsidiary figure; the crucifixion scene, for example, commonly includes Mary and John at the cross. Indeed, Mary is even a subsidiary figure in the Souillac miracle of Theophilus, where the devil is much more prominent in the scene than Mary.

The image of the Virgin and Child enthroned on the right portal of the west facade of Chartres (the Royal Portal) is the first major

---

popular until the thirteenth century, when, for example, scenes from her own life were added to the right portal of the west facade of Notre-Dame of Paris (Sauerländer, *Gothic Sculpture*, p. 405). An early exception is the right portal of the west facade of Chartres cathedral (mid twelfth century) where some scenes from the early life of the Virgin are portrayed on the relief friezes of the capitals (Adolf Katzenellenbogen, *The Sculptural Programs of Chartres Cathedral: Christ-Mary-Ecclesia* [New York: Norton, 1964; first published 1959], p. 25).

5. G. A. Wellen, *Theotokos. Eine ikonographische Abhandlung über das Gottesmutterbild in frühchristlichen Zeit* (Utrecht: Het Spectrum, 1961).

6. Marie-Louise Thérel, "Les portails de la Charité-sur-Loire. Etude iconographique," *Congrès archéologique de France, Nivernais*, CXXVe session (Paris, 1967), pp. 86–103; Meyer Schapiro, "The Sculptures of Souillac," in *Medieval Studies in Memory of A. Kingsley Porter* (Cambridge: Harvard University Press, 1939), 2: 359–87. Another early death and assumption scene is on the tympanum of Saint-Pierre-le-Puellier at Bourges (ca. 1160) (Philippe Verdier, *Le couronnement de la Vierge: Les origines et les premiers développements d'un thème iconographique*, Conférence Albert-le-Grand, 1972 [Montreal: Institut d'études médiévales; Paris: J. Vrin, 1980], p. 115 and pl. 8). Two capitals also show scenes of the Virgin's death: an image of the resurrection of the Virgin (Christ takes Mary's body from the tomb) on a capital from Clermont-Ferrand and an image of the death and assumption of the Virgin on capitals from the abbey of Fontevrault.

7. Thérel, "La Charité-sur-Loire," p. 101.

example in architectural sculpture of the Virgin and Child as an isolated unit rather than as part of an Adoration of the Magi scene (plate 2).[8] The Virgin and Child are seated on a throne, flanked by two angels. On the lintels below are scenes documenting the incarnation of Christ: the Annunciation, Visitation, Nativity, Annunciation to the Shepherds, and the Presentation in the Temple. The Seven Liberal Arts are portrayed in the archivolts. The Chartres image was very influential and was repeated on many subsequent facades, notably on the west facade of Notre-Dame in Paris. Although the isolation of the figures at Chartres was new, it was hardly more than a variation on the image from the Adoration of the Magi such as that at Vézelay. Other Adoration scenes with a centrally placed frontal image of the Virgin and Child are found at the monastery of Saint-Aubin d'Angers and at Bourges, the latter image subsequent to, and obviously influenced by, Chartres. Thus, although the Chartres portal portrayed the Virgin and Child in a new way, the traditional Romanesque meaning of the image as the representation of Christ's incarnation through his human mother was maintained. The context of the image confirms this meaning, since the three west portals together span the whole of Christ's life:. the Infancy cycle on the right, with the Ascension of Christ and Christ in Majesty in the left and central portals.[9]

The Royal Portal was decorated between about 1145 and 1155. Although its iconography was traditional, stylistically it was one of the first monuments of Gothic art. The portal's original contribution is the intellectual clarity of its sculptural statement. Chartres is an important link in the transition from Romanesque to Gothic, in that, through its stylistic lucidity, it effectively distills or crystallizes the meaning of the Romanesque iconography of the Virgin that it uses, and transmits this iconography to the newly developing Gothic art of northern France.[10] The image of the Virgin and Child enthroned continued to be produced in Gothic art through approximately the first quarter of the thirteenth century.

8. This type of image is often referred to as "the Virgin in Majesty," a term I find somewhat misleading, since the child-Christ is an essential part of the image.

9. Jan van der Meulen has recently argued that the northern portal represents the Creation of the World rather than the Ascension of Christ. In this interpretation the figure of Christ would represent the Deity, implying the Trinity: *The West Portals of Chartres Cathedral*, vol. 1: *The Iconology of the Creation* (Washington, D.C.: University Press of America, 1981).

10. Katzenellenbogen, pp. 7, 46.

One other type of sculptured image of the Virgin and Child was popular in twelfth-century France—free-standing wood sculptures of the Virgin and Child, sometimes referred to as *sedes sapientiae* or the Throne of Wisdom. The earliest known image of this type dates from about 946, and there is continued evidence of these statues through the eleventh century.[11] However, of the approximately one hundred statues surviving in France, only sixteen are from before 1100, and only one more from the first half of the twelfth century.[12] Despite the relative lateness of their production, their style, provenance, and iconography clearly mark them as Romanesque (plate 3).[13] Ilene Forsyth describes the format and intent of these statues:

> The statue presents an enthroned Mother and Child. It is normally small, somewhat under life-size, yet monumental in portraying the *sedes sapientiae*, the Throne of Wisdom, a complex concept wherein the Virgin is seen in majesty, hence called *Maiestas*, and is understood as both the Mother of God and the *cathedra* or seat of the Logos incarnate. As a mother, she supports her son in her lap, yet as the Mother of God she serves as a throne for the incarnation of Divine Wisdom. Thus Christ's humanity and divinity are equally apparent in the image so that it expresses clearly and simply the profound meaning of the Incarnation.[14]

The statues look much like idols and have a powerful effect on the viewer, combining both intimacy and a hieratic aloofness.[15]

These wooden statues are clearly related in style and meaning to the twelfth-century representations of the Virgin and Child that we

11. Ilene H. Forsyth, *The Throne of Wisdom: Wood Sculptures of the Madonna in Romanesque France* (Princeton: Princeton University Press, 1972), pp. 95–99. (The earliest statue does not survive and is known only from literary evidence.) Forsyth's book is an excellent study of these sculptures.

12. Ibid., pp. 9, 133, 134. Forsyth devotes most of her book to a detailed discussion of the early statues, giving only twenty pages to those from the twelfth century (in addition to the Register of Principle Examples, which gives a brief description of all the twelfth-century statues). Forsyth probably emphasizes the early period because of her desire to fill the gap in our knowledge of early medieval wood sculpture (ibid., p. 4). While minimizing the significance of the small number of early examples, she also admits that the statues may have become more popular in the second half of the twelfth century.

13. As can readily be seen from the map in Forsyth's book, the largest number of surviving statues come from the Auvergne. Forsyth, however, prefers to stress the fact that statues survive from all areas of France (pp. 18, 134).

14. Ibid., pp. 1–2.

15. Ibid., p. 2.

have seen in architectural sculpture. Mary and Christ are presented as a closely related unit. Christ is always seated in Mary's lap, creating a figural symbiosis; neither one could, or did, exist without the other. Mary is the larger of the two figures, and it is understandable that the statues were and are often referred to as statues of Mary. But the form of the statue tells us clearly why it is that Mary is important—it is because of her role as the mother of Christ. Mary is significant because she bore Christ, and in the Metropolitan statue (plate 3) the largeness of Mary's hands emphasizes the gesture with which Mary presents her son to the world. This aspect of Mary as bearer of Christ is emphasized rather than any kind of sentimental relationship between mother and child. Although he is smaller in size, Christ, not Mary, is the central focus of these statues. The Christ figure is usually portrayed frontally, at the center of the main axes of the composition. Mary, though larger, serves as the throne for her son.[16]

This same relationship between Mary and Christ, and the relative importance of the two, governs the Romanesque and early Gothic tympana that portray the Virgin and Child. The Chartres portal states the relationship particularly clearly, given the context of the west facade as a whole, with each tympanum centered on a frontally positioned figure of Christ, framed by figures turned toward him (angels in the lateral tympana, the symbols of Angel and Eagle in the center). In this setting, the image of the Virgin and Child, with its theological message of the Incarnation, emphasizes the human side of Christ's nature, a theme that was in accord with the twelfth-century desire to stress the humanity of Christ.[17]

The Gothic imagination departed from this portrayal of Mary. Although the Virgin and Child image continued to be produced into the thirteenth century, a new image of Mary was created in the last third of the twelfth century that soon surpassed the Virgin and Child in popularity, and continued, with important modifications, to be one of the most common themes of Gothic art through the fifteenth century. This is the image commonly referred to as the Triumph of the Virgin.

16. Ibid., p. 23.
17. See R. W. Southern, *The Making of the Middle Ages* (New Haven, Conn.: Yale University Press, 1953), pp. 236–37. The prominence of the Virgin and Child image in the early Christian centuries could also have been related to controversies about the human nature of Christ (Rohault de Fleury, 1: 311–12).

The Early Gothic Image: The Triumph of the Virgin

The Triumph of the Virgin shows Mary and the adult Christ seated next to each other on a throne; the Virgin wears a crown. Although a few representations of this scene can be found in England and Italy in the first half of the twelfth century, the theme did not prove to be popular in those countries.[18] In contrast, as soon as the image appeared in France on the central tympanum at Senlis, it was repeated quickly in the succeeding monuments of Gothic art, and it was through these French examples that the image was then popularized throughout Europe.[19]

18. For a discussion of the English examples (which actually show the coronation of the Virgin by Christ rather than the Triumph of the Virgin), see George Zarnecki, "The Coronation of the Virgin on a Capital from Reading Abbey," *Journal of the Warburg Institute* 13 (1950): 1–12. Zarnecki dates this capital at about 1130–1140. The other known early English example of the Coronation is a tympanum from Quenington Church, Gloucestershire, dated about 1150. The early Italian representation is a mosaic at S. Maria in Trastevere, in Rome, dated about 1140. Emile Mâle believes that Abbot Suger was the source of this Roman mosaic (*Rome et ses vieilles églises* [Paris: Flammarion, 1942], pp. 202–9); see also Philippe Verdier, "Suger a-t-il été en France le créateur du thème iconographique du couronnement de la Vierge?" *Gesta* 15 (1976): 227–36. Even if this Roman example is of native inspiration, the theme did not become popular in Italy until much later. (On the Italian development, see Verdier, *Couronnement*, pp. 153–62.)

19. The most thorough discussion of the development of the triumph/coronation of the Virgin is the *thèse* of Anne Marie Conan, "Essai sur l'iconographie du Couronnement de la Vierge en France pendant le moyen âge dans la sculpture, la peinture, et les miniatures" (Thèse Ecole du Louvre, Paris, 1948). I am grateful to the author for permission to consult her thesis. Verdier's *Couronnement* is a meticulous survey of the sources and early development of the image, with a discussion of many related images; the book is graced with an excellent selection of photographs, and the bibliography included in the footnotes is extensive. Other useful summaries are those by R. Jullian, "Evolution des thèmes iconographiques: Le Couronnement de la Vierge," in Paul Guth et al., *Le siècle de Saint Louis* (Paris: Librairie Hachette, 1970), pp. 153–60; Emile Mâle, *The Gothic Image: Religious Art in France of the Thirteenth Century*, trans. Dora Nussey (New York: Harper Torchbooks, 1958; first published in English in 1913), pp. 231–58. The most useful analysis of the individual sculptures is found in Sauerländer, *Gothic Sculpture*. The most thorough treatments of Senlis are found in three dissertations: Pia Wilhelm, "Die Marienkrönung am Westportal der Kathedrale von Senlis" (Diss., Hamburg, 1941); Franklin Monroe Ludden, "The Early Gothic Portals of Senlis and Mantes" (Ph.D. diss., Harvard, 1955); Diane Cynthia Brouillette, "The Early Gothic Sculpture of Senlis Cathedral" (Ph.D. diss., University of California, Berkeley, 1981). See also Willibald Sauerländer, "Die Marienkrönungsportale von

Dating from about 1170,[20] the Triumph of the Virgin portal at Senlis is the only decorated twelfth-century portal of the church (plate 4). In the lintels we see the scenes of the death and resurrection of the Virgin.[21] The death scene (on the left) has suffered some damage, but the main elements can be made out. The apostles are gathered around a bed, on which the Virgin lies dead. Two angels take away her soul, in the form of a small body, and they hold a crown above her head. In the resurrection scene, on the right, Mary rises from her tomb with the help of angels who push, tug, and lift her body. Another angel holds a crown above her head. In the scene of the Triumph itself, we see Christ and Mary, both crowned, seated next to each other on a throne. They turn slightly toward each other. Christ raises his right hand, presumably in a gesture of blessing; the Virgin holds an open book in her right hand and a scepter in her

Senlis und Mantes," *Wallraf-Richartz Jahrbuch* 20 (1958): 115–62; Marcel Aubert, *Monographie de la cathédrale de Senlis* (Senlis: E. Dufresne, 1910); Marcel Aubert, "Le portail occidental de la cathédrale de Senlis," *Revue de l'art chrétien* (1910): 157–72; Emile Mâle, "Le portail de Senlis et son influence," *La revue de l'art ancien et moderne* 29 (1911): 161–76.

20. Sauerländer, *Gothic Sculpture*, p. 408. Verdier dates the Senlis tympanum as 1160–1170 (*Couronnement*, p. 120), Brouillette as 1165–1170 (p. 126).

21. Authors do not always distinguish carefully between the scenes of the death, resurrection, and assumption of the Virgin. The death of the Virgin, an image imported from Byzantine art, shows the Virgin lying on a bed. She is usually surrounded by the Apostles, who have gathered around her. Commonly, Christ or an angel takes away her soul, usually in the form of a miniature body. In the resurrection scene, the Virgin is being lifted from her tomb, usually by angels. The assumption shows Mary actually on her way to heaven: the most common image shows her in a standing position in an aureole, held up by angels. The scene of the resurrection was usually chosen for the lintel scene to accompany the death and coronation, whereas in earlier manuscripts the assumption was more common. Perhaps this is because the horizontal emphasis of the resurrection iconography is more suited to a lintel than the vertical orientation of the assumption. One complication to this categorization is that in some manuscript representations of the death of the Virgin, the soul is seen leaving the body and on its way to heaven. This image often accompanies the liturgy for the feast of the assumption of the Virgin, and one can assume the artist meant to portray the assumption as well as the death of the Virgin. But theologically there is a distinction between her soul going to heaven (as might anyone's) and her body going to heaven, an honor reserved for Mary and Christ. The fact that the soul is portrayed as a small body enhances the confusion. Jean Fournée distinguishes between representations of the assumption of the soul of the Virgin and the assumption of her body ("Les orientations doctrinales de l'iconographie marial à la fin de l'époque romane," *Centre international d'études romanes* [1971], no. 1, pp. 23–56). The portrayal of the bodily assumption of Mary, unlike her death, was a creation of western iconography.

left.[22] They are enclosed in a prominent heart-shaped arcade and are flanked by angels. Another angel hovers in the point of the arcade, and above the angel is a descending dove, symbolizing the Holy Spirit. The archivolts are inhabited by the ancestors of Jesus and Mary, the Tree of Jesse. The outer archivolt contains patriarchs and prophets, who refer to the prophecies of the coming of the Messiah. The jamb statues relate primarily to Christ—they are Old and New Testament figures who refer to the sacrificial nature of Christ's death.[23]

The subject of the Senlis portal was soon repeated in other churches of northern France. Mantes and Laon, dating from the end of the twelfth or the beginning of the thirteenth century, show compositions similar to Senlis.[24] These compositions are all examples of the Triumph of the Virgin, and should not be confused with the Coronation of the Virgin, a later image that shows the Virgin in the process of being crowned. The Coronation scene shows something being done to the Virgin, and suggests a passivity that is absent from Senlis and these early offspring. The emphasis of these compositions is not on the crowning of Mary but on the elevation of the Virgin and her equal rank with Christ.[25] The power or authority of the Queen of Heaven is also stressed; the Virgin of Senlis holds a book, symbol of knowledge, and a scepter, symbol of authority. At Mantes and Laon the Virgin holds a scepter and Christ a book.[26] Mary and Christ are shown as the co-rulers of heaven. The joining of this scene with the lintel scenes of the death and resurrection of the Virgin justifies the emphasis on the Virgin in the name "Triumph of the Virgin."

The contrast between the new Gothic image of the Triumph of the Virgin and the essentially Romanesque image of the Virgin and Child is striking. Both twelfth-century images show Mary enthroned,

22. According to Wilhelm, the scepter, which has been broken off and is now barely recognizable, was visible in earlier photographs (p. 21, n. 24).

23. Sauerländer, *Gothic Sculpture*, p. 407. For a full description of all elements of the portal, see Wilhelm, pp. 15–23 and Brouillette, pp. 121–312.

24. Sauerländer dates the Mantes portal at about 1180 and Laon at 1195–1205 (*Gothic Sculpture*, pp. 408, 428).

25. Regula Suter-Raeber, "Die Marienkrönung im 12. und frühen 13. Jahrhundert," *Zeitschrift für schweizerische Archäologie und Kunstgeschichte* 23 (1963/64): 205–6. This is an excellent article, especially useful for its analysis of the sources of the image of the Triumph of the Virgin.

26. Brouillette, p. 450. The attributes at Mantes are now destroyed.

and they portray the Virgin with majesty, and even awe, although the latter quality is emphasized more in the Virgin and Child. The earlier image, however, shows the Virgin within the context of the Infancy cycle of Christ, and shows her as the mother of Christ—she is important because of her role as bearer of the Savior. In the Gothic image we see Mary in the context of a cycle devoted to her own death and resurrection. Christ, now the adult Christ, is seated next to Mary instead of on her lap. Mary now appears to have power in her own right rather than only as a direct function of her motherhood.[27] We see a shift in emphasis from Mary as earthly mother of the child-Christ to Mary as heavenly companion of the adult-Christ, with a new hieratic equivalence between Mary and Christ.

An appreciation of the originality of the image of the Triumph of the Virgin is enhanced by an understanding of the literary sources and artistic precursors of the image. A contrast with the history of the image of the Death and Assumption of the Virgin is particularly illuminating, since these images were to become, in sculpture, so closely linked to the scene of the Triumph.

Most of the major images of medieval art illustrate a specific literary passage, whether from the Old or New Testaments, the Apocrypha, saints' lives, or some other text. The Death and Assumption of the Virgin are among these. The story of Mary's death was told by Gregory of Tours (d. 594), and also in a letter mistakenly attributed to Jerome, but written no earlier than the seventh century. Both of these sources were often included in the liturgy for the feast of the Assumption.[28] The story was further popularized in the thirteenth century by Jacobus de Voragine and Vincent of Beauvais.[29]

The pictorial tradition for the scenes of the death, resurrection, and assumption of the Virgin includes a rich complement of manuscript illuminations going back to the ninth century. However, there are few examples of these scenes in architectural sculpture before the Senlis lintel: tympana at La Charité-sur-Loire and Saint-Pierre-le-

27. A Triumph of the Virgin tympanum is, however, sometimes accompanied by a tympanum on an adjacent portal devoted to the Adoration of the Magi, as is the case at Laon and Chartres. This might be a reminder that Mary's triumphal end is closely related to her role as the mother of Christ (Katzenellenbogen, p. 66).

28. Mâle, *Gothic Image*, pp. 246–47, 262.

29. Jacobus de Voragine, *The Golden Legend* (London: Longmans, 1941), "The Assumption of the Blessed Virgin Mary (August 15)," pp. 449–65; Vincent of Beauvais, *Speculum historiale*, 7. 75–78.

Puellier at Bourges, and two capitals, one at Clermont-Ferrand and one at Fontevrault (all dating from the twelfth century).[30] In addition to this lag between manuscript illumination and architectural sculpture, there seems to have been a related lag between popular practice and ecclesiastical acceptance, as evidenced by the contrast between the widespread celebration of the feast of the Assumption and the later theological delineation and acceptance of a doctrine of bodily assumption. Although liturgical evidence of the celebration of the feast in the West goes back to the seventh century,[31] the first discursive theological treatment of the subject dates from the early twelfth century. This treatise, a sermon falsely attributed to Augustine, was used in two sermons written before the middle of the twelfth century—one by Abelard and one by Nicolas of Clairvaux. From the second third of the century, exponents of the bodily assumption become more numerous.[32] The chronology for the development of the death and assumption of the Virgin would thus seem to be: (1) liturgical witnesses to belief in the assumption of the Virgin (with liturgical books often decorated with a picture of the assumption); (2) theological elaboration beginning in the early part of the twelfth century and accelerating at mid-century; (3) large-scale sculptural representations in France beginning with Senlis, about 1170. This appearance at Senlis, and its quick imitation elsewhere, would seem to indicate that the time was then ripe for general acceptance of the idea. It could, at this point, be placed on the single decorated entrance of a church, a public proclamation of belief.

In contrast to the rich literary, artistic, and liturgical tradition of the scenes of the death and assumption, the background of the Triumph of the Virgin is impoverished. The Triumph had no narrative source comparable to the accounts of Gregory of Tours and pseudo-Jerome. At best, the scene was indirectly related to a few passages

30. See above, n. 6. The iconography of the death and assumption, and its connection with the Coronation of the Virgin, is considered at length by Verdier, *Couronnement*, pp. 49–79, 113–52.
31. D. B. Capelle, "Le témoignage de la liturgie," *Bulletin de la société française d'études mariales* 2 (1949): 49–50.
32. H. Barré, "La croyance à l'Assomption corporelle en Occident de 750 à 1150," *Bulletin de la société française d'études mariales* 2 (1949): 63–123; M.-D. Chenu, "La croyance à l'Assomption en Occident de 1150 à 1250," ibid., 3 (1950): 13–32; R. J. Hesbert and E. Bertaud, eds., *L'Assomption de Notre-Dame: Textes choisis*, vol. 1: *Des origines au XVIe siècle* (Paris: Librairie Plon, 1952).

from the Psalms and the Song of Songs that were often included in the liturgy for the Assumption of the Virgin, and whose bridal and regal imagery was interpreted allegorically to refer to Mary.[33] The pictorial tradition for the Triumph is meager but complex. Reference to the crowning of the Virgin is sometimes found in manuscript illuminations of her death and assumption: sometimes a divine hand extends a crown downward toward the Virgin,[34] sometimes a divine hand actually crowns the personified soul of the Virgin as it is carried up to heaven by an angel,[35] and sometimes Mary is shown already crowned.[36] This type of scene is used at Senlis in the lintel, where we see a crown held above Mary's soul and above her resurrected body. But these types of coronations were clearly not the prototype for the Senlis Triumph of the Virgin.

Visual antecedents for the Triumph of the Virgin are found only outside the context of the death and resurrection, the context into which it has been placed at Senlis. The closest prototypes are illustrations from the Song of Songs.[37] Some of the twelfth-century images of Christ (the *Sponsus*) and his *Sponsa* that decorate its opening verse bear a striking resemblance to the Senlis Triumph.[38] These images,

33. Mâle, *Gothic Image*, pp. 254–55; Katzenellenbogen, p. 57; Wilhelm, pp. 4–11, 22–23. The most common verses used were Song of Songs 4: 8, Psalm 21: 3, Psalm 45: 9.
34. For example, the Benedictional of Saint Ethelwold (ca. 980), British Museum Add. ms. 49598, fol. 102v.
35. Gradual of Prum (tenth century), Paris, Bibl. nat. ms. lat. 9448, fol. 60v.
36. Missal from Saint-Martin of Tours (beginning of the twelfth century), Tours, Bibl. municipale, ms. 193.
37. Besides the images from illustrations of the Song of Songs, at least two manuscript illuminations show an actual crowning of Mary outside of the context of her death and assumption, but neither of these seem to be prototypes for the Senlis image. One is a scene from the *Hortus Deliciarum* (identified by Straub and Keller as "L'Eglise conduite par les apôtres devant le Christ": *Herrade de Landsberg, Hortus Deliciarum*, texte explicatif commencé par le chanoine A. Straub et achevé par le chanoine G. Keller [Strasbourg, 1899], p. 34). They note that the person who sketched this scene (the manuscript itself was destroyed by fire in 1870) unfortunately neglected to copy the messages on the scrolls held by Christ and by the woman. These perhaps would have given us a better idea of whether the image was intended to be Mary and/or the Church. Suter-Raeber considers this an image of Mary crowned (p. 198, n. 6) and includes this and an illumination from Pierpont Morgan ms. 44 (fol. 16; ca. 1170), the latter much closer to the image of the Triumph of the Virgin, as examples of the standing-type of the Coronation of the Virgin, a tradition she follows to the tympanum at Lausanne, where the Virgin is shown standing off to the side.
38. The similarity of these images to the Triumph of the Virgin has been discussed by Suter-Raeber, Verdier (*Couronnement*, pp. 83–103), Wilhelm (pp. 31–35, 70–78),

many of which cannot be precisely dated and so may in some cases postdate rather than antedate Senlis, show the bride and bridegroom either seated[39] or standing,[40] often embracing, with the bride sometimes crowned, sometimes not. One example that comes very close in appearance to the scene of the Triumph of the Virgin is shown in plate 5.

The identity of the bride figure is not always made explicit in these images. The tradition in the Christian commentaries on the Song of Songs was to interpret the bridegroom as Christ and the bride as the Church or the individual soul. Some passages might also be interpreted as referring to Mary, and we have seen lines from the Song of Songs used in the liturgy of Marian feasts, but it was not until the first half of the twelfth century that commentators interpreted the whole work, rather than just parts of it, to refer to Christ and Mary; the first two writers to do so were Rupert of Deutz (d. 1129) and Honorius Augustodunensis (d. ca. 1156).[41] The traditional interpretation was prevalent in the first half of the century, but the new, totally Marian interpretation became common in the second half. We should not expect that the manuscript illuminators of the Song of Songs necessarily meant the Bride to be either Mary or the Church; medieval exegesis certainly allowed a symbol to signify more than one thing. Some of the manuscripts do, however, identify the bride. In one illumination the figures are labeled "Sponsa-Ecclesia" and

---

and Brouillette (pp. 264–65). Katzenellenbogen discusses extensively the literary parallels between Mary and the Church and the liturgical application of the Song of Songs to Mary, but he misses a strong support for his case in not citing these manuscript images.

39. Bede's commentary on the Song of Songs, Cambridge, King's College ms. 19, fol. 21v (twelfth century), reproduced in Engelbert Kirschbaum, ed., *Lexikon der christlichen Ikonographie* (Rome: Herder, 1968-), 1:320; Bible, Paris, Bibl. nat. ms. lat. 116, fol. 12 (twelfth century).

40. Stuttgart, Landesbibliothek, cod. 55, fol. 180v (first third of the twelfth century), reproduced in Karl Löffler, *Schwäbische Buchmalerei* (Augsburg: B. Filser, 1928); Anselm of Canterbury, *Explanationes in Cantica*, Admont, ms. 37 (255), fol. 12 (twelfth century), in Paul Buberl, *Die illuminierten Handschriften in Steirmark*, pt. 1: *Die Stiftsbibliotheken zu Admont und Vorau* (Leipzig: Hiersemann, 1911); Paris, Bibl. nat. ms. lat. 16745, fol. 112v (twelfth century); Missal of Henricus Presbiter de Midel, in the collection of the Earl of Fürstenberg-Stammheim, 12 (1150–1160), reproduced in Suter-Raeber. The standing version is more frequent that the seated one (Verdier, *Couronnement*, p. 83).

41. Johannes Beumer, "Die marianische Deutung des Hohen Liedes in der Frühscholastik," *Zeitschrift für katholische Theologie* 76 (1954): 411–39.

"Christus-Sponsus"; in another, the identification of the bride as the
Church is made clear by the attribute she holds—a model of a
church; in another, Christ beckons to a figure of the Church standing on his right as he pushes away a figure of the Synagogue on his
left.[42] In a missal from Stammheim, an elaborate literary array accompanies the illustration. Although most of the texts quoted are from
the Song of Songs and other books of the Old Testament, two refer
directly to Mary: on the left, Moses holds out a scroll which reads,
"Honora patrem et matrem," and, a more explicit reference, the scroll
of the figure in the lower right reads: "Gloriosa semper Virgo Maria
celo ascendit."[43] A similar transitional image, but on a monumental
scale, is the mosaic in the apse of S. Maria in Trastevere in Rome
which dates from about 1140.[44] The two figures are seated on a
throne, and the bridegroom has his right arm around the shoulders
of his bride, a gesture emphasized by the text from the Song of Songs
on a scroll held up by the bride: "His left arm will be under my head
and his right arm will embrace me."[45] Such an embrace is perhaps
more appropriate to the Church than to Mary, yet two peripheral
texts refer directly to Mary: the prophets Isaiah and Ezekiel appear
on the lateral walls of the apse, the one holding a scroll which reads:
"Behold, a virgin will conceive and bear a son," and the other:
"Christ the lord is captured in our sins."[46]

The identification of Mary and the Church because of their similar
roles as virgin mothers was old, but the identification of the two in
the context of the love poem of the Song of Songs stresses a different

42. Stuttgart, Landesbibliothek, cod. 55, fol. 180v (first third of the twelfth century),
reproduced in Löffler; Paris, Bibl. nat. ms. lat. 16745, fol. 112v (twelfth century); Bible of
Saint Etienne Harding, Dijon, Bibl. mun. ms. 14, fol. 60 (1109), reproduced in Charles
Oursel, *Les miniatures cisterciennes à l'abbaye de Cîteaux au temps du second Abbé Saint
Etienne Harding (1109-vers 1134)* (Mâcon: Protat Frères, 1960). On the relationship to
the iconography of church and synagogue, see Verdier, *Couronnement*, pp. 33–39.

43. Missal of Henricus Presbiter de Midel (see above, n. 40). For a description of
this picture, see Suter-Raeber, p. 207.

44. See above, n. 18.

45. Song of Songs 8: 3. With his left hand Christ holds an open book on his knee. It
reads: "Veni electa me, ponam in te thronum meum," a quotation mixing the Song of
Songs and Psalm 45 and found in this form in the liturgy for the feast of the Assumption (Mâle, *Rome*, p. 201; Verdier, *Couronnement*, p. 41).

46. Is. 7: 14; Lamentations 4: 20. For a full description of this image, see Verdier,
Couronnement, pp. 40–47. Even with these quotations, it is possible to interpret the
bride figure as the Church rather than Mary. For a brief summary of the problem, see
Jullian, p. 154.

role—both are *sponsa Christi*, the bride of Christ.[47] The twelfth-century Marian commentaries on the Song of Songs self-consciously identified Mary both as mother and as bride of Christ. Some twelfth-century sermons commemorating the assumption of Mary also refer to Mary explicitly as both mother and bride. Abelard does so in a striking comparison between Eve and Adam, and Mary and Christ (the new Eve and new Adam):

> Let women consider carefully with how much glory the Lord elevated their inferior sex and how natural it must seem that both the heavenly and the earthly paradise pertain to them. Indeed, although in the latter [earthly paradise] the female sex was first created in body and soul, to the former [heavenly paradise] she is this day raised in soul as well as in body. Eve was created out of the Old Adam, but the New Adam, Redeemer of the Old, was produced out of Mary. The former [Eve] expelled him who was at once her husband and father [Adam] from paradise. Today, he who is at once her bridegroom and son [Christ], lifts the latter [Mary] to a more happy paradise.[48]

Nicolas of Clairvaux also refers to Christ as Mary's *sponsus* and *filius*. He describes Mary, after her arrival in heaven, as "reclining on the golden couch of divine majesty, resting in the arms of her *sponsus*, who is indeed her son."[49]

This evidence from sermons on the Assumption brings us back to the context of the events following the death of Mary. The similarity of the image of Christ and his bride illustrating the Song of Songs and the image of the Triumph of the Virgin has already indicated the plausibility of the one as source for the other. An even more direct link between the two images can be made by joining the artistic evidence to the liturgical evidence, that is, verses from the Song of

47. For discussion of the parallel between Mary and the Church see: H. Barré, "Marie et l'Eglise du vénérable Bède à saint Albert le Grand," *Bulletin de la société française d'études mariales* 9 (1951): 59–143; Hervé Coathalem, *Le parallelisme entre la sainte Vierge et l'Eglise dans la tradition latine jusqu'à la fin du XIIe siècle, Analecta Gregoriana,* vol. 74, Sectio B, no. 27 (Rome, 1954); J. Lécuyer, "Marie et l'Eglise comme Mère et Epouse du Christ," *Bulletin de la société française d'études mariales* 10 (1952): 23–41; Antonio Piolanti, "'Sicut Sponsa ornata monilibus suis': Maria come 'Sponsa Christi' nella teologia fino all'inizio del sec. XIII," *Euntes docete* 7 (1954): 299–311.

48. Sermon on the day of the Assumption of the Virgin, *Patrologiae cursus completus: Series latina*, ed. J.-P. Migne (Paris, 1841–64) 178: 542 [hereafter abbreviated *P.L.*].

49. *P.L.*, 144: 722.

Songs being applied to Mary in the liturgy of the feasts of her
Nativity and Assumption. The further evidence from sermons on the
assumption, in which verses from the Song of Songs are cited, and
the Virgin is, in her moment of Triumph, referred to as the bride as
well as the mother of Christ, provides another link between the Song
of Songs and the Triumph of the Virgin.

Having considered the iconography of the assumption of Mary
and of the bride and bridegroom of the Song of Songs, we are better
able to understand both the originality and the meaning of the image
of the Triumph of the Virgin as found at Senlis. This image combined two different traditions: the long tradition of the death and
assumption of the Virgin, an essentially narrative image, with the
newer tradition of the *sponsus* and *sponsa*, a more mystical, allegorical
image. If the sculptors had only been interested in describing the
narrative event of Mary's crowning in heaven, there were precedents
within the manuscript tradition of the death and assumption that
could have been used. Instead, the new image was placed above the
scenes of the death and resurrection, thus identifying it undeniably
as Mary, but the image of the triumph itself was taken from another
source, one that carries to Senlis the relationship of the two lovers
of the Song of Songs, the bridegroom and bride, Christ and the
Church. The symmetry of the two figures in the image at Senlis suggests not only the equality of lovers but also a mutuality of power, as
Christ and Mary are portrayed also as King and Queen. Nicolas of
Clairvaux, in his sermon on the Assumption, describes the glorious
reception of Mary by the angels and the extraordinary power which
she has:

> This is the sublime day, glittering with a very brilliant sun, in
> which the regal Virgin is carried up to the throne of God the
> Father, and is seated on the throne of the Trinity itself; she even
> invites the angels to look at her. A whole crowd of angels presses
> to see the *queen* sitting *on the right* of the Lord of virtues, *in
> clothing of gold*, always immaculate in body, *covered with a robe of
> many colors*, adorned with a multitude of virtues.

> O what great dignity, what special power to lean upon Him
> whom the angelic powers look upon only reverently.[50]

50. *P.L.*, 144: 717, 722. Nicolas's mention of Mary sitting on the throne of the Trinity confirms a resemblance of the image of the Triumph of the Virgin to representa-

The Triumph of the Virgin is thus a complex image that presents Mary as Queen and Bride, rather than as mother, that emphasizes the power and reciprocity possible in those relationships, and that elevates the Virgin as the subject of her own cycle of death, resurrection, and triumph rather than as a subsidiary subject in the story of Christ's birth, death, and resurrection.

The Coronation of the Virgin and the Standing Virgin and Child

Two developments dominated the sculptured image of the Virgin in the twelfth century. First of all, the image of the Adoration of the Magi, in which Mary had the subsidiary narrative role of displaying the Christ child, developed into the hieratic image of the Virgin and Child enthroned. The unit of Mary and Child was sometimes emphasized in Adoration of the Magi scenes, but it was not until mid-century at Chartres that the two were actually isolated, creating an image that was repeated in many late Romanesque and early Gothic monuments. This change put an increased emphasis on Mary, although it kept her clearly within the traditional context of mother and child. The second development, more innovative than the first, was the creation of a new sculptural cycle devoted to the death, resurrection, and triumph of the Virgin, an image forged from two separate manuscript traditions of illustrations of the death and assumption of the Virgin and of the *sponsus* and *sponsa* of the Song of Songs. This new cycle took Mary out of the old context of mother and child, to show instead two adults seated on the same throne, both equally the object of the viewer. Instead of mother and child, we see the bride and the bridegroom. As the bride and bridegroom are made equal in their love, the King and Queen of Heaven appear nearly equal in their power. Both sit upright in a frontal pose, turned slightly toward each other. The main differentiation between the two figures in the early versions of the image is that Mary receives the blessing of Christ.

But the powerful, triumphant, exultant image of the Virgin Mary as seen at Senlis barely survived the twelfth century. Although the versions of Mantes and Laon were closely modeled after Senlis, two

---

tions of the Trinity in manuscript illuminations (Verdier, *Couronnement*, pp. 20, 26). This resemblance might further enhance the assertion of Mary's dignity and power contained in the Triumph of the Virgin image.

early thirteenth-century versions at Chartres and Braine show slight but significant variations in the disposition of Mary and Christ. The Chartres sculpture (north facade, central portal) was done shortly after 1204 (plate 6).[51] The content of the portal varies little from the composition at Senlis. The death and resurrection are on the lintel; the Triumph of the Virgin is in the tympanum; angels, the Tree of Jesse, and Old Testament figures are in the archivolts; and the jamb figures are also similar to those at Senlis. There is, however, a concern, also evident at Laon, to relate the figures of Christ and Mary more closely. At Senlis the two main figures were separated by the compartmental design of the heart-shaped arch. This form was never imitated, and at Laon and Chartres the artist has related the figures by gesture as well as by a differently shaped arcade. At Laon, Mary turns her head further toward Christ and gestures to him with her left hand. At Chartres, a new relationship is stated. Although both figures are, as at Senlis, basically frontal but turned slightly toward each other, at Chartres the Virgin bends her head and lifts her arms toward Christ in gestures of humility and submission that would have been out of place in the heavy, regal solemnity of Senlis.[52] The gestures contrast with Senlis and Laon, where Mary held a book and a scepter, symbols of authority and power. A book and a scepter were also often used as the attributes of the Church. Perhaps the lack of such attributes at Chartres indicates a shift away from the allegorical implications of the Senlis image (Mary=Church=Bride of Christ) toward a more narrative account, with Mary understood more univocally as herself.[53]

The gesture of humility is more pronounced at the Premonstratensian church of Saint-Yved of Braine (ca. 1205–1215). As at Senlis, Mary is already crowned, but while Christ is still frontal, Mary is shown in profile, bending over, and her hands are joined in prayer as

51. Sauerländer, *Gothic Sculpture*, p. 430. The dating of the left and right north portals is uncertain, as is the existence of a coherent, unified meaning for the three portals together. See ibid., p. 435; and Katzenellenbogen, pp. 56–78.

52. Mâle, "Le portail de Senlis," p. 172; Katzenellenbogen, p. 98.

53. Katzenellenbogen deciphered an elaborate unified meaning of Chartres's three north portals, in which the understanding of Mary as the Church is central (pp. 56–78). This may be the case, but it is still interesting that Mary has been stripped of those symbols usually associated with the Church, and is now shown not in triumph but in humility, an attitude perhaps more easily applied to Mary herself than to Mary-as-Church.

she receives Christ's blessing. The early thirteenth-century Ingeborg Psalter contains a similar presentation of the image.[54]

The next important step in the development of the image occurred at Notre-Dame of Paris, about 1210–1220 (west facade, left portal; plate 7). The Paris portal is innovative in both style and iconographical content. The effect is a wholly unified portal, building up dramatically to the image of the Coronation of the Virgin. In the bottom third of the tympanum we see six Old Testament figures, three patriarchs or prophets and three kings. They flank an image of the Ark of the Covenant in the Tabernacle. In the middle third is a conflation of the scenes of the death and resurrection of Mary. Christ and the apostles, usually shown in the death scene, are here witnesses to the resurrection, as they watch two angels lift up Mary's body. Most important to us is the change in the scene of the Triumph of the Virgin. It is, in fact, no longer the scene of her triumph accomplished but the scene of the preceding coronation. An angel reaches down to place the crown on Mary's head, while Mary and Christ themselves are in positions similar to those in previous Triumph scenes. Christ is frontal, with his head turned slightly toward Mary as he blesses her. With his left hand, he extends a fleur-de-lis to Mary. The lower half of Mary's body is frontal, but the upper half turns and leans toward Christ and her hands are together in prayer, an attitude expressing "wonder, gratitude, and modesty."[55] A second version of Mary crowned by an angel was placed on the north transept of Notre-Dame in about 1260 (the Porte Rouge). Christ is shown in a similar stance, though his left hand rests on a book instead of extending a fleur-de-lis to Mary. Mary's posture has become more submissive; the bottom part of her body is no longer frontal, and she is in a somewhat awkward half-sitting, half-kneeling position.

One other change occurs by about 1230. At Strasbourg, double portals on the south transept illustrate the death, assumption, funeral, and coronation of the Virgin, but here we see her crowned by Christ himself.[56] The posture of the Virgin is akin to that at

54. Chantilly ms. 9, fol. 34 (ca. 1200); reproduced in Florens Deuchler, *Der Ingeborgpsalter* (Berlin: Walter de Gruyter & Co., 1967).

55. Mâle, *Gothic Image*, p. 256.

56. The lintel scenes of the funeral and assumption are nineteenth-century, but they replaced medieval versions of these same scenes. At Strasbourg Mary is shown seated to the left of Christ, which is odd, but not unique (Conan, pp. 50–51).

Chartres—the body quite straight with the head bent toward Christ and the hands raised with the palms facing outward. This type of coronation can also be found in a manuscript illumination which perhaps predates the Strasbourg image.[57]

With the introduction of the Coronation of the Virgin, the image of the Triumph of the Virgin almost completely disappeared, but its progeny—the Coronation of the Virgin—became one of the most common images of the thirteenth and fourteenth centuries, and its popularity would be difficult to exaggerate. The coronation scene was henceforth shown either with Christ or with one or more angels crowning Mary, although the version with Christ crowning predominates in architectural sculpture. Both versions were extremely popular in the small ivory carvings that proliferated in the fourteenth century. Mary continued to be shown with varying degrees of humility, but never again in the upright, triumphal manner of Senlis. Although humility had been one of Mary's characteristics in twelfth-century theological writings,[58] her humility is emphasized increasingly in the later Middle Ages and can be seen vividly in the art of the period.[59] Indeed, by the end of the fourteenth century the Coronation of the Virgin scene itself further emphasized Mary's humility by showing her on her knees before Christ (and later the Trinity) to receive her crown.[60]

Thus, although the images of the Triumph and Coronation of the Virgin are similar enough that many scholars term them both the "Coronation," the meaning shifted profoundly, though subtly, from one image to its successor. The visible changes are slight—a bend to Mary's head or torso and the addition of the act of crowning—and yet the emotional content of the earlier Triumph of the Virgin is closer to the dignity, majesty, and regality of the Chartrian Virgin and Child than it is to the humble and submissive thirteenth-century versions of the Coronation of the Virgin. Instead of the symmetry

57. Psalter, Paris, Bibl. nat. ms. lat. 238, fol. 62v (end twelfth century or beginning thirteenth century); reproduced in V. Leroquais, *Les psautiers manuscrits latins des bibliothèques publiques de France*, 3 vols. (Macon, 1940–41). Zarnecki mentions two other early manuscript examples of the Coronation of the Virgin (Zarnecki, p. 10).

58. Jaroslav Pelikan, *The Christian Tradition: A History of the Development of Doctrine*, vol. 3: *The Growth of Medieval Theology (600-1300)* (Chicago: University of Chicago Press, 1978), p. 164.

59. M. Warner, chapter 12.

60. Mâle, *Gothic Image*, p. 258, n. 1.

and equality of the two figures in the early versions of the Virgin's Triumph, we find that Christ's authority over Mary is portrayed, an authority particularly emphasized when Christ is shown crowning Mary. As Mary is shown more in profile while Christ remains frontal, as Mary bends further over while Christ remains erect, the image celebrates the Virgin's humility and modesty rather than her dignity and power. It is as though the marriage that began with the equality of the bride and bridegroom has seen the husband assume authority over his wife.

One other major development in the iconography of the Virgin occurred at the turn of the century, that of the trumeau statue which shows the Virgin standing with the Child in her arms.[61] As the Coronation of the Virgin developed from the Triumph of the Virgin, this new image can be considered the thirteenth-century remodeling of the image of the earlier seated Virgin and Child. Although the seated image of the Virgin and Child continued to appear in tympana and as free-standing statues into the thirteenth century, the standing trumeau type became dominant. Even the seated statues changed character in the thirteenth century. Instead of the hieratic, metaphysical majesty of the twelfth-century statues, in the thirteenth-century version Mary appears as a gentle mother.[62]

The standing figure dictates a different relationship between Mary and Christ. One of the first of these statues is found at Amiens as the trumeau to the Coronation portal (plate 8). Mary is still frontal, as in the *sedes sapientiae*, but she no longer is the seat for Christ. The infant-Christ of the Amiens trumeau is in striking contrast to the "miniature adult" Christ of the *sedes sapientiae*. At Amiens, Christ rests on Mary's arm, just above her left hip, rather than being placed in front of her on her lap. His feet rest in the cross fold of Mary's mantle, and the lines made draw one's vision in a circle, which encompasses the gentle relationship between the two figures. And Mary herself, in the fact that she is now standing rather than serving

61. Sauerländer mentions a trumeau Virgin at Moutiers-Saint-Jean which dated from the third quarter of the twelfth century, but it has not survived (*Gothic Sculpture*, p. 34). The earliest known image of a standing Virgin and Child occurs in an early version of the Tree of Jesse image in a twelfth-century Cistercian manuscript (Bibliothèque de Dijon ms. 129, fol. 4v; reproduced in Oursel, plate 40).

62. Forsyth, p. 4.

as the seat for Christ, has become the dominant figure in the image. In this early Amiens trumeau the Virgin retains much of the majesty of the Romanesque figures—she is frontal, crowned, and stands solidly on the serpent, whom she has conquered by giving birth to the Redemptor.[63] The transcendence of the Romanesque image is also retained in the other-worldly stare with which both Mary and Christ look out past the viewer.

By the second third of the thirteenth century, the image has undergone another change, which dominates for the rest of the thirteenth and fourteenth centuries. In the famous Vierge dorée of the south portal of Amiens, the basic composition is the same, but the tone has been dramatically altered (plate 9).[64] In the earlier Amiens statue, the gesture of Mary's right hand and the outward-directed stares of the figures made that statue a kind of presentation of the child, as were the Romanesque *sedes sapientiae* statues. In contrast, the Vierge dorée gestures with her right hand toward Christ. She tilts her head toward Christ and looks at him, full of a new tenderness. The child returns her glance. The sway of Mary's hip and the tilt of her head break the frontality of the figure. The Virgin has become less of a queen and more of a princess, less a God-bearer and more an earthly mother. Instead of a majestic *Regina Coeli*, we see "a lithe young girl who carries the Child with ease, and gazes at Him with a gracious smile. Angels hold her nimbus, and the high crown seems too heavy for the youthful head. She has become a woman and a mother."[65] This type of characterization of the Virgin, human and intimate rather than solemn, continues into the fourteenth century.

The development from seated to standing Virgin and Child is parallel to the change from the Triumph to the Coronation of the Virgin. Both developments show the increasing humanization of the character of the Virgin. This is clearly part of a change in style and expression that affected all Gothic sculpture. The hieratic nature of

63. For a detailed study of the artistic portrayal of the relationship between Eve and Mary, see Ernst Guldan, *Eva und Maria. Eine Antithese als Bildmotiv* (Graz-Köln: Böhlau, 1966).

64. Sauerländer dates the Vierge dorée between 1259 and 1269 (*Gothic Sculpture*, p. 495). Robert Suckale believes the statue could have been executed as early as 1240 (*Studien zu Stilbildung und Stilwandel der Madonnenstatuen der Ile-de-France zwischen 1230 und 1300* [Diss., Ludwig-Maximilians-Universität, Munich, 1971]).

65. Mâle, *Gothic Image*, p. 236. See also Sauerländer, *Gothic Sculpture*, p. 36; and J. de Mahuet, "Essai sur la part de l'Orient dans l'iconographie mariale de l'Occident," *Bulletin de la société française d'études mariales* 19 (1962): 157–59.

the twelfth-century images of the Virgin and Child and the Triumph of the Virgin would have been out of place in the thirteenth-century trend toward humanization and toward more narrative imagery.[66] Whereas the Romanesque image elicits from the observer worship and awe, the Gothic image invites participation, even identification. The other-worldly stare of the Romanesque figures as they look out beyond the viewer enforces the abstract nature of the image; the image of the seated Virgin and Child states the doctrine of the incarnation of Christ through a human mother, but tells us little about the relationship between son and mother. On the other hand, the later Gothic images are more concrete, with the figures engaged with each other through their eyes and through gestures. They explore particular aspects of the relationship between Christ and his mother: the Coronation of the Virgin through the metaphor of bridegroom and bride, the trumeaux figures through the metaphor of a mother and her child. The Gothic images, then, in keeping with their more humanized style, draw more directly on cultural stereotypes of roles and characteristics appropriate to women, with the Coronation of the Virgin stressing the qualities of humility and submission and the trumeaux stressing tender motherhood.

The Triumph of the Virgin was a transitional image in this development. The image retained, particularly in its earliest form at Senlis, the awesomeness and abstract quality of Romanesque sculpture, yet it put a new emphasis on the Virgin by placing her in the context of her own death, resurrection, and triumph rather than in the context of the incarnation of Christ. The image also explored the content of the relationship between Mary and Christ by drawing on the metaphor of the bride and bridegroom.

The transformation of the Triumph of the Virgin into the Coronation illustrates the multiple meanings that can be called forth from a symbol. Both images utilized the metaphor of Mary as the bride of Christ. But the human experience of marriage yields several different implications of the bride/bridegroom relationship.[67] The image of the bride is itself a fundamentally ambivalent image, expressing a

66. Sauerländer, *Gothic Sculpture*, p. 28. For the distinction between a devotional, or hieratic, image and a narrative image, see F. P. Pickering, *Literature and Art in the Middle Ages* (London: Macmillan, 1970), p. 227.

67. Daniel P. Maltz, "The Bride of Christ Is Filled with His Spirit," in *Women in Ritual and Symbolic Roles*, ed. Judith Hoch-Smith and Anita Spring (New York: Plenum Press, 1978), pp. 27–44.

transitory state between virgin and wife/mother. As we have seen above, the image of the bride can express the equality of two lovers (as in the Triumph of the Virgin), but it can also express the humility of the bride in her submission to her bridegroom (as in the Coronation of the Virgin). It is the quality of humility, along with the tender motherhood emphasized in the trumeaux figures, that continued to dominate the imagery of the Virgin through the rest of the Middle Ages and into the modern era.

The Virgin Mary and Attitudes toward Women

What, then, can the iconography of the Virgin Mary, and the changes in iconography from the twelfth to the thirteenth centuries, tell us about medieval attitudes toward women? What does the proliferation of female religious imagery mean about contemporary perceptions of women? In secular literature, we saw that we could not make a one-to-one correspondence between literary image and actual women, as literature is a purposeful reshaping of reality, but that by examining basic patterns of interaction between men and women in the stories, we could come to an understanding of the complexity of attitudes toward women. Yet the female characters portrayed in *chanson de geste* and romance, imaginary as they are, are at least clearly recognizable as humans, even if humans in an idealized or fantasized world. When dealing with the figure of the Virgin Mary, it is less clear whether or not the creator or the audience of the image was thinking of ordinary females at the same time as they were thinking of the mother of God.

Given the silence of the artistic image, literary texts can help illuminate the variety of relationships envisioned between the Virgin Mary and women. Some authors held up Mary as a model for female behavior. Abelard, for example, in his sermon on the Assumption of the Virgin, exhorted women to consider how their attainment of paradise is made natural because of their commonality with Mary.[68] Other twelfth-century sermons held up Mary's special virtues, in par-

---

68. See above, p. 59. For an excellent discussion of Abelard's extensive writings on women, see Mary Martin McLaughlin, "Peter Abelard and the Dignity of Women: Twelfth Century 'Feminism' in Theory and Practice," in *Pierre Abélard, Pierre le Vénérable: Les courants philosophiques, littéraires et artistiques en occident au milieu du XIIe siècle* (Colloques Internationaux du Centre National de la Recherche Scientifique, Abbaye de Cluny 2 au 9 juillet 1972) (Paris: C.N.R.S., 1975), pp. 287–334.

ticular, her virginity, her humility, and her obedience, as models for
women.[69] Other sources demonstrate an effort to consider the Virgin
Mary, unusual as she may have been, in the same category as ordinary
women. For example, in the twelfth-century formulation
of church doctrine on marriage, both canonists and theologians
struggled to fit the marriage of Mary and Joseph, unusual in that it
excluded sexual intercourse, into their definitions of marriage, drawn
up in order to facilitate the church's dealings with problematic mar-
riages of ordinary humans.[70]

But despite this recognized similarity between Mary and other
women, her singularity is more commonly emphasized, as is seen in
many of the prayers to the Virgin composed throughout the Middle
Ages. Not only is the phrase from Luke, "Blessed art thou among
women" (Luke 1: 28, 42), repeated in many prayers, but the phrase
is often elaborated upon to stress her uniqueness before all other
women. Bede, for example, substituted the preposition *prae* for the
in or *inter* of the Vulgate:

Et tu beata prae omnibus,
Virgo Maria, feminis . . .[71]

Another early prayer maintains the preposition *inter*, but explains
further: "Ecce beata tu inter mulieres, integra inter puerperas, domina
inter ancillas, regina inter sorores . . ."[72] Some of the later prayers are
more elaborate. One particularly fervent eleventh-century prayer includes the following:

Virgin Mary, holy and immaculate bearer of God, most kind,
most merciful and most holy, glorious mother of my Lord and
illustrious beyond the stars, *you who alone without equal have been
a woman pleasing to Christ*, you alone with your aid have brought
health to a desperate world, pure and most worthy virgin of virgins and most powerful of all women, *lord [domina] of all women*,
for whom nothing is difficult in the presence of God, come to
the aid of a miserable sinner, an unjust man, a person full of sin.[73]

69. Jean Longère, *Oeuvres oratoires de maîtres parisiens au XIIe siècle: Etude historique
et doctrinale* (Paris: Etudes Augustiniennes, 1975), 1: 222.

70. Penny S. Gold, "The Marriage of Mary and Joseph in the Medieval Ideology of
Marriage," in *Sexual Practices and the Medieval Church*, ed. James Brundage and Vern
Bullough (Buffalo: Prometheus Books, 1982), pp. 102–17.

71. Barré, *Prières*, p. 53 (for full reference to this work, see n. 1).

72. Ibid., p. 31; a seventh-century prayer.

73. Ibid., p. 140. I have underlined phrases that recall the passages from Luke.

A prayer by Anselm of Canterbury calls on the Virgin: "Oh woman extraordinarily singular and singularly extraordinary . . ."[74]

The terminology used to describe Mary in the prayers makes clear in what way Mary is "extraordinarily singular": she is the bearer of God, and she is at the same time mother and virgin. The opening lines of prayer after prayer call upon her as *mater/genetrix/virgo*:

Sancta Maria gloriosa Dei genetrix et semper virgo . . .
Sancta Maria genetrix mater Domini nostri Ihesu Christi
    semper virgo . . .
Virgo sancta mater Christi . . .
Gloriossima et precellentissima Dei genetrix Maria, virgo
    perpetua et immaculata . . . [75]

A phrase from a tenth-century prayer explicitly ties Mary's uniqueness to her simultaneous motherhood and virginity: "Holy Mary bearer of God, mother of my lord Jesus Christ, alone without example mother and virgin . . ."[76]

Thus Mary's singularity is found in the fact that although she has many of the virtues applicable to women—motherhood and virginity as well as humility and obedience—she has them to a much greater degree than other women, and in a combination (motherhood and virginity) impossible for anyone else. A letter of Pope Gregory VII to Matilda of Tuscany gives an example of this combination of likeness but uniqueness; Gregory is comparing Mary to human mothers:

May you believe beyond all doubt that, as she [Mary] is higher and better and more holy than all human mothers, so she is more gracious and tender towards every sinner who turns to her. Cease therefore, every sinful desire and, prostrate before her, pour out your tears from an humble and a contrite heart. You will find her, I surely promise you, more ready than any earthly mother and more lenient in her love for you.[77]

---

74. "O femina mirabiliter singularis et singulariter mirabilis . . ." (ibid, p. 304).

75. Ibid., passim.

76. "Sancta Maria Dei genetrix, mater domini mei Ihesu Christi, sola sine exemplo mater et uirgo . . ." (ibid., p. 121); see also Pelikan, p. 163.

77. *The Correspondence of Pope Gregory VII: Selected Letters from the Registrum*, trans. Ephraim Emerton (New York: Columbia University Press, 1932), p. 24; letter dated 16 February 1074. Peter Damian also described the singularity of the Virgin as an extreme case of the virtues of virginity and maternity (Jean Leclercq, "S. Pierre Damien et les femmes," *Studia Monastica* 15 [1973]: 45).

Mary is identified as a woman, with the qualities of a woman, and yet the comparison between Mary and other women emphasizes how far she surpasses other women. Marina Warner emphasizes this disparity of virtue in the title of her book, *Alone of All Her Sex*, a title derived from lines in an early Christian poem found in the liturgy.[78] Warner notes that the argument "that all women resemble the Virgin Mary . . . is very rare, for every facet of the Virgin had been systematically developed to diminish, not increase, her likeness to the female condition. Her freedom from sex, painful delivery, age, death, and all sin exalted her *ipso facto* above ordinary women . . ."[79] At least one twelfth-century writer based his argument for her Assumption on these differences between Mary and other women,[80] and it is the contrast between her perfection and the sinfulness of the petitioner that is the motivating core to many of the prayers to the Virgin.[81] The reason for these prayers, as for those to the other saints, is for Mary to pray for the petitioner, to intercede with Christ on the petitioner's behalf. It is because of their very unusual qualities that Mary and the other saints are in a position to pray for earthly sinners. In the context of prayer, then, Mary and the saints are not role models for ordinary humans but rather are exemplars of exceptional virtue who make us more aware of our own sins.[82] Finally, the developing interest in the twelfth century in such doctrines as the Assumption and the Immaculate Conception is an expression of a feeling of Mary's differences, not just from women but from all humans.[83]

As the above material illustrates, the perceived relationship be-

78. M. Warner, p. xvii.

79. Ibid., p. 153.

80. Pseudo-Augustine, *De assumptione beatae Mariae virginis*, chap. 4: "Maria ab Evae maledicto libera," *P.L.*, 40: 1144–45; translated in Hesbert, pp. 114–15.

81. For example, Barré, *Prières*, p. 189 (a late eleventh- or early twelfth-century French prayer).

82. Compare the similar conclusion reached by Ian Maclean, on the basis of sixteenth-century counter-Reformation texts: "Far from being the glory of her sex, [the Virgin Mary] is not of her sex in its malediction, tribulation, and imperfection. She incarnates certain moral virtues which are consistent with the social and religious rôle of women . . . , but does not ever become a model of behaviour, so remote is she from others of her sex" (*The Renaissance Notion of Woman: A Study in the Fortunes of Scholasticism and Medical Science in European Intellectual Life* [Cambridge: Cambridge University Press, 1980], p. 23).

83. On the controversy over the Immaculate Conception, which began in the late eleventh century and continued through the twelfth and thirteenth centuries, see the *Dictionnaire de théologie catholique* 7: 995-1042.

tween the Virgin and women in general was a complex one, ranging from Abelard's position of equivalence, to Gregory VII's expression of similar but better, to the position of essential difference that is a basic implication of the doctrine of the Immaculate Conception. Mary thus presented a rich ambivalence to her medieval interpreters, calling forth associations of comparison to what was seen as the particular virtues of women (virginity, motherhood, humility, obedience), as well as associations of contrast with the particular failings of the "weaker sex" (lust, disobedience).

The artistic images of the Virgin also express complexity, variety, ambivalence. We have described four major twelfth- and thirteenth-century images of Mary: the seated Virgin and Child (found in the context of the Infancy of Christ), the transitional Triumph of the Virgin (situated in the context of the Death and Assumption of the Virgin), the Coronation of the Virgin, and the trumeau figure of the standing Virgin and Child. We have seen that the Romanesque images were abstract statements, eliciting worship and awe, whereas the Gothic images were more narrative and humanized, inviting identification. The Romanesque images seem to say less about Mary as woman than do the later ones, which, in their more humanized style, incorporate cultural stereotypes of women. The mother and child of the Vierge dorée portrays an ideal of the human relationship between mother and child, and is in this sense fundamentally different from the seated mother and child of Chartres and the wooden statues. These latter expressed for the viewer the religious doctrine of the Incarnation, a doctrine that has little to do with the nature of women (whether humble, triumphant, or tender) or with the nature of actual mother-child relationships.

The core ambivalence thus carried by images of the Virgin Mary is that as hieratic icon (seated Virgin and Child), the image channeled those attitudes expressive of Mary's singularity among women (as the vehicle of the Incarnation of Christ); while as humanized, narrative image (Coronation of the Virgin, trumeaux statues), the image channeled those attitudes expressive of Mary's embodiment of female virtue (humility, submission, tender motherhood). The image of the Triumph of the Virgin was a transitional image that maintained some of the awesome, hieratic qualities of Romanesque images, while also participating in the Gothic introduction of emotion and humanity. The development from Romanesque to Gothic image

Pl. 1. Vézelay. Tympanum (west facade, right): Adoration of the Magi; Lintel: Annunciation, Visitation, Annunciation to the Shepherds, Nativity. Ca. 1120. © ARCH. PHOT/VAGA, New York/S.P.A.D.E.M.

Pl. 2. Chartres. Tympanum (west facade, right): Virgin and Child in Majesty; Lintel: Annunciation, Visitation, Nativity, Annunciation to the Shepherds, Presentation in the Temple. 1145–1155. © ARCH. PHOT/VAGA, New York/ S.P.A.D.E.M.

Pl. 3. Virgin and Child, French, school of Auvergne. Second half twelfth century. The Metropolitan Museum of Art, Gift of J. Pierpont Morgan, 1916. (16.32.194)

Pl. 4. Senlis. Tympanum (west facade, center): Triumph of the Virgin;
Lintel: Death and Resurrection of the Virgin. Ca. 1170. © ARCH. PHOT/
VAGA, New York/S.P.A.D.E.M.

Pl. 5. Bible, Paris, Bibl. nat. ms. lat. 116, fol. 12, Christ and *sponsa*. Twelfth
century. Phot. Bibl. nat. Paris. *(upper right)*

Pl. 6. Chartres. Tympanum (north transept, center): Triumph of the Virgin;
Lintel: Death and Resurrection of the Virgin. 1205–1210. © ARCH. PHOT/
VAGA, New York/S.P.A.D.E.M. *(lower right)*

CANTICORVM · Q̄ DIC

HE BRAICÆ · SIRASS

sc
me
ori
Qu
lio
ube
uir
gra
ung
opt
Ole
effu
nor

ruum· ideo adolescentule dilexerunt

Pl. 7. Paris, Notre Dame. Tympanum (west facade, left): Coronation of the Virgin; Lintel: Old Testament figures, the Resurrection of the Virgin. 1210–1220. © ARCH. PHOT/VAGA, New York/S.P.A.D.E.M.

Pl. 8. Amiens, west portal: Standing Virgin and Child. 1220–1230. © ARCH. PHOT/VAGA, New York/S.P.A.D.E.M. *(right)*

Pl. 9. Amiens, south portal: The Vierge dorée. Ca. 1250. © ARCH. PHOT/
VAGA, New York/S.P.A.D.E.M.

thus did not necessarily illustrate a fundamental shift in attitudes toward women; rather, as artistic purposes and styles changed, the expressions appropriate to each style also changed. The humble-submissive Virgin of the Coronation and the tender-mothering Virgin of the trumeaux are then explained by the fact that as the style of art became more humanized, the Virgin took on the characteristics predominantly assigned to earthly women.[84] Similarly in literature, the different purposes and styles of *chanson de geste* and romance allowed for the expression of differing views of women. Furthermore, the images of the Coronation of the Virgin and the standing Virgin and Child themselves compactly express a union of conflicting attitudes. The Coronation image carries forward the glorification of the Virgin first embodied in the Senlis tympanum devoted to her death, resurrection, and reign in heaven, while at the same time, with a bend of the head, adding the quality of humble submission. The trumeau statue of the Vierge dorée similarly carries forward the focus on the Virgin achieved in the earlier Amiens statue by her portrayal as standing rather than seated. But with a turn of the head and a sway to the hips, the later image adds in the quality of gentle tenderness.

The proliferation of images of the Virgin during the twelfth and thirteenth centuries demonstrates in itself neither a positive nor a negative attitude toward women. Rather, it shows a preoccupation with working out an understanding of the relationship between male and female. The artistic (and theological) images of the Virgin were, like the images of women in secular literature, the creations of men, and can be understood as fulfilling the emotional needs of the monks and clerics who created them.[85] The Virgin serves as a perfect embodiment of the conflicting ideals of virginity and motherhood that men believed in for women, and celibate men might feel particularly

84. Very suggestive along these lines is a recent study by Caroline Walker Bynum on maternal imagery in Cistercian writing, which, as she demonstrates, has little to do with attitudes toward actual mothers but rather applies cultural stereotypes of mothers to other situations, in particular, to the nurturing role of the abbot: "Jesus as Mother and Abbot as Mother: Some Themes in Twelfth-Century Cistercian Writing," in *Jesus as Mother: Studies in the Spirituality of the High Middle Ages* (Berkeley and Los Angeles: University of California Press, 1982), pp. 110–69.

85. Bynum, "Introduction," *Jesus as Mother*, p. 18. Bynum notes that whereas devotion to the Virgin Mary is found predominantly in writing by men, female writers tend to focus on aspects of Christ's humanity (the infant Jesus, the sacred heart, the wounds of Christ, etc.).

attached to such female imagery exactly because of their isolation from real women.[86] Rosemary Ruether has suggested that the Virgin was a kind of fantasy love object, compensating for the lack of real sexual relations, and that the creation of this ideal love object contributed to a negative attitude toward the real women who were forbidden objects of desire.[87]

As in literature, we see in art that the proliferation of female images is not in itself necessarily a sign of "improvement" in attitudes toward women; we must look past the quantity of images to the content of the images. Romanesque images, abundant as they are, say little directly about attitudes toward women. Gothic images of the Virgin, even more prolific and more focused on the Virgin Mary herself, serve to underline existent cultural norms of humility, submission, and tenderness, with the exception of the short-lived Triumph of the Virgin image that emphasized equality and power. Yet the later images also express an ambiguity similar to many of the prayers and theological writings discussed above: Mary shares the qualities of humility and tenderness with ordinary women, while she is also portrayed in a unique relationship with Christ as his bride, his mother, and his queen.

Complexity, variety, and ambivalence—these are what characterize female imagery, whether secular or religious, literary or artistic. The experience of women—real-life ladies and virgins—will be examined through the study of monastic movements and property relations. We will see that this experience was shaped according to a pattern

86. W. Lloyd Warner, *The Living and the Dead: A Study of the Symbolic Life of Americans* (New Haven: Yale University Press, 1959), pp. 379, 386–87. Although created according to the purposes of men, these images can speak also to women, but the relationship of women to female images created by men can be a problematic one. Rather than providing a positive role model for women, the medieval cult of the Virgin, as expressed in Mary's theological isolation from human femaleness, emphasized the weakness, inferiority, and subordination of actual women (Eleanor C. McLaughlin, "Equality of Souls, Inequality of Sexes: Women in Medieval Theology," in *Religion and Sexism: Images of Woman in the Jewish and Christian Traditions*, ed. Rosemary Radford Ruether [New York: Simon and Schuster, 1974], p. 246). For a sensitive treatment of this issue in the context of Jewish symbolism, see Riv-Ellen Prell-Foldes, "Coming of Age in Kelton: The Constraints of Gender Symbolism in Jewish Ritual," in *Women in Ritual and Symbolic Roles*, pp. 75–99.

87. Rosemary Radford Ruether, *Mary—the Feminine Face of the Church* (Philadelphia: Westminster Press, 1977), p. 72.

similar to that found in secular and religious images. Varying from one monastery to another, from region to region, and over time, this experience was indeed diverse. But an undercurrent of ambivalence runs throughout and can be traced in the many ambiguities and contradictions of women's lives as nuns and as property holders.

·3·

Religious Life
The Monastic Experience

The Christian monastic experience for women was characterized by a basic contradiction entirely absent from the male experience. On the one hand, monastic life offered one of the few nondomestic outlets for women's capabilities and talents and provided an opportunity for both education and a certain degree of autonomy. The availability of this option is often held up by Christian apologists, and by some feminists as well, as evidence of the benefit to women of the spread of Christianity in the Middle Ages. On the other hand, female religious in the Christian tradition rarely, if ever, were able to achieve full autonomy or independence from male scrutiny, and women's ability to enter and enjoy the religious life was circumscribed by an ideology of feminine weakness that implied that female religious were unable to manage their own affairs. The dependence of female monastics on men could take several forms. All nuns were (and still are) reliant on priests, necessarily male, for performance of the sacraments. Thus all nunneries had to make arrangements for the regular service of one or more priests.[1] Material as well as spiritual service was often considered to be necessarily done by men, as some kinds of physical labor were seen in the Middle Ages, as today, as inappropriate to women. Men, either clerical or lay, frequently handled the business matters of nuns, particularly those requiring travel, as en-

---

1. I use the term nunnery only for the sake of convenience; it is not a medieval term. The term *monasterium* could refer to either a male or female community, as could the term *conventus*.

closure was thought more necessary for nuns than for monks.[2] The assumed and acknowledged dependence of nuns on these three areas of service—spiritual service, the service of physical labor, and business management—opened the way for male supervision as well. This can be seen in the case of spiritual service when an abbot, from whose monastery sacramental service was provided, was made the spiritual head of a female community, superior in authority to the abbess or prioress. It can be seen also on the material side when a master or procurator was appointed, often by an external male authority, to supervise the temporal concerns of a nunnery. The complex of temporal and spiritual needs is often referred to as the *cura monialium*, the care of nuns, a term that points out the gender imbalance in medieval monasticism, with nuns seen as in need of the care of men but with monks capable of a life independent of women.

Thus, a basic structure delimiting the female monastic experience in the Middle Ages was this contradiction between the opportunity for women to become nuns and to gain the educational, spiritual, and administrative experience potentially available in such a setting, and the limitations on that opportunity imposed by an ideology proclaiming feminine weakness and by practice that made nuns dependent on men.

Yet within this basic structural contradiction, there was room for much variation in the balance between opportunity and limitation, and certain chronological patterns can be discerned. That is, there were periods when opportunities for women to enter the monastic life were particularly abundant, and others when opportunities were closed off. There were times when ideological and institutional opposition to female religious was particularly strong, and others when opposition was low. The first half of the twelfth century, a period of intense monastic revival and experimentation, was also a time of resurgence in women's participation in monastic life in France, when opportunity was open and opposition minimal. This chapter will ex-

---

2. For the connection between enclosure and dependence on men, see Louis J. Lekai, *The Cistercians: Ideals and Reality* (Kent, Ohio: Kent State University Press, 1977), pp. 350–51. A useful discussion of enclosure and its effects can be found in Jane Tibbetts Schulenburg, "Strict Active Enclosure and Its Effects on the Female Monastic Experience (500-1100)," in *Distant Echoes: Medieval Religious Women*, vol. 1, ed. John A. Nichols and Lillian Thomas Shank (Kalamazoo, Mich.: Cistercian Publications, 1984), pp. 51–86.

plore the nature and parameters of the female monastic experience by (1) a brief review of the history of female monasticism before the twelfth century; (2) a description of the response of several of the important reforming orders to the religious enthusiasm of women; and (3) a detailed examination of the one reforming order that made the needs of women its central concern, the order of Fontevrault. Attention will be paid throughout to the dialectic of opportunity and opposition, to the various arrangements with men made by nunneries for the fulfillment of their spiritual and material needs, and to an assessment of the relative success of these arrangements in satisfying the demand of medieval women for a variety of religious experience.

Historical Survey

The first nunneries in France were founded in the sixth century, shortly after the conversion of the Franks, and the number of establishments increased through the sixth and seventh centuries.[3] The canonization of many of the women involved in founding these nunneries has left this period with France's largest number of female saints. A similar blossoming of nunneries is evident in England after the conversion of the Anglo-Saxons at the end of the sixth century. Monastic foundations became the main centers of learning, and women, as well as men, were educated.

The next frontier of Christianity was again on the continent, with the conversion of the Saxons at the end of the eighth century. Again, conversion was followed by the establishment of many nunneries. These nunneries, among them Gandersheim and Essen, were of great sociopolitical as well as intellectual influence. As in France, the women who ran the nunneries were of prominent families and their entrance into monastic life effectively broadened rather than limited their secular influence by giving them control over the material assets of the nunnery.

In this early period of Christian monasticism, cooperation between monks and nuns seems to have been the norm. The institution of the so-called double monastery was particularly successful in En-

3. Lina Eckenstein, *Woman under Monasticism* (Cambridge: Cambridge University Press, 1896), pp. 45–79; Suzanne Fonay Wemple, *Women in Frankish Society: Marriage and the Cloister, 500 to 900* (Philadelphia: University of Pennsylvania Press, 1981), pp. 154–65.

gland. In this kind of community, nuns lived in close association with a group of monks, both sexes in fact belonging to one community, under the rule of an abbess. Sexually mixed communities existed in France as well, but with a less consistent organizational structure than in England. In particular, although many such communities on the continent were governed by an abbess, in others an abbot was in control.[4] The question of the purposes and success of double monasteries will be considered below, in the context of their twelfth-century revival. They are important here as evidence of the ready acceptance of female religious in the early period.

The tenth and eleventh centuries witnessed a drastic decline in opportunities for religious women in all countries, particularly France and England. This did not correspond with a general monastic decline, since it was in these centuries that Cluny was established and built up its network of monasteries. Yet only one Cluniac monastery was established for women before the beginning of the twelfth century, at Marcigny, founded at the suggestion of Hugh, abbot of Cluny, in order to provide a retreat for women whose husbands had become monks of Cluny.[5]

Few new nunneries were founded in these centuries. In England, many of the great nunneries of the eighth and ninth centuries were taken over by men, among them Whitby, Ely, and Wimbourne. The final blow in England came with the Norman conquest. The establishment of nunneries decreased further, and those that were established were set up as priories, subject to the rule of an abbot, whereas the Anglo-Saxon foundations had been abbeys, with the abbess in complete control.[6]

Various causes may have contributed to this decline. Some of these factors are equally applicable to male communities, and so, while helping to explain difficulties faced by nunneries, do not tell us why female communities were less successful than male in overcoming

4. Mary Bateson, "The Origin and Early History of Double Monasteries," *Transactions of the Royal Historical Society*, n.s. 13 (1899): 164; John Godfrey, "The Double Monastery in Early English History," *Ampleforth Journal* 79 (1974): 22. Wemple discusses in detail the variety of arrangements in the Frankish communities (pp. 160–74).

5. R. W. Southern, *Western Society and the Church in the Middle Ages* (Baltimore: Penguin Books, 1970), pp. 310–11. On Marcigny, see Noreen Hunt, *Cluny under Saint Hugh 1049–1109* (London: Edward Arnold, 1967), pp. 186–94. For Carolingian legislation restricting the range of religious opportunities open to women, see Wemple, pp. 165–74.

6. Eckenstein, pp. 201–5.

these difficulties. Such factors include the invasions of the ninth and tenth centuries and the interference of the laity in monastic affairs.[7] Ecclesiastical attacks on double monasteries, evident from as early as the sixth century, continued through this period and may have forced a change in arrangements at existing communities and discouraged the foundations of new communities.[8] An understanding of the life cycle of social movements, and religious movements in particular, can also help us understand the decline of nunneries in the tenth and eleventh centuries, as well as the problems encountered by female monastic movements after their vigorous revival in the twelfth century.

In his study of the sociology of religion, Max Weber noted a pattern of inclusion of women in the early, prophetic stage of a religion, but the exclusion of women and the dominance of men in the subsequent stage of "routinization and regimentation."[9] Weber also noted that the inclusion of women in the early stage contributed to the missionary strength of a religion, as women were attracted by the prospect of equal status with men. Weber saw this pattern of progressive hostility to women in Pauline Christianity, but it seems equally applicable to the declining participation of women in tenth- and eleventh-century monasticism.[10] Unfortunately, although Weber described the pattern, he did not explain why increasing organization should lead

7. Jean Verdon, "Recherches sur les monastères féminins dans la France du Nord aux IXe-XIe siècles," *Revue Mabillon* 59 (1976): 69.

8. Southern, p. 310; Wemple, p. 170; Bateson, pp. 144, 163–64. Southern also suggests that the increasing emphasis in the tenth and eleventh centuries on the careful and constant performance of the liturgy as the central monastic duty would emphasize the importance of monks, "who could most efficiently perform these duties" (p. 310). Yet surely nuns prayed also, and donations to nunneries as to monasteries demonstrate the expectation of prayer on behalf of the donor. For a case in which the demonstrated liturgical precision of a group of canonesses prevented the takeover of their church by canons, see Joan Morris, *The Lady Was a Bishop: The Hidden History of Women with Clerical Ordination and the Jurisdiction of Bishops* (New York: Macmillan, 1973), pp. 11–12.

9. Max Weber, *The Sociology of Religion*, trans. Ephraim Fischoff (Boston: Beacon Press, 1963; first published 1922), p. 104.

10. A similar pattern can perhaps be discerned in some of the religious movements of the Protestant Reformation; see Natalie Z. Davis, "City Women and Religious Change in Sixteenth Century France," in *Society and Culture in Early Modern France* (Stanford, Calif.: Stanford University Press, 1975), pp. 65–95. Southern alludes to the effects of increasing organization when he states that "as society became better organized and ecclesiastically more right-minded, the necessity for male dominance began to assert itself" (p. 310). The notion of ecclesiastical "right-mindedness" is inappropriate, as it assumes the illegitimacy of early medieval nunneries.

to the exclusion of women. Why are women not incorporated into the organizational structures that develop out of the earlier, amorphous stage of a religious movement?

To understand this exclusion, we must remember that the ideology of the general society, whether we are speaking of early Christianity, the high Middle Ages, or any later period in European history, was characterized by a strong component of hostility to women, expressed through legal, social, and intellectual restrictions. Many religious movements, in the context of their general critique of the larger society, might be willing to include women. Even if considering practical terms only, women's participation might be welcome in the initial phase of religious expansion when any and all help was urgently needed. We have seen that women made important contributions in the recently converted areas of Gaul, England, and Saxony. But once the movement has become well established, such an expansive effort is no longer necessary and might even be cumbersome as the movement consolidates its gains through an elaborated organizational structure.[11] At this stage, as the movement settles into the niche it has succeeded in carving out for itself, societal hostility toward women may be allowed to assert itself, and in the case of monastic movements, the duty of providing liturgical and other services for nuns may seem more burdensome than it is worth, with energies spent in supporting women seen to be better applied elsewhere. It is also possible that the initial enthusiasm of the early stage of a religious movement enables participants to forget the ordinary strictures on a close and equal association between men and women. It seems, then, that when a religious movement is new, and in some sense "anti-establishment," women's participation is acceptable; but when the movement becomes an organization, when it becomes part of that establishment, the participation of women is perceived as no longer appropriate.

The Reform Movements

With only one major exception (the order of Fontevrault), a pattern similar to that outlined above can be found in the experience of

11. For analyses of the stages through which most social movements progress, see the essays by Herbert Blumer, C. A. Dawson and W. E. Gettys, and Mayer N. Zald and Roberta Ash in *Studies in Social Movements: A Social Psychological Perspective*, ed. Barry McLaughlin (New York: Free Press, 1969).

women in each of the new monastic orders founded during the late
eleventh to thirteenth centuries: after an initial period favorable to
female participation came a reaction and retrenchment, an unwilling-
ness to provide for the surge of women desiring monastic life.¹² The
examples of two major twelfth-century orders, the Cistercians and
Premonstratensians, are instructive.

The Cistercian order's response to women was characterized by a
disjunction between, on the one hand, local encouragement (or at
least tolerance) of the establishment of nunneries following the Cistercian rule, and, on the other hand, at the official level of the legislation of the order, an obliviousness to these nunneries that was even-
tually replaced by outright hostility.¹³ By the mid-twelfth century,

12. For more detailed descriptions of this sequence in the various orders, see
Micheline de Fontette, *Les religieuses à l'âge classique du droit canon: Recherches sur les
structures juridiques des branches féminines des ordres* (Paris: J. Vrin, 1967); Southern,
pp. 309–31; Herbert Grundmann, *Religiöse Bewegungen im Mittelalter: Untersuchungen über die geschichtlichen Zusammenhänge zwischen der Ketzerei, den Bettelorden
und der religiösen Frauenbewegung im 12. und 13. Jahrhundert und über die geschichtlichen
Grundlagen der deutschen Mystik* (Hildesheim: Georg Olms, 1961; first published in
1935); Brenda Bolton, "Mulieres Sanctae," in *Women in Medieval Society*, ed. Susan
Mosher Stuard (Philadelphia: University of Pennsylvania Press, 1976), pp. 141–58;
Eleanor C. McLaughlin, "Equality of Souls, Inequality of Sexes: Women in Medieval
Theology," in *Religion and Sexism: Images of Woman in the Jewish and Christian Tradi-
tions*, ed. Rosemary Radford Ruether (New York: Simon and Schuster, 1974), pp.
233–51. Another order that, to a certain extent, followed the pattern of Fontevrault was
the Gilbertine order in England, founded by Gilbert of Sempringham; see Rose
Graham, *S. Gilbert of Sempringham and the Gilbertines: A History of the Only English
Monastic Order* (London: E. Stock, 1901); and Sharon Elkins, "Female Religious in
Twelfth Century England" (Ph.D. diss., Harvard University, 1977).

13. The following works survey the subject of Cistercian nuns and their reception
by the order: Louis J. Lekai, *The Cistercians: Ideals and Reality* (Kent, Ohio: Kent
State University Press, 1977), chap. 22; Jean de la Croix Bouton, "L'établissement des
moniales cisterciennes," in *Mémoires de la société pour l'histoire du droit et des institutions
des anciens pays bourguignons, comtois et romands*, fasc. 15 (1953): 83–116; Ernst G.
Krenig, "Mittelalterliche Frauenklöster nach den Konstitutionen von Cîteaux, unter
besonderer Berücksichtigung fränkischer Nonnenkonvente," *Analecta sacri ordinis
cisterciensis* 10 (1954): 1–105; Sally Thompson, "The Problem of the Cistercian Nuns in
the Twelfth and Early Thirteenth Centuries," in *Medieval Women*, ed. Derek Baker
(Oxford: Basil Blackwell, 1978), pp. 227–52; John A. Nichols, "The Internal Organization of English Cistercian Nunneries," *Cîteaux. Commentarii Cistercienses*, (1979):
23–40; Coburn V. Graves, "English Cistercian Nuns in Lincolnshire," *Speculum* 54
(1979): 492–99; Sister Michael [Elizabeth] Connor, "The First Cistercian Nuns and
Renewal Today," *Cistercian Studies* 5 (1970): 131–68; Frederick Mark Stein, "The Religious Women of Cologne: 1120–1320," (Ph.D. diss., Yale University, 1977).

nunneries following Cistercian customs had appeared all over Europe. One contemporary commented on the enthusiasm with which women, despite their sex, adopted all the harshness of the Cistercian discipline: they were

> striving to conquer not only the world but their own sex as well; of their own free will they embraced violently, nay joyfully, the Order of Cîteaux, which many robust men and youths fear to enter. Laying aside all linen garments and furs, they wore only woolen tunics. They did not only women's work, such as spinning and weaving, but they went out and worked in the fields, digging, cutting down and uprooting the forest with axe and mattock, tearing up thorns and briers, laboring assiduously with their hands and seeking their food in silence. Imitating in all things the monks of Clairvaux, they proved the truth of the Lord's saying, that to the believer all things are possible.[14]

This rapid and spontaneous growth took place without any formal accommodation by the Cistercian order. These nunneries were founded with the cooperation of individual Cistercian abbots, but no formal place in the structure of the order was accorded to them. No mention of the nunneries was made in the official acts of the order. Although the existence of these unofficial Cistercian communities must have appeared anomalous within the carefully articulated organization of the order, this female demand for the Cistercian way of life may have been appealing to the zeal for expansion that was also an important aspect of the Cistercian movement.[15] This inclusion of large numbers of women during the initial period of enthusiastic expansion is reminiscent of women's participation in the monastic movements of the sixth to eighth centuries.

Although the nunneries claiming Cistercian affiliation were not mentioned in the statutes of the order until the thirteenth century, the twelfth-century statutes were scattered with references to the necessity of avoiding contact with women, with the frequency of such warnings increasing sharply in the last decade of the century.[16] These

14. Herman of Tournai, ca. 1150; cited by Lekai, p. 349.
15. Ibid., pp. 315–16.
16. J. Canivez, ed., *Statuta capitulorum generalium ordinis cisterciensis ab anno 1116 ad annum 1786* (Louvain: Bureaux de la Revue d'Histoire Ecclésiastique, 1933–41). Twenty-three warnings date from the 1190s; at least six others can be found in the statutes of the years 1134, 1154, 1157, 1180, and 1185.

latter statutes either limited or prohibited the entrance of women
into the monasteries, or indicated punishment for such breaches of
conduct. The statutes usually prohibited the entrance of women in
general terms,[17] but occasional details indicate that there were two
usual sources of the problem: female servants whose tasks tended to
bring them in contact with the monks, and local women who were
allowed entrance for participation in a ceremony.[18] One statute, for
example, assigned punishment for members of a community that had
let women into the oratory on the occasion of the anniversary of the
death of Louis VII, who was buried there. Another punished a monastery that habitually let in women for the celebration of the church's
dedication day. Even the simple presence of women in a nearby
house could be cause for a reprimand.[19] In a similar vein, Bernard of
Clairvaux warned the abbot of a Premonstratensian abbey against
the danger of his monks using a mill where they were forced to be in
the company of women, and urged them to either forbid access to
women, or to monks and lay-brothers, or to give up the mill entirely.[20] And another Cistercian writer of the mid-twelfth century,
Idung of Prüfening, boasted of the strict Cistercian enclosure that
prohibited any female guests in the monastery.[21]

Although these prohibitions and reprimands concern the monasteries' dealings with secular rather than religious women (the words
feminae or *mulieres*, as opposed to *moniales*, are used throughout),
the concern to prevent even the most innocent contact with women
is a strong indication of the seriousness with which the order viewed
the possibility of contamination of its monks, and, seeing this concern, we can hardly expect the order to have been enthusiastic about
taking communities of nuns into its very structure. Not long after
this crescendo of statutes against contact with women, the Chapter
General began to promulgate legislation closely restricting the reli-

17. For example, 1185, Statute 34; 1192, 55.

18. 1134, 7; 1197, 6.

19. 1190, 55; 1191, 22 (see also 1191, 5; 1193, 28); 1194, 31 (a case concerning women in
the nearby house of a bishop).

20. Epistola 79, *Sancti Bernardi Opera*, vol. 7: *Corpus Epistolarum, 1–180*, ed. J.
Leclercq and H. Rochais (Rome: Editiones Cistercienses, 1974); Letter 81 in *The
Letters of St. Bernard of Clairvaux*, trans. Bruno Scott James (London: Burns Oates,
1953).

21. Idung of Prüfening, *Cistercians and Cluniacs: The Case for Cîteaux. A Dialogue
between Two Monks; An Argument on Four Questions* (Kalamazoo, Mich.: Cistercian
Publications, 1977), p. 75.

gious women in existing Cistercian nunneries and to prevent the foundation of new female communities. This ended the order's silent toleration of the many communities claiming Cistercian affiliation.[22] Beginning in 1213, statutes appeared explicitly limiting the freedom and numbers of Cistercian nunneries, culminating in a decree of 1228 that no more nunneries were to be allowed to join the order.[23] The order's desire to abandon its women was caused not only by the men's fear of women as sexual temptresses, but also by their resentment of the material commitment monks were expected to make to nearby nunneries. In 1222, for example, the Chapter General had begged Pope Honorius III "not to compel us to send our monks and lay-brothers to live with nuns and to provide them with temporalities."[24]

Despite these adverse rulings, the Chapter General was not able to effect a diminution in the numbers of Cistercian nunneries, and in the course of the thirteenth century Cistercian nunneries actually came to outnumber monasteries in some areas of Europe.[25] Some, but not all, of the nunneries founded before the prohibition had officially incorporated into the order, and they continued as such, but many of the nunneries were only quasi-Cistercian, following Cistercian customs but not considered Cistercian by the order. This grass roots growth was possible because of local support for these commu-

22. Some authors interpret an 1134 statute (no. 29) prohibiting the blessing of nuns by abbots or monks as an early prohibition of Cistercian nuns. But the statute has also been interpreted as meaning that such a blessing would be usurping the power of the bishop. I follow the editor of the statutes in this latter interpretation, and note that Idung of Prüfening mentions that the consecration of a nun is so important that only a bishop should officiate (Idung, p. 173). See Connor, pp. 142–43; and S. Thompson, p. 227, for discussion of this question. Thompson rests much of her argument on the evidence this statute supposedly provides of early official prohibition of nuns. The statute reads: "Prohibitum est ne quis abbatum vel monachorum nostrorum monacham benedicere, infantulum baptizare, vel etiam in baptismo tenere praesumat, nisi forte in articulo mortis fuerit, et presbiter defuerit." Surely the inclusion of the baptism of infants in the same statute confirms that it was a question of jurisdiction rather than absolute prohibition.

23. 1228, 16; Southern, pp. 316–17. Southern lists the relevant statutes, p. 316, n. 18. As noted by Southern, the only explicit reference to a Cistercian nunnery before 1213 was a statute of 1191 concerning the abbesses of some Spanish nunneries. See also M. de Fontette, pp. 28–61; Grundmann, pp. 203–8.

24. 1222, 30.

25. Southern, p. 317; Lekai, p. 352. See also Simone Roisin, "L'efflorescence cistercienne et le courant féminin de piété au XIIIe siècle," *Revue d'histoire ecclésiastique* 39 (1943): 342–78. For a detailed illustration of how little effect the decrees of the General Chapter had in one diocese, see Stein, pp. 119–48.

nities, both by ecclesiastical and lay officials.[26] One might be tempted, in the face of the continuing success of these nunneries, to dismiss the institutional rejection as unimportant. But this rejection was significant and had at least two effects. First of all, the uncertain status of these nunneries within the order meant that privileges normally given to Cistercian communities—like exemption from taxes and exemption from episcopal visitation—might not be extended to these nunneries.[27] Second, this institutional rejection must have had an important, though less tangible, effect on the self-image of the women in the communities. These were women who lived according to Cistercian customs, wore Cistercian dress, and who thus considered themselves Cistercian, and yet who were not officially incorporated into the order and so could not participate in official affairs, and could not enjoy a sense of membership in the institution that was clearly of great importance to them. The uncertain status of these Cistercian nunneries is a signpost not simply of the secondary status of the nuns, but of the fact that they were viewed as peripheral and not to be counted as part of the strength of the movement. Rather than looking positively at new female communities as a healthy growth of the order, the men in charge of the order looked upon them as anomalous, burdensome, and dangerous.

Another example of the difficulties women faced in being accepted by predominantly male orders is the development of the Premonstratensians.[28] In contrast to the Cistercians, women were self-consciously included in the early Premonstratensian foundations. Norbert of

26. For Cologne, see Stein, pp. 119–48. For evidence from England, see Graves. Brian Patrick McGuire argues that friendships between Cistercian monks and nuns flourished in the first half of the thirteenth century: "The Cistercians and the Transformation of Monastic Friendships," *Analecta Cisterciensia* 37 (1981): 1–63

27. S. Thompson, p. 248. Cistercian nunneries were sometimes accorded these privileges despite official disavowal of their Cistercian status. Graves shows that English Cistercian nunneries were recognized as Cistercian by English kings and bishops and were extended exemption from payment of the tenth, even though the abbot of Cîteaux wrote to the dean of Lincoln Cathedral that the houses were not members of the order (Graves, pp. 496–99).

28. Concerning Prémontré, see Hugues Lamy, *L'Abbaye de Tongerloo, depuis sa fondation jusqu'en 1263*, in *Recueil de travaux publiés par les membres des conférences d'histoire et de philologie de l'Université de Louvain*, fasc. 44 (Louvain, 1914); A. Erens, "Les soeurs dans l'ordre de Prémontré," *Analecta Praemonstratensia* 5 (1929): 5–26; M. de Fontette, chap. 1; Ursmer Berlière, "Les monastères doubles aux XIIe et XIIIe siècles," Académie Royale de Belgique, Classe des lettres et des sciences morales et politiques, *Mémoires* (ser. 2) 18, fasc. 3 (1923). A map illustrating the spread of the Premonstraten-

Xanten, the founder of the order, was a wandering preacher who attracted both male and female followers. In establishing a community for these followers at Prémontré (founded in 1121), Norbert provided for both men and women. However, the Premonstratensian organization was similar to the Cistercian in one very important respect: the men in the order were given authority over the women. Norbert's community was basically one of male canons, with women attached. This left the women in a vulnerable secondary position, and, about six years after Norbert's death in 1134, the General Chapter ordered that the women were to leave the mixed communities and set up their own communities at a distance.[29] The resulting female establishments were still dependent on the male communities, and there exist several papal bulls exhorting the men to aid the women. Toward the end of the twelfth century the official stance hardened. Citing the danger of the times and the burden of the church, the order prohibited the admission of any more women.[30] This decree was confirmed by Innocent III in 1198.

In the thirteenth century there was some opposition to this ruling. In the beginning of the century, the General Chapter ruled to allow a particular community, Bonoeil, to receive sisters again. In 1240 legislation regulating admission of women was drawn up, limiting the number of women in each community to twenty; this seems to have become the general rule for the whole Order, and the legislation was approved by Innocent IV in 1247. But antagonism toward women had not disappeared. During the pontificate of Honorius III (1216–1227), the General Chapter decided to solicit from the pope a privilege *de non recipiendis sororibus*. In 1270 the General Chapter decided to suppress communities of women that were annexed to male communities; women were only to be received in separate nunneries.[31] The expulsion of women from the community at Marchthal in 1273

---

sians, and distinguishing male, female, and double communities, may be found in *Grosser Historischer Weltatlas*, vol. 2: *Mittelalter* (Munich: Bayerischer Schulbuch-Verlag, 1970), p. 81.

29. Erens, p. 8. For a description of the migrations of women that followed the expulsion, see Berlière, pp. 24–25.

30. The original statute is lost, but it is referred to in a supplement to the statutes of the General Chapter: "Quoniam instant tempora periculosa et Ecclesia supra modum gravatur, communi consilio capituli statuimus ut amodo nullam sororem recipiamus. Si quis autem hujus statuti transgressor exstiterit, abbatia sua sine misericordia privetur" (Erens, p. 10, citing E. Martène, *De antiquis ecclesiae ritibus*, 3: 925).

31. Berlière, pp. 24–26.

was the occasion for the following comments from Abbot Conrad on the necessity of the action:

> We and our whole community of canons, recognizing that the wickedness of women is greater than all the other wickedness of the world, and that there is no anger like that of women, and that the poison of asps and dragons is more curable and less dangerous to men than the familiarity of women, have unanimously decreed for the safety of our souls, no less than for that of our bodies and goods, that we will on no account receive any more sisters to the increase of our perdition, but will avoid them like poisonous animals.[32]

We thus see repeated in the Premonstratensian case the fear of women and their sexual temptation as one of the causes of the order's abandonment of women. The other cause, that of resentment of the material burden of providing for women, is implied in the late twelfth-century statute that prohibited the admission of women on the ground of the danger of the times and the burdens of the church. Since the primary orientation of the order was toward men, and the power of the order was in the hands of men, the needs of women were perceived not only as secondary but as burdensome, and after an initial period of acceptance, persistent attempts to exclude women were made.[33] For the Premonstratensians, as well as for other orders, "the spiritual well-being of the male religious [was] used as the justification for the refusal to permit women to aspire to the religious life."[34]

Unlike the Cistercians, the Premonstratensians purposefully included both men and women in their early communities, yet within about twenty years of the foundation of the order steps were taken to

32. English translation from Southern, p. 314. The Latin text is in Erens, p. 10, n. 20. Conrad further stated that the prohibition was to hold for fifty years, with his successors then to reconsider it if they wished. There is some question as to the authenticity of this document; see Erens, p. 10; and Berlière, p. 26, n. 1.

33. The predominance of men was not just a question of numbers. A man was in charge of the "independent" female Premonstratensian communities as well as of the mixed communities (Erens, pp. 17–18). There is even a question as to whether the women were actually professed nuns; Berlière points out that they did not chant the office (p. 23). Cluniac nunneries were headed by a male prior (Dom Philibert Schmitz, *Histoire de l'ordre de Saint-Benoît*, vol 7: *Les moniales* [Liège: Maredsous, 1956], p. 51; Hunt, p. 189); Cistercian nunneries were assigned a male *procurator* for supervision of material concerns (Connor, p. 146).

34. E. McLaughlin, "Equality of Souls," p. 242.

isolate the women from the men. As we saw for the Cistercians, there was a growing concern about the situation toward the end of the twelfth century, and women were denied further entrance to the order. For the Cistercians, the subsequent juridical development was fairly uniform: the Chapter General continued to order the exclusion of women, although this did not effect a halt in the establishment of Cistercian nunneries. The Premonstratensian development showed more controversy at the administrative level, but as with the Cistercians, female Premonstratensian communities continued to exist.

Many other examples can be found of monastic movements that in their early stages incorporated women. The monastery of Savigny was founded in about 1112 by Vital de Mortain, a disciple of Robert of Arbrissel, the founder of Fontevrault. By 1147, some thirty other communities were affiliated with Savigny, including three abbeys of women.[35] Another disciple of Robert of Arbrissel, Raoul de la Fûtaye, founded the community of Saint-Sulpice in the second decade of the twelfth century. Like the early Premonstratensian communities (and like Fontevrault, its model), Saint-Sulpice comprised a community of women as well as one of men, and an abbess was in charge of both. By mid-century there were about thirty affiliated priories.[36]

Other orders show the acceptance/rejection pattern of Cîteaux and Prémontré. The order of regular canons of Arrouaise, founded in about 1090, accepted women through most of the twelfth century. But again, the turn of the twelfth and thirteenth centuries was a turning point: in 1197 a move was made to limit the number of women in the order, and in the mid-thirteenth century women were totally prohibited from joining.[37] The pattern of the Franciscan and Dominican orders differed only in that women were resented almost immediately, even by the founders of the orders.[38]

These two mendicant orders were not founded until the beginning

35. Jacqueline Buhot, "L'abbaye normande de Savigny, chef d'ordre et fille de Cîteaux," *Moyen âge* (ser. 3) 7 (1936): 16.

36. P. Piolin, "Le moine Raoul et le bienheureux Raoul de la Fustaye," *Revue des questions historiques* 42 (1887): 505–6. Piolin does not mention whether the same arrangements held at the priories as well.

37. Ludo Milis, *L'ordre des chanoines reguliers d'Arrouaise: Son histoire et son organisation, de la fondation de l'abbaye-mère (vers 1090) à la fin des chapitres annuels (1471)*, 2 vols. (Bruges: De Tempel, 1969), 1: 118, 248, 515–17. See also Berlière, pp. 31–32.

38. The following account of women in the Franciscan and Dominican orders is taken from Bolton, pp. 149–52. Detailed accounts of the struggle between these or-

of the thirteenth century—the period when other orders had already
begun to exclude women. Although Francis encouraged Clare, he
did not want to be personally involved with her convent of Saint-
Damian, nor, in general, did he want his followers to be burdened
with the care of women, and he vigorously opposed an attempt by
Cardinal Hugolino to commit the Friars to some form of service to
the women's communities.[39] Throughout the thirteenth century the
papacy, concerned for the care of these nuns, struggled with the order on this issue.

Dominic was more positively disposed to providing for women in
a religious life, particularly at the beginning of his career, and he
founded several nunneries in the first two decades of the century. But
he seems to have changed his mind toward the end of his life and
discouraged his followers from becoming involved with women.[40]
Whatever Dominic's own attitude may have been, the Dominicans,
like the Franciscans, resisted the demands of women, and of the papacy in their support, through the thirteenth century.

Micheline de Fontette points out that despite the male opposition
to female participation, women persisted in joining religious communities and in somehow finding the support they needed: "Neither
juridical subjection, nor material and spiritual dependence, nor the
latent hostility of the superior authorities of the orders, none of these
prevented them [the female communities] from multiplying with un-
paralleled vigor and from covering Europe with their monasteries."[41]
Yet other evidence would indicate that some women, rather than
squeezing themselves into the strictures of these orders, sought out
less orthodox movements that willingly accepted them. In the twelfth
century women were active in heretical movements, notably with
the Albigensians and Waldensians.[42] In the thirteenth century many

ders and the papacy on the issue of women can be found in M. de Fontette, chaps. 5
and 6, and in Grundmann, pp. 208–318.

39. Bolton, pp. 149–50. Rosalind and Christopher Brooke suggest that Francis perceived Clare as a possible barrier to his acceptability in high circles ("St Clare," in *Medieval Women*, pp. 283–84).

40. Bolton, pp. 150–51.

41. M. de Fontette, p. 154.

42. Gottfried Koch, "Die Frau im mittelalterlichen Katharismus und Waldensertum," *Studi medievali* (ser. 3) 5 (1964): 741–74; idem, *Frauenfrage und Ketzertum im
Mittelalter: Die Frauenbewegung im Rahmen des Katharismus und des Waldensertums
und ihre sozialen Wurzeln (12.-14. Jahrhundert)* (Berlin: Akademie-Verlag, 1962).
Huguette Taviani discusses the egalitarian attitudes and behavior of eleventh-century

women joined the beguines, a movement with a similar geographic distribution to the Premonstratensians, who were then questioning the inclusion of women in their order.[43] Given the situation in the orthodox orders, the establishment of houses of beguines may have been a way of providing for the numerous women who could not find religious opportunities elsewhere.[44] In addition, the growth of beguine communities was not hampered by male resentment of material support, as they were less expensive to found and maintain, with little external support needed because of the beguines' own economic efforts.[45]

Brenda Bolton has asked why, given the widespread enthusiasm among women for the monastic life, no specifically female monastic orders were established. Bolton cites the male opposition to nunneries and the male responsibility for material and spiritual care entailed by female communities as the primary disincentive to separate

heretics: "Le mariage dans l'hérésie de l'An Mil," *Annales: Economies, sociétés, civilisations* 32 (1977): 1074–89. M. C. Barber estimates that about one-third of Cathar perfects were women: "Women and Catharism," *Reading Medieval Studies* 3 (1977): 51. Eleanor McLaughlin, on the other hand, suggests that too much has been made of the participation of women in heretical movements, and states that they disappeared from prominent roles after the early years: "The *perfectae* disappeared as the *perfecti* became more like bishops than religious" ("Women, Power, and the Pursuit of Holiness in Medieval Christianity," in *Women of Spirit: Female Leadership in the Jewish and Christian Traditions*, ed. Rosemary Ruether and Eleanor McLaughlin [New York: Simon and Schuster, 1979], p. 124). Richard Abels and Ellen Harrison also note a decline in *perfectae*, attributing it to the impossibility of continuing the convent-type life of *perfectae* after the establishment of the Inquisition in the 1230s and 1240s ("The Participation of Women in Languedocian Catharism," *Mediaeval Studies* 41 [1979]: 233–40). This excellent article challenges the assertion of extensive female participation in heresy, yet shows that the percentage of perfects who were female could be as high as 45% (p. 225). The authors resist interpreting this figure as high, emphasizing instead that it is lower than the assumed 50% of the population that would be female. They mention but quickly pass over the fact that this level of participation would undoubtedly be higher than that in Catholic society (ibid.).

43. For a good, brief discussion of the beguines, see Southern, pp. 319–31. The standard work in English is Ernest W. McDonnell, *The Beguines and Beghards in Medieval Culture, with Special Emphasis on the Belgian Scene* (New Brunswick, N.J.: Rutgers University Press, 1954). See also Otto Nübel, *Mittelalterliche Beginen- und Sozialsiedlungen in den Niederlanden: Ein Beitrag zur Vorgeschichte der Fuggerei* (Tübingen: J. C. B. Mohr, 1970).

44. Berlière, p. 32. On the evidence of Cologne, Stein suggests that the growth of the beguines should not be attributed solely to the lack of opportunity in the religious orders but should be seen also as a preference, by many, for the beguine way of life.

45. Stein, p. 174.

female orders, as it was to female communities attached to those of men. Yet Bolton briefly suggests another reason that is perhaps more important: there was no *need* for specifically female orders;[46] or, rather, there had been, in most places, no need for female orders in the period of great monastic expansion in the twelfth century because, as we have seen, most of the new orders accepted women as well as men, accommodating them either in mixed or separate communities. Only toward the end of that century and the beginning of the next were sustained efforts made to exclude women. At that point, it might well have become desirable to establish orders for these women, and the beguine movement was a grass roots phenomenon expressing this need. But as Bolton points out, the prohibition of all new movements promulgated by the Lateran Council in 1215 inhibited the formation of female orders, as did the death in 1216 of Innocent III, who had been a very strong supporter of religious women, and of the Poor Clares in particular. In the thirteenth century, then, opportunities for women in orthodox orders were severely limited:

> Left to themselves, the women reverted, becoming branches of the male orders, some vigorous shoots such as the community of St. Damian and the Cistercian nuns and Beguines in Flanders, and others, such as the incorporated Dominican and Franciscan convents, proliferating like suckers and risking always severance from the main life-giving trunk of the church.[47]

But the thirteenth-century situation should not distract us from the contrasting picture of the twelfth century, and particularly its first half, when the new movements had the vigor and abundant energy of new growth, and thus often welcomed rather than resisted women. The inclusion of women, though controversial by 1200, was unexceptional earlier in the century.

There also existed an important exception to the lack of specifically female orders in the twelfth century—the order of Fontevrault. In addition, Fontevrault was the order that most prominently avoided the acceptance/rejection pattern of contemporary movements. The history of this order holds significant lessons about women in monastic life, since although it was in the above ways unique, it was in other important ways typical of twelfth-century monasticism. Its

46. Ibid., p. 153.
47. Ibid., p. 154.

growth and success in the early twelfth century should come as no surprise to us, but the fact that it continued to provide for women through the difficult times of the late twelfth and thirteenth centuries needs to be explained. An analysis of the reasons for its success will help explain the failure of other movements to provide a positive response to the desire of medieval women for a monastic vocation.

The Order of Fontevrault

Fontevrault was founded in 1100 or 1101 by Robert of Arbrissel, a native of Brittany who had been born around 1060 into a poor peasant family.[48] Robert's early career was shaped by the spirit of Gregorian reform prevalent in the late eleventh-century church. After studying in Paris, Robert returned to Brittany, entering the service of Sylvester, bishop of Rennes. He spent four years there as archpriest, "making peace between quarrelers, liberating churches from slavery to the laity, separating the incestuous unions of priest and laity, opposing simony, and manfully opposing all sins."[49] But these reforming activities were not uniformly popular, and when Bishop Sylvester died, Robert was forced to leave. He taught in Angers for a short time, but then became caught up in the contemporary enthusiasm for eremeticism.[50] Accompanied by another priest, Robert went

48. René Niderst, *Robert d'Arbrissel et les origines de l'ordre de Fontevrault* (Rodez: G. Subervie, 1952), p. 38. The following details of Robert's life are taken from the two saint's lives devoted to Robert. The first was written by Baldric, bishop of Dol, shortly after Robert's death in 1117. The second, concerned only with the events leading up to Robert's death, was written by a Fontevrist monk after Baldric's biography was written, but sometime before 1120. I have used the edition of the texts in Migne, *P.L.*, 162: 1043–78. A thorough discussion of the dating, authorship, reliability, and usefulness of the various sources of Robert's life, including the two saint's lives, can be found in Johannes von Walter, *Die ersten Wanderprediger Frankreichs: Studien zur Geschichte des Mönchtums*, vol. 1: *Robert von Arbrissel* (Studien zur Geschichte der Theologie und der Kirche, vol. 9, no. 3) (Leipzig: Dieterich, 1903), pp. 9–94. See also Jean-Marc Bienvenu, "Les deux *Vitae* de Robert d'Arbrissel," in *La littérature angevine médiévale. Actes du colloque du samedi 22 mars 1980* (Maulévrier: Hérault, 1981), pp. 63–76; and *L'étonnant fondateur de Fontevraud; Robert d'Arbrissel* (Paris: Nouvelles Editions Latines, 1981). Unfortunately, I was unable to consult M. Bienvenu's *thèse:* "Les premiers temps de Fontevraud (1101–1189). Naissance et évolution d'un ordre religieux," thèse de Doctorat d'Etat, Paris-Sorbonne, 1980.

49. Baldric, *Vita*, *P.L.*, 162: 1048–49.

50. This aspect of Robert's life, and the lives of others like him, is described by L. Raison and R. Niderst, "Le mouvement érémitique dans l'Ouest de la France à la fin du XIe siècle et au début du XIIe siècle," *Annales de Bretagne* 55 (1948): 1–46.

into a deserted area in the forest of Craon to devote himself to contemplation. As so often happened with hermits, however, his isolation did not last long—he soon had visitors, many of whom wanted
to remain with him. In order to provide for them, he founded a con-
gregation of canons who were to live by the rules of the primitive
church. Robert developed a reputation for his skillful preaching, and
when Urban II was in Anjou in 1095, it was arranged that Robert
would preach at the dedication of a church in Angers. The pope was
impressed with his zeal, and enjoined him to preach. Robert then
began his career as an itinerant preacher, a way of life he continued
until his death. He was so successful in this role that he gave up the
community of canons at Craon in order to have more time for
preaching. As he traveled, he was joined by many people of both
sexes.[51] Again, Robert founded a community for the people who had
gathered around him, this time at a deserted place called Fontevrault,
at the intersection of the boundaries of Anjou, Poitou, and Touraine.
Robert's biographer Baldric attributes the foundation to Robert's
fear that some people within the enlarging crowds might act in-
discreetly. Noting, however, that "women should live with men,"
Baldric describes Robert's decision to look for a deserted place where
they could live "scrupulously, without scandal." [52]

Thus just as Norbert of Xanten would soon accommodate his
mixed group of followers, Robert of Arbrissel established a community that included both women and men. Contact between the men
and the women was, however, strictly limited, and labors were divided according to sex. The women were assigned a silent life in the
cloister; the men were subject to labor: spiritual for the clerics and
physical for the laymen. In this way, Robert "commended the more
tender and weaker sex to psalm-singing and contemplation, while he
applied the stronger sex to the labors of the active life." [53] These

---

51. " . . . sexus utriusque plures adjuncti sunt ei" (Baldric, *P.L.*, 162: 1051).

52. "Videns autem subsequentium multitudinem dilatari, ne aliquid ageretur incon-
sulto, quoniam mulieres cum hominibus oportebat habitare, ubi possent sine scan-
dalorum scrupulositate conversari et vivere, deliveravit perquirere, et si quod desertum
contigisset reperire" (Baldric, *P.L.*, 162: 1051).

53. "Mulieres tamen ab hominibus segregavit, et inter claustrum eas velut damnavit,
quas orationi deputavit; homines vere laboribus mancipavit. Non sine discretione id
agere videbatur, quia sexum teniorem et imbecilliorem commendabat psalmodiae, et
theoriae; fortiorum autem applicabat exercitiis vitae actualis. Laici et clerici mi[x]tim
ambulabant; excepto quod clerici psallbant, et missas celebrabant, laici laborem spon-
tanei subibant" (Ibid., col. 1052).

people were not only of both sexes but of all conditions: "Many men of every condition came; women assembled, both poor and noble, widows and virgins, young and 'old, whores and those who spurn men."[54] The numbers of men and women at Fontevrault are not known. It seems clear, however, that women outnumbered men. Baldric notes in his *Vita* that after building the oratory, they built cloisters, yet "three or four did not suffice for such a great gathering of women."[55] The special importance of women in the community is also indicated by Robert's choice of a woman, Hersende, to govern the community as prioress when he recommenced his life as a wandering preacher. Petronilla of Chemillé, who was later chosen abbess, was at this time assigned the office of procurator.

During the next fifteen years, Robert traveled through most of western and southwestern France, preaching, setting up priories of Fontevrault, and receiving donations for the growing order.[56] The events of the last year of Robert's life, as described by his second biographer, Andrea, are particularly interesting, as they reveal clearly the purpose that Robert had in founding Fontevrault.[57] The first sec-

54. "Multi confluebant homines cujuslibet conditionis; conveniebant mulieres, pauperes et nobiles, viduae et virgines, senes et adolescentes, meretrices et masculorum aspernatrices" (ibid., col. 1053; see also col. 1055). Robert was drawing married women as well as widows and virgins: Niderst, p. 25, n. 22; Andrea, *Vita, P.L.*, 162: 1075; J. de Petigny, "Lettre inédite de Robert d'Arbrissel à la comtesse Ermengarde," *Bibliothèque de l'Ecole des Chartes*, ser. 3, 5 (1854): 209–35.

55. Baldric, *P.L.*, 162: 1054.

56. Niderst, pp. 41–50. There is general agreement on the number of priories founded by mid-century (about twenty by the time of Robert's death in 1117 and another twenty by the time of the death of Petronilla, the first abbess of Fontevrault, in 1149). But estimates on the number founded after 1149 vary considerably, ranging from eighteen to one hundred additional priories. It is sometimes difficult to distinguish a priory from a simple domain, that is, a parcel of land worked or supervised by one or more members of the order (Françoise Grelier, "Le temporel de l'abbaye de Fontevrault dans le haut-Poitou, des origines à la réforme du XVe siècle," [Thèse, Ecole des Chartes, 1960], pp. 121–39).

57. Andrea, *P.L.*, 162: 1057–78. The identity of the author is not certain. For a discussion of the question of the authorship, see von Walter, pp. 17–25. Andrea's story appears to be addressed to the men at Fontevrault rather than to the men and women or women alone. There is no opening salutation, but toward the middle of the *vita*, the author exclaims: "Licet mihi, fratres, dicere virum hunc . . ." (col. 1068). In contrast, Baldric's *vita* is addressed explicitly to the abbess and nuns of Fontevrault. His *vita* begins: "Baldricus, Dei gratia Dolensium sacerdos, licet indignus, ancillae Christi Petronillae, venerabili monasterii Fontevraldensis abbatissae, omnibusque ejusdem coenobii sanctimonialibus sub ejus regimine, salutem" (col. 1043). The different topics

tion of Andrea's biography focuses on two events: first, Robert's request that the brothers of Fontevrault pledge to remain in the community under the rule of women; and, second, Robert's choice of an abbess to govern the community.[58] Andrea tells the following story, using long "quotations" from Robert himself.

Robert, gravely ill at Fontevrault, calls the brothers to his bedside. He tells them that he is about to die and that he would like to ascertain whether the brothers want to continue in their purpose at Fontevrault, that is, for the sake of their souls, to obey the command of the handmaidens (*ancillae*) of Christ. He reminds them that whatever he has established, he has subjected to the rule of these women. If the men do not want to stay at Fontevrault, he gives them permission to join another order. With an almost unanimous voice, the brothers declare that there is no better life possible, and they pledge to remain.[59]

Not many days later, Robert sends for several bishops and abbots. When assembled, he tells them that he is near death and that he has called them to Fontevrault to help him in the choice of an abbess. Robert instructs them that all he has built has been for the nuns, that he has given them full power over his goods, and that he has committed himself and his disciples, for the salvation of their souls, to the service of the nuns. On this account, with their advice, he would like to appoint an abbess while he is still alive, lest after his death someone might presume to oppose his goal. Robert then discusses the choice of the abbess. He considers the question of whether he should appoint a lay convert (*laica conversa*) or a virgin.[60] The dignity of the

---

emphasized by the two authors may perhaps, then, be related to the different audiences intended. It is also a commentary on the separateness of the male and female communities that one *vita* would be addressed to the women and one to the men, although Andrea refers to the life written by Baldric, and indicates that his purpose is to fill out the description of the events surrounding Robert's death (col. 1057).

58. These events comprise roughly the first quarter of the *vita*; the rest of the *vita* describes Robert's journeys during the seven months between the choice of the abbess and his death at the priory of Orsan.

59. *P.L.*, 162: 1058–59. The pledge is first described as being almost unanimous, but later as unanimous. This is a matter of some interest as a nonunanimous pledge could be taken as a sign of some dissatisfaction among the men. Such dissatisfaction was a distinct problem at various times from the fifteenth century onward (F. Deshouillières, "Le prieuré d'Orsan en Berry," *Mémoires de la société des antiquaires du Centre* 25 [1901]: 51–137).

60. *P.L.*, 162: 1060. The exact meaning of *conversa* and *virgo* are not clear. In this context, the distinction emphasized is someone who has joined the community later in

order would seem to demand governance by a virgin, but Robert expresses concern that someone who had been brought up within the cloister would not have the worldly knowledge needed to run a monastic order, and he is concerned that the community he has built not deteriorate. A Martha-type woman is needed for an abbess; let Mary gaze longingly at heaven.[61] The assembled men agree wholeheartedly. Seven months later Robert chose as abbess Petronilla of Chemillé, who had been one of his early followers.[62] In announcing his choice, Robert mentions that she had been married once and that to him nothing seems more in accordance with the authority of abbess.[63] This is apparently not meant simply as a loophole for Petronilla— Andrea tells us that Robert had it written into the rules of Fontevrault that the abbess should never be someone who had been brought

---

life as opposed to someone brought up from childhood in a monastery. For a discussion of the difficulty of establishing a precise meaning for the word *conversa*, see Berlière, pp. 27–31; Duane J. Osheim, "Conversion, *Conversi*, and the Christian Life in Late Medieval Tuscany," *Speculum* 58 (1983): 371–73. Abelard expressed a similar preference for an experienced woman as abbess in his letter to Heloise, answering her request for a Rule for the nuns of the Paraclete: Letter 7 (8), edited by T. P. McLaughlin, "Abelard's Rule for Religious Women," *Mediaeval Studies* 18 (1956): 252–53; trans. Betty Radice, *The Letters of Abelard and Heloise* (Baltimore: Penguin Books, 1974), pp. 200–201.

61. *P.L.*, 162: 1060. In contrast, Mabilia, elected abbess of the Benedictine house of Le Ronceray d'Angers in about 1122, was praised as "virg[o] Deo ab infantia consecrat[a]" (*Cartulaire de l'abbaye du Ronceray d'Angers (1028–1184)*, ed. Paul Marchegay [Paris: A. Picard, 1900], p. 19).

62. It is not clear why the choice was delayed seven months. Andrea also does not indicate whose counsel was sought in the selection of Petronilla. He only says that Robert made the choice "not without the counsel of religious men [*virorum*]" (ibid., col. 1061).

63. "Licet enim monogama fuerit, cogente tamen necessitate, nulla mihi convenientior videtur huic praelationi" (ibid.). A seventeenth-century "translation" of this passage adds an apologetic tone not present in the original:

Qu'il est vray qu'elle a esté une fois mariée: mais que cét empeschement a esté levé, comme quelques-uns d'eux qui y ont assisté, sçavent tres-bien, dans l'assemblée de Messeigneurs les Prelats, qui tous unanimement ont conclu, qu'on peut élire une Abbesse qui ait passé par cét Estat. Qu'elle estant instruite & depuis plus long-temps, & mieux que toutes les autres Dames, de ses Maximes, de son Esprit, & de ses desseins, elle les pourra facilement perpetuer dans l'Ordre.

[Sébastien Ganot, *La vie du bien-heureux Robert d'Arbrissel, fondateur de l'ordre de Fonteurauld* (La Fleche, 1648), p. 211]

Robert was being considered for canonization in the seventeenth century, and his association with women was the cause of much defensive writing like the above. (See Reto R. Bezzola, *Les origines et la formation de la littérature courtoise en Occident (500-1200)*, *Bibliothèque de l'Ecole des Hautes Etudes*, vol. 313[2] [1960], p. 283, n. 1.)

up in the cloister; many churches, he notes, had been ruined by such inexperienced abbesses. Robert did not choose to perpetuate his own role by appointing a male master of the order, either instead of or in addition to an abbess. In contrast, Gilbert of Sempringham, whose Gilbertine houses in England for men and women are frequently compared to Fontevrault, personally selected a male successor, and the position of master was included in the Institutes of the order, thus institutionalizing male control.[64]

The two saint's lives of Robert thus give us a picture of a self-consciously ordered community of men and women. The sexually mixed composition of the crowds that followed Robert in his first years as a wandering preacher may have been due to the general attraction of such figures (similarly, Norbert of Xanten); but whatever the reason for the initial mixture, his biographers show Robert purposefully organizing a continued association. The principles are clear: Robert's works have been done for the sake of women; the men should, for the sake of their souls, carry on their service for the women; the governance of both the men and the women of the community should be carried out by the abbess. Baldric also mentions a concern for the physical separation of the women from the men. The Rule of the community reinforces this picture.

Three versions of the Rule for Fontevrault have survived.[65] None of these appears to be the original rule drawn up by Robert, as described by Andrea. Andrea reported that, beside a regulation concerning the election of the abbess, Robert also dictated regulations directing both the men and the women with respect to speech, acts, food, and clothing. Yet none of the existing rules contain consideration of all four things. Rule I (following the order in Migne) consists of forty-four rules for women and twenty-seven rules for men. Rule II contains seven rules for women and seven for men. Rule III is composed of eight rules for women. Von Walter judges that Rule II is a fragment of the original rule, and dates from 1116 or 1117. He considers Rule I to be a reworking of the original rule, completed sometime before 1155, and probably before Petronilla's death in 1149. Rule III seems to be a later form of Rule I and may date from around 1150.[66] This chronology is only an estimation, but it is worth explor-

64. Elkins, "Female Religious," pp. 241, 271.
65. *P.L.*, 162: 1079–86.
66. Von Walter, pp. 65–82.

ing the differences between Rule II, judged to be closest to the original, and Rule I, the most detailed elaboration of the rules, judged to date sometime after Rule II.

Rule II contains a strong statement of the spiritual and secular jurisdiction of the abbess over Fontevrault and all its dependents:

Petronilla, chosen by master Robert and constituted abbess by the common will and by the devoted request of the nuns as well as of the religious brothers, is to have and maintain the power of ruling the church of Fontevrault and all the places belonging to that church, and they are to obey her. They are to revere her as their spiritual mother, and all the affairs of the church, spiritual as well as secular, are to remain in her hands, or be given to whomever she assigns, just as she decides.[67]

This rule also states that the male members of the community (*presbyteri, clerici, laici*) have promised to serve under the bond of obedience to the nuns, and that this subjection should be followed not just at Fontevrault but at the other communities in the order as well. The governance of the nuns in everyday matters can be seen in three of the statutes for the men: the men are to be content with what is given to them by the nuns; they are to bring their leftover food to the door of the nuns' quarters where it will be distributed to the poor; the men are to receive nothing from the outside without the permission of the abbess.[68] The nuns were not strictly confined to the cloister; one provision, for example, ordains that the cloistered nuns should always maintain silence, except for those who attend to business on the outside.[69] Another statute assumes the external travels of the prioress, noting that she should be received and obeyed in all the communities of the order.[70] Only one statute refers to the segrega-

67. "Ut Petronilla electa a magistro Roberto et constituta abbatissa communi voluntate, et devota petitione tam sanctimonialium quam religiosorum fratrum habeat, obtineatque potestatem regendi ecclesiam Fontis Ebraldi, et omnium locorum eidem ecclesiae pertinentium, et obediant ei; venerentur eam ut suam matrem spiritualem, in ejusque prudentia omnia ecclesiae negotia tam spiritualia quam saecularia permaneant, aut quibuscunque attribuerit, et prout constituerit" (*P.L.*, 162: 1083–84, Statute 5).

68. Ibid., col. 1085, Statutes 7, 9, 11, 14.

69. Ibid., col. 1083, Statute 3. Enclosure was more strict at contemporary Cluniac and Cistercian nunneries (Roger Gazeau, "La clôture des moniales au XIIe siècle en France," *Revue Mabillon* 58 [1974]: 295).

70. *P.L.*, 162: 1084, Statute 6. We also know from Andrea's *vita* that the abbess and prioress of Fontevrault traveled extensively (*P.L.*, 162: 1068 ff.). Petronilla's travels can

tion of the men and women. This is an injunction that sick nuns are never to be anointed or receive communion, except in the church, a rule presumably intended to prevent the possibility of a priest entering the nuns' quarters.[71]

All but two of the statutes of Rule II are included in Rule I, either unchanged, or with slight changes. The rule that described the authority of abbess Petronilla is omitted, as is a prohibition of meat-eating. Of the numerous statutes included in Rule I, but not found in Rule II, many concern dress, a topic not touched upon in Rule II. More important to us here are the additional rules directed at restricting contact between men and women in the community. Nine of the forty-four rules for women and one of the twenty-seven rules for men deal with such restrictions.[72] Most of these are concerned with preventing contact between the sexes during the various religious offices. For example: "When the priest comes to celebrate mass, the door to the choir will not be open to the nuns, unless for communion, and when they do receive communion, the abbess, dean, or cellaress should always watch over them."[73] The one new men's statute is concerned with the possibility of women entering the male quarters: "The brothers are not to receive women [*mulieres*] into their houses to do their work."[74]

Other added rules spell out a stricter discipline for women than was apparent in Rule II. For example, the statute is repeated that enjoins the cloistered nuns to silence, while excepting those who need to do business outside, but a rule is added specifying that they are to maintain the honesty and seriousness of the cloister as much as they can, within and without. No nun is to go outside the cloister to do anything, unless ordered by the abbess; no nun can go outside with-

---

also be gauged by the many scattered charters bearing her signature (Niderst, pp. 67–74).

71. *P.L.*, 162: 1083, Statute 5.

72. Ibid., cols. 1079–82, Statutes XXVIII-XXX, XXXIII-XXXV, XXXVIII, XL, XLI (women), and col. 1083, XIV (men). In von Walter's edition of Rule I, which is superior to Migne's, these statutes are numbers 28, 29, 32–36 (women) and 15 (men).

73. *P.L.*, 162: 1081, Statute XXXIII (von Walter, p. 192, Statute 32). Compare canon 27 of the Second Lateran Council (1139), which forbids canons or monks to sing in the same choir with nuns (J. D. Mansi, *Sacrorum conciliorum nova et amplissima collectio* [Venice, 1776], 21: 533).

74. *P.L.*, 162: 1083, Statute XIV (von Walter, p. 194, Statute 15). This sounds like the Cistercian prohibitions of contact with women, and probably refers to servants rather than nuns.

out the company of at least two men, one religious and one secular, and there is to be no speaking *en route* except by the abbess or prioress.[75]

These surviving fragments of the Rule of Fontevrault confirm the picture formed by the saint's lives of Robert of a religious community based upon a well-thought-out relationship between men and women. Even though reliant on men for the conducting of religious services, it was the women who, in their lives of contemplation, were the focus of the community. The men were there to serve the nuns, both spiritually and materially. Robert's choice of a woman to be the superior of the community, and the complete charge of both men and women given to the abbess by the Rule, confirm the predominant importance of the female element at Fontevrault.

Because its male and female communities were in close proximity and because a woman held administrative authority over both communities, Fontevrault is often referred to by scholars (though not by its contemporaries) as a "double monastery." Although double communities of men and women, governed by an abbess, had been common in the earlier Middle Ages, they had died out in the tenth and eleventh centuries, and Fontevrault has been seen as a twelfth-century revival of this form. The term "double monastery" is misleading, however, and a detailed investigation of the foundation and development of Fontevrault can help clarify the use of the term. The term is often used with the implication that the two communities, joined for convenience under the authority of one person, were of equal importance. But the term "double" disguises the fact that most of these communities were originally founded for the benefit of either men or women rather than both. The Anglo-Saxon double monasteries seem to have been primarily communities for women. A. H. Thompson remarks that "it is difficult to regard these religious houses . . . as anything but nunneries in connection with which there were communities of brethren to do such work and perform such services as the nuns could not do or perform themselves."[76] In

<hr />

75. *P.L.*, 162: 1079–80, Statutes III, XXVI, XVIII, XIX (von Walter, pp. 190–91 (Statutes 3, 26, 18, and 19); the full text of Statute 26 is found only in von Walter's edition.

76. Alexander Hamilton Thompson, "Double Monasteries and the Male Element in Nunneries," in *The Ministry of Women: A Report by a Committee Appointed by His Grace the Lord Archbishop of Canterbury* (London: Society for Promoting Christian Knowledge, 1919), p. 148.

these early foundations, as at Fontevrault, where the nuns were also the predominant element, it was the norm to have an abbess rule over both men and women. Yet there were other communities referred to as "double monasteries" that were in origin male communities to which a group of women became attached. Such an association might begin gradually, by the offering of protection for a female recluse, or large numbers of women might be associated from an early date, as was the case in the Premonstratensian order.[77] Not surprisingly, this type of "double monastery" had an abbot as head. The use of the term "double monastery" thus disguises a variety of organizational structures, a variety influenced by the original purpose and mode of foundation of the communities. The importance and role of women in these communities could be very different, as in some cases the community was at its foundation organized around the needs of women and women were in charge of governance, while in others women were taken into predominantly male communities, perhaps because they sought a religious life and could not find suitable nunneries. In the former, men were attached to a female community for the convenience and support of the women; in the latter, women were attached to a male community as a favor to the women and for their protection. Between these two extremes was a variety of establishments responding to local needs and pressures. Rather than speaking of these communities as "double monasteries," it is more exact to recognize the diversity of arrangements and purposes by referring to the general phenomenon of religious men and women living in close proximity to each other, and by specifying the particular purpose and arrangements at the communities in question.[78] Fontevrault, as we have seen above, was a community intended by its founder to be centered on women. The men were an important part of the community, but their importance rested upon their subservient role: they were there to serve the women.

A wide range of documents—chronicles, letters, as well as charters from the monastery itself—confirm this picture of the relative roles

77. Stephanus Hilpisch, *History of Benedictine Nuns*, trans. Sister M. Joanne Muggli, ed. Leonard J. Doyle (Collegeville, Minn.: St. John's Abbey Press; 1958), pp. 23–24. Benedictine monasteries commonly had such an attached group of nuns (Schmitz, 7: 45–50); see Stein, pp. 37–38, for examples in twelfth-century Cologne.

78. On this point, see Sharon Elkins, "Double Monasteries of Twelfth Century England" (paper delivered at the Seventeenth International Congress on Medieval Studies, Kalamazoo, 1982).

of men and women at Fontevrault. In fact, sources from outside the monastery rarely even mention the men at Fontevrault. All letters addressed to Fontevrault were addressed to the abbess, the abbess and the nuns, or the nuns; the salutations never include the men.[79] The content of these letters, and of letters written about, as well as to, Fontevrault, only infrequently mention the men of the community.[80]

Occasional mentions of Fontevrault in chronicles give us another view of how outsiders perceived the institution. Here again, Fontevrault is most frequently described as a community of nuns. William of Malmesbury, writing not long after Robert's death, identified Fontevrault clearly as an establishment for women:

> [Robert of Arbrissel] was the most celebrated and eloquent preacher of these times: so much did he excel, not in frothy, but honeyed diction, that from the gifts of persons vying with each other in making presents, he founded that distinguished monastery of nuns at Font-Evraud, in which every secular pleasure being extirpated, no other place possesses such multitudes of devout women, fervent in their obedience to God. For in addition to the rejection of other allurements, how great is this! that they never speak but in the chapter: the rule of constant silence being enjoined by the superior, because, when this is broken, women are prone to vain talk.[81]

William of Newburgh's account, written in the 1190s, similarly mentions only women, and another English chronicle records that Henry II and Richard I were buried with "the nuns of Fontevrault." A treatise on the various monastic orders, written in 1154, mentions only nuns at Fontevrault. Another chronicle notes that Robert of Arbrissel drew to him many people of both sexes, and one chronicle, oddly, mentions only male followers.[82]

79. For example, letters from Honorius II (*P.L.*, 166: 1268), Lucius II (*P.L.*, 179: 864, 924), Paschal II (*P.L.*, 163: 296, 419), Calixtus II (*P.L.*, 163: 1121), Innocent II (*P.L.*, 179: 72, 304, 320, 634, 635), Eugenius III (*P.L.*, 180: 1037, 1396, 1413).

80. Some letters do mention *fratres* at Fontevrault: from Calixtus II (*P.L.*, 163: 1122), Lucius II (*P.L.*, 179: 865), Gelasius II (*P.L.*, 163: 504), Honorius II (*P.L.*, 166: 1268), Eugenius III (*P.L.*, 180: 1037).

81. *Chronicle of the Kings of England*, trans. J. A. Giles (London, 1904), p. 471. The Latin can be found in the Rolls Series, no. 90, vol. 2, p. 512 (Book 5, §440). Giles translates the word *egregium* as "noble"; I have changed this to "distinguished."

82. *Historia rerum Anglicarum*, Rolls Series, no. 82, 1: 51–52; *Ex Radulphi Coggeshalae Abbatis chronico Anglicano*, in *Recueil des historiens des Gaules et de la France*, 18: 62, 85; Robert of Torigny, *Tractatus de immutatione ordinis monachorum* (*P.L.*, 202:

Internal documents—most voluminously, charters of donation and disputes over property—make it clear that the large population of monks at Fontevrault was there to serve the nuns, just as Robert had ordained. The following analysis of the relative roles of the monks and nuns as seen from within Fontevrault is based on a study of the hundreds of charters that survive.[83] Of these hundreds, only a handful of charters mention men as the recipients of a gift. The donations are usually made to "God, blessed Mary, and the nuns of Fontevrault," or to "God, blessed Mary, and the church of Fontevrault."[84] The huge proportion of donations addressed to the nuns of Fontevrault rather than to the monks, or to the nuns and monks together, demonstrates that outsiders (here the people donating

---

1312); The *Annals* of Saint-Sergius of Angers, entry for the year 1116, in *Chroniques des eglises d'Anjou*, ed. Paul Marchegay and Emile Mabille (Paris, 1869), p. 143; The Chronicle of Saint-Maxentius of Poitiers records that in the year 1100 Robert began to build the monastery of Fontevrault and to support churchmen (*patres*) and monks in many places (ibid., p. 420).

83. The cartulary of Fontevrault, of which less than half (about 400 charters) still exists, is in two pieces; the bulk of it is in the Bibliothèque nationale in Paris (nouv. acq. lat. 2414), and nine folios are in the Archives départementales of Maine-et-Loire, bound with a nineteenth-century copy of the part of the cartulary that is in the BN (Maine-et-Loire, 101H225). (For an account of the history of the cartulary, see R. I. Moore, "The Reconstruction of the Cartulary of Fontevrault," *Bulletin of the Institute of Historical Research*, London University 41 [1968]: 86–95.) The bulk of the charters in the cartulary date from the first half of the twelfth century. I have supplemented these with other charters dating through 1249, both original charters deposited in the archives of Maine-et-Loire (hereafter abbreviated M&L), and a large collection of extracts of charters made at the end of the seventeenth century and now preserved in Paris (Bibliothèque nationale, Collection Gaignières, *Extraict des titres originaux de l'abbaye de Fontevraud en Anjou au diocèse de Poitiers*, 1699; ms. lat 5480; abbreviated as BN5480; this manuscript is paginated rather than foliated). When referring to charters from the cartulary of Fontevrault, my reference will be F, for Fontevrault, followed by the number of the charter in the nineteenth-century copy (M&L 101H225), followed by a folio number, if it is from BN nouv. ms. lat. 2414, or a page number if it is from the nine manuscript leaves in M&L 101H225 (these leaves are paginated, 1–18); thus, for example, F781, fol. 75r. This system should facilitate reference to either the original in Paris or the copy in Angers. Folio references are to the folio on which the given charter begins, although the quotation itself might come from the next folio.

84. Donations made to both the women and the men of Fontevrault (all from the first half of the twelfth century): F720, fol. 52r; F743, fol. 62r; F746, fol. 63v; F754, fol. 66v; F787, fol. 77r. Donations made to the men only: BN5480, p. 77 (1199); BN5480, p. 49 (1232); BN5480, p. 83 (1237). Eleanor of Aquitaine founded a chapel of St. Laurence at Fontevrault and donated revenues for the maintenance of a chaplain (BN5480, p. 465); later gifts from others provided further support for that chaplain: M&L 101H55; BN5480, p. 226; BN5480, p. 286.

property) viewed Fontevrault as a community of women rather than as a special community of both men and women.[85] But the salutations might also be considered an insider's point of view, since the language with which a charter was worded must frequently have been the work of the scribe, or perhaps a representative of the church who dictated to the scribe. The salutations of the donations might, then, present a good image of the self-definition of the community.

Whether the salutations present an inside or an outside perspective, the circumstances of the drawing up of the charters makes even more significant the predominance of the nuns in the salutations, as the monks were more involved in these business transactions than the nuns. It is likely that the charters were drawn up by monks rather than nuns, as the few charters we have that indicate the scribe name a man.[86] Furthermore, the donors were more likely to have had direct dealings with the monks of the community than with the nuns (other than the abbess or prioress). The witness lists included in many of the charters from the first half of the twelfth century show the abbess and prioress of Fontevrault appearing with regularity as witnesses (in thirty-three charters out of 305 from the first half of the century). Even if not serving as witness, one of them is often mentioned as having arranged the donation, as having paid a *quid pro quo* to the donor, or as having received the donation (or consent to the donation) *in manu*. But other nuns appear rarely—only three of the 305 charters were witnessed by nuns other than the abbess or prioress. In contrast, monks of the community appear as witnesses even more frequently than the abbess and prioress, in sixty-three charters. The monks also did other business involved in seeing a donation through to completion—they might measure the land to be given, or go to a donor's home to secure consent from a wife and children who had not come to the ceremony at the monastery.[87] In fact, it was not uncommon for the donation itself to be made away from the monastery, closer to the donor's home.[88]

---

85. In contrast, donations to Gilbertine houses in England, houses frequently compared to Fontevrault, are commonly addressed to "the nuns and their brethren, cleric and lay," or to "the canons and nuns": F. M. Stenton, *Transcripts of Charters Relating to the Gilbertine Houses of Sixle, Ormsby, Catley, Bullington, and Alvingham* (Horncastle: W. K. Morton and Sons for the Lincoln Record Society, 1922), p. 77 and passim.

86. For example, F574, fol. 2r; F760, fol. 68v.

87. F830, fol. 89v; F910, fol. 133r; F580, fol. 6v.

88. F719, fol. 51v; F780, fol. 74v; F772, fol. 72r: a monk of Fontevrault present on all three occasions, and the abbess in F780.

The handling of business affairs as presented by these charters shows that most nuns had little to do with business matters. Many tasks were taken care of by the monks, who often traveled outside the community on business. But the dominant figure on these journeys was the abbess or the prioress, who often coordinated the whole transaction. In one case in which a dismissal of a claim was made "in the hand" of a monk Gaufridus, we are told that it was done this way "because the abbess was not there"—that is, the expectation was that the abbess would have received the dismissal, but in her absence the monk substituted for her.[89] Although the abbess and prioress were busy with the economic concerns of the abbey, the other women in the community were left free for their spiritual duties, the life of contemplation, while the monks took care of the necessary work involved in keeping up with the stream of donations. The ready availability of the monks made it unnecessary for the nuns to travel outside the community on business matters. Such travel had been allowed for in the rule of the community, so it was not that a strict cloistering of the nuns required that business be carried out by the monks. Rather, at Fontevrault, despite the fact that the nuns were not strictly cloistered by their rule, it was seen as preferable to have the monks do this necessary but spiritually unrewarding work.[90]

Two examples illustrate the utility of having monks available to carry on business outside the abbey. In 1114 Geoffrey of Vendôme, the abbot of an important monastery in a neighboring province, came to Fontevrault to give a salt revenue from the domain of his abbey. In return, the anniversary of Geoffrey's death was to be observed at Fontevrault. The charter records that this transaction was made "in the chapter of Fontevrault, in the presence of lord Geoffrey abbot and of lord Robert our master, with the assent of all the sisters."[91] We see, then, some business, involving Geoffrey, one of the monastic celebrities of the area, taking place at Fontevrault in the

89. F719, fol. 51v. The action took place away from Fontevrault.

90. Compare Abelard's recommendations to Heloise regarding the role of monks in taking care of the external needs of nuns (T. P. McLaughlin, pp. 257–58; *The Letters of Abelard and Heloise*, pp. 209–10). The situation was quite different at Le Ronceray d'Angers; there the resident canons and priests, as well as lay male officials, carried out business for the community, but the nuns themselves participated much more frequently than was the case at Fontevrault ("Women and Men in Monastic Business: The Case of Le Ronceray d'Angers," paper by the author presented at the Sixth Berkshire Conference on the History of Women, 1984).

91. F698, fol. 43v.

chapter of nuns; no monks are mentioned. However, when the concession of this revenue was later confirmed at the chapter of the monastery of Vendôme, two monks from Fontevrault were present.[92] The important business, including the reception of the abbot, was done in the presence of the nuns, and then the necessary but time-consuming task of seeing the transaction through to its confirmation (a task that also entailed travel away from Fontevrault) was taken care of by the monks.

In another example, the monks took care of the groundwork for a transaction that was later confirmed at Fontevrault by the chapter of nuns. Sometime during the second quarter of the twelfth century, abbess Petronilla gave a house to a couple and their heirs, who were to pay a certain amount in dues for it to Fontevrault. The transaction was witnessed by nine men, including the prior, two monks, and two priests of Fontevrault. This transaction apparently took place away from the abbey, since we are told that a short time later the abbess confirmed the gift in the chapter, with the nuns consenting.[93] The chapter of nuns clearly acted as the formal governing body, before which business matters were brought for conclusion. A donation confirmed in the chapter might have involved much preparation by the monks, as well as by the abbess or prioress, but it was in the chapter of nuns that the act would be finally formalized.[94]

What of the internal governance of the community? Did that work out as Robert had hoped, with the monks "content with what is given to them by the nuns"? Unfortunately, documents recording internal affairs are virtually nonexistent; many directions must have been given orally rather than in writing, or else the documents that were generated were not deemed worthy of preservation. Two documents survive from the first half of the thirteenth century that illus-

92. Ibid.; an abbreviated version (lacking mention of Fontevrist monks at Vendôme) in *P.L.*, 162: 1095–96.

93. F575, fol. 3r.

94. The chapter at which such ceremonies took place was apparently only for nuns, not nuns and monks: "capitul[um] piae et justae congregationis sanctimonialium" (F692, fol. 41v). However, on at least one occasion, the nuns and monks met together in chapter. In 1119 Calixtus II visited Fontevrault and confirmed the possessions and privileges of the abbey. The charter of confirmation mentions his attendance at the chapter "of brothers as well as sisters": "Sequenti sane die in capitulum venientes, in pleniorii [sic] tam fratrum, quam sororum conventu . . ." (*P.L.*, 163: 1122). But it seems likely that the men joined the assembly just for the special occasion of hearing Calixtus, which perhaps explains the use of the comparative form of *plenus*.

trate the relative roles of the abbess, nuns, and monks in decisions that affected the whole community. A charter from 1210 records a transfer of revenue from the nuns to the monks: "I abbess Adele and the convent of Fontevrault announce that on the petition of our brother Harduinus, we give to God and blessed John the Evangelist and the convent of our clercs and brothers of the Habit of Fontevrault, ten *solidi* to be rendered annually to the prior."[95] Ten sous is a very small sum. Perhaps some circumstance made this particular revenue especially important to the monks, or perhaps this was a type of transaction that went on all the time at Fontevrault, without usually being recorded or preserved. The second document records a decision made in 1241 by a later abbess Adele with the assent and counsel of the prioress, prior, and the whole chapter (of nuns, presumably), regulating the mixture of grains with which bread was to be made for the whole community—nuns and brothers, both cleric and lay.[96] Scanty as these documents are, it is reassuring to find at least this much confirmation of Robert's intentions that the abbess would govern both the men and the women, even with respect to the details of material life.[97]

95. BN5480, p. 340.
96. BN5480, p. 439.
97. The fifteenth-century reformed rule of Fontevrault details a decision-making process for the community. When an important decision had to be made, the prioress was to call together all the nuns. After getting their advice, she could, if she so desired, ask for advice from secular experts or from some of the brothers. But if she did ask for advice from the brothers, they were to give it in humility and subjection, and not push their advice in an impudent manner (*Regula ordinis Fontis-Ebraldi. La reigle de l'ordre de Font-Evrauld* [Paris, 1642], p. 198). As the tone indicates, the fifteenth-century monks might not have been as willing to devote themselves to the nuns as the twelfth-century members of the order. Certainly by the seventeenth century, the whole arrangement must have seemed odd. At least two treatises were written that were largely apologies for the organizational subjection of men to women at Fontevrault: *Noviciat des enfans de la Vierge dicts religieux de l'ordre de Fontevrauld*, faict par le Solitaire de la Sacrée Vierge mère de Dieu (Poitiers, 1634); *De la puissance et jurisdiction des religieux pères confesseurs de l'ordre de Fontevrauld au sainct sacrement de poenitence* (Poitiers, 1634). F. Uzureau briefly discusses the seventeenth-century male objection to their "subjection" to women in "La réforme de l'ordre de Fontevrault," *Revue Mabillon* 9 (1923): 145. For information on one community's regulation of economic relations between its nuns and canons in the second half of the eleventh century, see N.-N. Huyghebaert, "Examen des plus anciennes chartes de l'abbaye de Messines," *Bulletin de la commission royale d'histoire* 121 (1956): 175–222. At Messines the men and women originally held all property jointly, but after a dispute between the abbess and the canons over revenues, the goods were partitioned (pp. 175–81).

What light is shed on the general situation of women in monastic life by the example of Fontevrault? Two basic observations can be made. On the one hand, by looking in detail at this one foundation, we have seen the kinds of needs for spiritual and material assistance, the *cura monialium*, that all nunneries had. All nunneries had to make some kind of arrangement for these services, and, until the end of the twelfth century, most of the predominantly male monastic orders were willing to participate in a more or less close relationship with female establishments. Besides the innumerable individual monasteries that accepted women as well as men,[98] the early establishments of the orders of Arrouaise, Prémontré, and even Cîteaux either included women, or had nearby communities of women closely associated with them. Within the Benedictine order, men set up communities early in the twelfth century in imitation of Robert of Arbrissel: Vital de Tierceville (who founded Savigny), Gerard de Sales (Cadouin), and Raoul de la Futaye (Saint-Sulpice). The order founded by Gilbert of Sempringham followed similar lines. Traditional Benedictine nunneries also had to have relationships with male clerics for spiritual services and with lay-brothers for material services.[99] Medieval hospitals were another type of religious organization that included close cooperation between male and female religious.[100] In this context, Fontevrault was not an unusual institution and was not viewed as such by contemporaries—rather, it was viewed as a prominent community of nuns. On the other hand, Fontevrault differed in important ways from other female communities, and these differences, I would suggest, were responsible for Fontevrault's

98. See Berlière, pp. 3–21.

99. One of the more extensive twelfth-century discussions of the appropriate working relationship between male and female religious can be found in the correspondence of Abelard and Heloise, particularly Letter 7(8) (see above, n. 60). For review of the question of the authenticity of the correspondence, see D. E. Luscombe, "The *Letters* of Heloise and Abelard since 'Cluny 1972,'" in *Petrus Abaelardus, 1079–1142: Person, Werk und Wirkung*, ed. Rudolf Thomas, *Trier theologische Studien*, vol. 38 (Trier, 1980), pp. 19–39; and John F. Benton, "A Reconsideration of the Authenticity of the Correspondence of Abelard and Heloise," in ibid., pp. 41–52. Abelard's views on women in the religious life have been analyzed by Mary Martin McLaughlin, "Peter Abelard and the Dignity of Women: Twelfth Century 'Feminism' in Theory and Practice," in *Pierre Abélard, Pierre le Vénérable: Les courants philosophiques, littéraires et artistiques en occident au milieu du XIIe siècle* (Colloques Internationaux du Centre de la Recherche Scientifique, Abbaye de Cluny 2 au 9 juillet 1972) (Paris: C.N.R.S., 1975), pp. 287–334.

100. Nübel, pp. 20–23.

continued existence and success as an institution even during the
thirteenth century, when other orders were making efforts to exclude
or restrict the participation of women.

Perhaps contributing to Fontevrault's success was the relatively
large number of men at Fontevrault, at least during its first two centuries of existence. We do not have extensive information on the
numbers of monks and nuns at Fontevrault and other communities,
but Fontevrault had what was probably an unusually large community of men. Seventy-nine different monks appear among the witnesses to charters from Fontevrault during the period 1100–1149. An
account of pensions to be paid to the monks and chaplains of Fontevrault, dating from 1228, lists some 120 names.[101] The large number
of co-resident men provided a sizable "staff" available to carry out
the various tasks necessary to the continued financial success of the
institution—and Fontevrault was highly successful in attracting donations. The large pool of help also meant that the burden of service
could be spread widely (few monks appear as witnesses more than
once or twice); perhaps this eased resentment that might otherwise
have been felt. And when we think of the variety and number of
business tasks and trips undertaken by the monks of Fontevrault, the
resentment expressed by Cistercian and Premonstratensian monks
and canons because of the "burden" of women becomes understandable.[102] But more information is needed before we conclude that the
simple fact of numbers was particularly important to the success of
Fontevrault. Scholars may have underestimated the number of men
usually resident at a nunnery.[103] On the other hand, the many priories of Fontevrault may not have had nearly as high a proportion of
monks as did the mother-house.[104]

101. M&L 101H225.

102. For a good description of the "burden" from the male Cistercian point of view,
see S. Thompson, p. 239.

103. For information on numbers of men and women in some Benedictine houses,
see Schmitz 7: 52.

104. Alfred Jubien gives some statistics on the population of ten priories of Fon-
tevrault in 1209:
Saint-Aignan: 60 nuns, 2 monks, 2 clercs
Le Breuil: 52 nuns, 9 monks
Saint-Croix: 75 nuns, 2 clercs, 2 laymen [*lais*]
L'Espinasse: 100 nuns, 2 clercs, 3 laymen
Le Paravis: 59 nuns, 3 priests, 1 clerc, 10 laymen
Vaupillon: 56 nuns, 1 priest, 11 laymen
Saint-Laurent: 76 nuns, 2 monks, 22 laymen

The major difference between Fontevrault and other orders was that in the early stage of its development, the founder and early members of Fontevrault formally institutionalized, through detailed written regulations, the relationship that was to exist between the men and the women of the community, with the women the focus of the community, and the men there to serve the women. In commenting on the exclusion of women from Arrouaise and other orders at the turn of the century, Ludo Milis refers to the importance of the organizational inclusion of women:

> Around 1200, many orders began a movement to abolish or diminish the female presence. It is likely that the origin of part of the discontent could be found in an inadequate organization: statutes appropriate to the sisters of Arrouaise were never drawn up; for the Norbertine sisters, there were only a few, added on to the Customary of the men.[105]

In the earlier Middle Ages—the sixth to ninth centuries—women were active in the monasticism of the frontier but were excluded from the later, more thoroughly organized, period of monastic development of the tenth and eleventh centuries. A similar pattern seems to have occurred in the twelfth and thirteenth centuries. The new frontier was both territorial and spiritual: territorial in the desire (expressed at Fontevrault as well as Cîteaux) to set up communities in a wilderness area, spiritual in the desire to push the boundaries of monastic spirituality beyond those of the previously institutionalized church. These frontiers dissipated more quickly than the frontier of initial conversion, corresponding to a more rapid reconsideration of women's place in these twelfth-century movements.

The women of Fontevrault apparently were spared this disruption because the inclusion of women was written into the legislation of the order, whereas elsewhere, women, having attached themselves as they could to a predominantly male structure, were easily viewed as peripheral, and were likely to be forced out as the organization of the

---

Boulauc: 70 nuns, a prior, 2 priests, 1 clerc, 31 laybrothers [*frères lais*]

Langages: 79 nuns, 4 monks, 4 laybrothers

Mommère: 60 nuns, 1 chaplain, 20 laybrothers

[*L'abbesse Marie de Bretagne et la réforme de l'ordre de Fontevrault d'après des documents inédits* (Angers, 1872), p. 11, n. 2]

Grelier also comments on the small numbers of men (often just two, three, or four) at many of the priories (p. 150).

105. Milis, pp. 516–17.

order was tightened. In other words, the early formalization, or institutionalization, of women's participation at Fontevrault prevented the attacks suffered in other orders. The participation of women at Fontevrault was not unusual for the first half of the twelfth century, but the formal structuring of an arrangement dominated by women was. The structured inclusion of men was also important to Fontevrault's success. In most other cases, arrangements were made with men on a more casual basis, using whatever resources were locally available. There were several variables in the arrangements: Would the fulfillment of the material and spiritual needs of the nuns be cast as service or supervision? Would they be fulfilled by an individual man or a community of men? Would that individual or community be co-resident with the nuns or at a distance? The particular arrangement could make a great difference in the reliability of services for the nuns. Those nuns dependent on priests from a separate, neighboring community, for example, had a less convenient and secure arrangement than nuns who could call on a resident chaplain or group of chaplains. Whether this male participation was structured as service or supervision also made a difference. The business trips undertaken by the monks of Fontevrault under the direction of the abbess or prioress were a different phenomenon from the Cistercian use of a male supervisor (*custos*) for temporal affairs.[106] The system at Fontevrault tended to avoid the antagonisms that could occur in more casual arrangements. The men at Fontevrault were part of the community and they identified with it. What was unique about Fontevrault was not that it had some men associated with the community but that it had a particularly large group of men actually integrated into the community by the original design of the founder. Robert of Arbrissel also firmly established the role of the men in the community as one of service, not supervision.[107] Although this may have been the intent at many other female commu-

106. Nichols, p. 30. For details on various arrangements, see also Lekai, pp. 350–52; Elkins, "Female Religious," p. 6; Nicolas Huyghebaert, "Les femmes laïques dans la vie religieuse des XIe et XIIe siècles dans la province ecclésiastique de Reims," *I laici nella "societas christiana" dei secoli XI e XII* (Atti della terza settimana internazionale di studio, Mendola, 2–27 agosto 1965) (Milan, 1968), p. 371.

107. For an interpretation that minimizes Robert's role in the structuring of the institutions of Fontevrault, see Jacqueline Smith, "Robert of Arbrissel: *Procurator Mulierum*," in *Medieval Women*, pp. 175–84. Smith is a good antidote to Bezzola and others who elaborate, with little evidence, on Robert's intentions in founding and

nities, it was rare in twelfth- and thirteenth-century institutions to have the power of the abbess so little curtailed by male authority of one kind or another. This undoubtedly enhanced the prestige of Fontevrault and contributed to its reputation as one of the foremost communities for women in France.

These institutional arrangements enabled Fontevrault to survive the period of monastic retrenchment that occurred at the end of the twelfth and the beginning of the thirteenth century, and to escape the knife of necessity or convenience that severed women from many monastic communities. The woman-centeredness of Fontevrault was not unique, but its firm institutional expression was, making it impossible to view the nuns at Fontevrault as burdensome, unimportant, or peripheral.

In the preceding chapter we saw that the image of the Virgin Mary was deeply appealing to the male religious mind of the twelfth and thirteenth centuries, but that even the Queen of Heaven was subject to notions of feminine humility and submissiveness. The attitudes toward actual female religious were even more clearly contradictory. On the one hand, Christianity had from the earliest centuries affirmed the validity and special virtue of the religious woman consecrated to virginity. On the other hand, unlike the Virgin Mary, the living, human woman could never, it seems, totally divest herself of a kind of sexual aura implicit in her femaleness. Eleanor McLaughlin notes that "the female religious, even though she had denied her sensuality and sex in embracing the virginal life, never escaped the male assumption that she was a danger, a source of contamination, and that, in addition, her sex made her incapable of resisting the temptations of any contact with the male or the world." [108] Women's sexuality was dangerous to the woman herself, and so necessitated her strict enclosure (stricter than that for men), an enclosure that would save her from confronting temptation that she would apparently be too weak to resist. [109] But women's sexuality was also dangerous as a potential

---

structuring Fontevrault, but I think she goes too far in the opposite direction, ignoring Robert's continuing involvement in the community after its foundation, as evidenced in Andrea's *Vita* and in many charters of donation.

108. E. C. McLaughlin, "Equality of Souls," p. 244 (article cited above, n. 12).

109. Ibid.; see also Idung of Prüfening, pp. 168–76 (the third question in *An Argument concerning Five Questions*), in which he argues that Benedict's rule was obviously not written for nuns because they need stricter enclosure than is outlined in the rule.

source of contamination to male religious. This latter danger is the-
oretically reciprocal, with men being a potential source of contamination to women and so to be avoided, but the reciprocity is incom-
plete in two ways: (1) women were in fact viewed as being more
identified with sexuality than men and, like Eve, were considered the
primary source of temptation; and (2) as we have seen throughout
this chapter, religious women were not free to abandon contact and
interaction with men, because their spiritual and material sustenance
was dependent upon the cooperation of men. Monks, themselves in
no way dependent on the spiritual or temporal services of women,
could successfully have a goal of total avoidance of contact with
women.

The ideology of feminine weakness and disability is an important
link in this dynamic of ambivalence. That is, Christianity affirms that
women can overcome sexuality through virginity and thus achieve a
spiritual vocation, but Christian doctrine maintains that women cannot be priests, and Christian practice dictated that women needed
not only the service of men but also their protection and supervision.
Yet because of the aura of sexuality around even these religious
women, the contact between men and women dictated by such service, protection, and/or supervision of nuns was too dangerous for
celibate men to safely perform, a danger most vociferously expressed
by the Premonstratensian abbot Conrad of Marchthal.[110]

But what about the periods of monastic cooperation between men
and women? It seems that in peak times of religious enthusiasm
monks and nuns could overcome sexual fears and work together as
brother and sister. But the more successful the movement, the more
recruits it attracted, the more difficult discipline may have become to
maintain, and the more resentful monks may have become of the increased demands for assistance. Fontevrault, which fully institutionalized the early stage of cooperation and service, was the one
movement that was able to avoid the pushing of women to the periphery so easily encouraged by the deep-seated male ambivalence toward women.

Woman, both as image and actor, was thus experienced in highly

110. Compare Idung, who emphasized that nuns needed male supervision (p. 176),
but who also praised the Cistercian prohibition on abbots giving direction to nuns
because of the spiritual injury (to the male) that might occur, an injury that would
outweigh the spiritual profit to be gained by the nuns (p. 107).

contradictory terms by male religious. As the Virgin Mary, she was a paragon of virtue, from whom all taint of sexuality had in this one case successfully been washed away (highlighted in the twelfth-century interest in the doctrine of the immaculate conception); as anonymous collectivity, women were feared as a source of sexual temptation and resented as a burden on monastic time; but finally as specific individuals, encountered as co-religionists, women were accorded affection, respect, and support as well as scorn, disgust, and neglect.[111] To be a religious woman living within this tangled web of contradictory attitudes was (and remains) a problematic experience.

111. Marie-Thérèse d'Alverny briefly makes a similar point with regard to medieval theologians: while they denigrated women in the abstract, they still could carry out affectionate and supportive relationships with individual women, Saint Jerome being the classic example ("Comment les théologiens et les philosophes voient la femme," *Cahiers de civilisation médiévale* 20 [1977]: 110, 129).

·4·

Secular Life
Control of Property

Having examined key images of women, both secular and religious, and having documented aspects of women's religious experience in the twelfth and early thirteenth centuries, we turn now to consider a central element of the secular experience of medieval women—their control of property. Although I believe no one factor to be the primary determinant of social and economic life, I agree with those who see rights in property and the control of its disposition as crucial elements in the structure and extent of women's secular power.[1] The voluminous records kept by medieval monasteries detailing the property transactions between these institutions and the communities surrounding them provide rich documentation regarding the basic structures of property control.

Analysis of these documents shows that women's experience was founded upon a central structural dynamic reminiscent of that found in *chansons de geste*. The fundamental unit in which possession and control of property were vested was the family, a social body of which women were necessary members. But within the family, a woman's position with respect to rights and control over property was normally secondary to those of male members. Thus, one commonly sees women included in property transactions, but usually at the pe-

---

1. For example, Joan Kelly-Gadol, "The Social Relations of the Sexes: Methodological Implications of Women's History," *Signs: Journal of Women in Culture and Society* 1 (1976): 819; Martin King Whyte, *The Status of Women in Preindustrial Societies* (Princeton: Princeton University Press, 1978), p. 170.

riphery. Yet there were circumstances (primarily widowhood) that could thrust a woman into a central role. The medieval household, bound together by property interests, was a unit whose hierarchical nature demanded one head, usually a man. But when deprived of that head by death, it was normal to place a woman in that role, rather than leave the family without a head or to search outside the household for a less closely related male.[2]

Several studies based on the quantitative analysis of medieval charters either focus on or include information about women and the family.[3] Except for a pioneering article by David Herlihy that surveys all of continental Europe,[4] these studies are based on single regions. The necessity and value of such regional studies is clear: the abundance of available charter evidence necessitates selection, and a selection by region is desirable because of the wide variation in conditions and circumstance in different parts of medieval Europe. These regional studies are also temporally more restricted than Herlihy's survey, which covers the eighth through twelfth centuries; some studies focus on one century, others may cover as much as two hundred years. Important and necessary as such regional studies are, the frag-

2. For this formulation of women's role in the hierarchy of the household, I am indebted to Barbara B. Diefendorf: "Widowhood and Remarriage in Sixteenth-Century Paris," *Journal of Family History* 7 (1982): 386. Also suggestive is Laurel Thatcher Ulrich's discussion of the wife as "deputy husband" in colonial New England: *Good Wives: Image and Reality in Northern New England, 1650–1750* (New York: Knopf, 1982), pp. 36–50, 238.

3. While the present study is based upon monastic charters, there are various other documents also relevant to property control. Wills and marriage contracts are, like charters, documents of practice that can be used to understand social behavior. Unfortunately, these two types of documents do not survive for northern France for the period under consideration. Legal codes have also not been utilized here. Binding legal codes, legislated by a central authority, do not exist for this period, and collections of customary law exist only from the very end of the period. Furthermore, laws express prescription or intention, rather than deed, and it is the actual practice of property control that concerns us here, although reference to customary law will be made insofar as a confirmation or contradiction of practice is evident.

4. David Herlihy, "Land, Family and Women in Continental Europe, 701–1200," *Traditio* 18 (1962): 89–121. For a general consideration of women's participation in monastic charters, see Marc A. Meyer, "Land Charters and the Legal Position of Anglo-Saxon Women," in *The Women of England from Anglo-Saxon Times to the Present: Interpretive Bibliographic Essays*, ed. Barbara Kanner (Hamden, Conn.: Archon Books, 1979), pp. 57–82.

mentary nature of the evidence makes synthesis of this material difficult. The substantially different questions posed by the authors and the differing categories of analysis used also hamper a unified comparison of the regional findings. Furthermore, most authors have focused their analysis on the medieval family, with information on women presented as one aspect of the family. When the central questions propelling a study concern the family, questions about the complexity of women's situation are sometimes left unasked.

This chapter presents a regional analysis of Anjou, centering on the question of the structure and extent of women's control of property, with comparisons made whenever possible to other regional studies. I have chosen Anjou because of its importance as a region within northern France, because it is a region for which a detailed study of women and property has not yet been done, and because of the convenience of making further use of the charters from Fontevrault. The Angevin evidence gathered covers a broad period of time (1000–1249), facilitating the identification of long-term trends. Evidence for the eleventh and twelfth centuries has been drawn from the cartularies of three Angevin institutions: Saint-Aubin d'Angers, Le Ronceray d'Angers, and Fontevrault.[5] Thirteenth-century evidence, more difficult to utilize because not collected in medieval cartularies, has been gathered for Fontevrault from archival sources.[6] The bulk of the following analysis is based on 832 charters of donation and sale from these three monasteries. Donations and sales have been singled out from the multitude of types of charters because they most directly reflect the control of property. Evidence from *ca-*

5. *Cartulaire de l'abbaye de Saint-Aubin d'Angers*, ed. Bertrand de Broussillon, 3 vols. (Angers, 1896–1903); *Cartulaire de l'abbaye du Ronceray d'Angers (1028–1184)*, ed. Paul Marchegay (Paris: A. Picard, 1900); cartulary of Fontevrault, Bibliothèque nationale ms. nouv. acq. lat. 2414 and M&L 101H225. (For a description of the cartulary of Fontevrault and my reference system for documents from Fontevrault, see Chapter 3, n. 83.) Charters from the cartulary of Saint-Aubin and Le Ronceray are abbreviated as "A" and "R," respectively, followed by the number of the charter in the published cartulary.

6. The two sources for the thirteenth century were original charters preserved in the Archives départmentales de Maine-et-Loire and the collection of extracts of charters preserved in Bibliothèque nationale ms. lat. 5840. Extracts and charters from before 1150 were excluded, as that period is amply covered by the cartularies. Only dated extracts were used in order to facilitate the matching of the extracts with the archival originals, done to eliminate duplicates. A comparison of these duplicates (about forty) demonstrates the reliability of these extracts; in only one case had relevant material been left out of the extract.

lumpniae, or challenges to such transfers, has generally been kept separate, as a claim to control of property is a different matter from actual participation in a transfer.[7] Donations and sales have been grouped together, since, despite the use of differing terms (*dare* or *donare* as opposed to *vendere*), a substantive difference in the nature of the transfer performed is not always clear. In addition to the promise of spiritual services made to donors, monasteries often made monetary payments, the frequency and size of which make it difficult to draw a firm line between gifts and sales.[8]

People could participate in these transfers in several ways, three of which are of particular relevance here: alienor, co-alienor, and concessor. An example will make these roles clear. In the following charter from the first quarter of the twelfth century, Raginaudus Burget is the alienor, his wife Milesendis is the co-alienor, and his son and his feudal lord are the concessors:

> I Raginaudus Burget and my wife Milesendis give to the congregation of nuns at Fontevrault two arpents of land, one arpent of woods, and a field, namely the half of the fields that is by the stream of Balneolus. Conceding to this donation are my son Odo Borrellus, and Hugo de Giseis, from whose fief the land came.
>
> Witnesses to the act are: Paganus de Rocha and Aimericus, brother of Hugo and son of Amelina.
>
> This act took place at the time that Louis was king of France, Fulk count of Anjou, and Rainaudus bishop of Angers.[9]

---

7. One charter sometimes contains an account of a donation, followed by an account of a later challenge to that donation. For this type of composite charter, the donation has not been included in the sample, since it is the challenge that motivated the redaction of the charter, and the document will be a more faithful record of this *calumpnia* than of the original donation, which may have occurred a long time before (for example, A247 and A250).

8. On the difficulty of distinguishing donations and sales, see Marc Bloch, *Feudal Society*, trans. L. A. Manyon (Chicago: University of Chicago Press, Phoenix Books, 1964), 1: 132; Mireille Castaing-Sicard, "Les donations toulousaines, Xe-XIIIe siècles," *Annales du Midi* 70 (1958): 57–64; Emily Zack Tabuteau, "Transfers of Property in Eleventh-Century Norman Law" (Ph.D. diss., Harvard University, 1975, pp. 32, 35, 72–76, 84–95).

9. Ego Raginaudus Burget et uxor mea Milesendis donamus congregationi sanctimonialium Fontis Euvraudi duo arpenta terre et unum de bosco et pratum, scilicet de defensis medietatem, concedente filio meo Odone Borrello, Hugone de Giseis, ex cujus feodo erat, id est super vadum de Balneolo, sub testibus istis: Pagano de Rocha, Aimerico fratre Hugonis Ameline filio; acta Lodovico Francorum rege, Fulcone Andegavorum comite, Rainaudo Andegavorum presule. [F907, fol. 131v]

The alienor and co-alienor are set off from the concessors by syntactic closeness, and by the use of the verbs *dare, donare,* or *vendere* rather than the verb *concedere* or other expressions of consent (*cum assensu, cum voluntate, annuente,* etc.). Yet, despite this linguistic distinction, it is difficult to discern a clear functional difference between the roles of co-alienor and concessor, and participants in these two roles will usually be discussed together as "consenters."[10]

It is tempting to deduce from the terminology used in the charters that alienors and consenters participated together in charters because of commonly held rights in the property being alienated. Since the main purpose of the action described in the charters was to transfer property, one expects that the various participants all had some specific rights in the property being transferred. But the event of a property transfer was more than an economic transaction; it was also a ritual in which religious benefits were being conferred and social and political ties were being confirmed. This multi-purpose nature of the acts can help explain the unsystematic way in which relatives and others were associated in these transfers. There are no clear rules according to which a given relative participated. Although consenters' hereditary, co-proprietary, or feudal rights are sometimes clearly spelled out in a charter, one cannot be sure that all people with such rights to that property have been included, or that all people included have such rights.[11] Great care must thus be taken in interpreting changes in women's participation in the charters. So many factors may be involved in determining participation that anything but the most dramatic changes must be interpreted with caution.[12] Yet, while the complex nature of these transactions makes analysis difficult, it also enhances the importance of the phenomenon being studied, as these transactions tell us not simply about the control of property but also

10. For a full discussion of the problems in distinguishing these roles, see Penny S. Gold, "Image and Reality: Women in Twelfth-Century France" (Ph.D. diss., Stanford University, 1977, pp. 219–32). Witnesses have not been included in this analysis, as their role was different from that of consenter. Most witnesses were disinterested third parties or personnel from the monastic community rather than people closely associated with the property being given or sold.

11. Gold, "Image and Reality," pp. 219–32. For the importance of interpreting the participation as more than economic, I am indebted to Stephen D. White, "The *Laudatio Parentum* in Northern France in the Eleventh and Twelfth Centuries: Some Unanswered Questions" (paper delivered at the Ninety-second annual meeting of the American Historical Association, Dallas, 28 December, 1977).

12. Ibid., p. 10.

about the place of women in a constellation of social relations, as evidenced in property transactions. The most striking characteristic of women's participation in property transfers is the stability of the basic structure of that participation during the whole period studied: women appear in small numbers as alienors but in large numbers as consenters. In Anjou, 11.9% of the donations and sales made in the period 1000–1249 were made by female alienors.[13] Although exact comparison with other studies is difficult, the Angevin data appear typical of the participation of women as alienors in northern France. Jean Verdon, using a variety of types of documents from the eleventh, the early fourteenth, and the fifteenth centuries, found a range from 4.9% to 15.3% in acts accomplished by a woman alone, or by a woman accompanied by her children.[14] David Herlihy, in his comprehensive study of the period 1001–1200, found that 8.6% of the transactions from northern France were made by women.[15] Robert Hajdu and Suzanne Wemple have used more restrictive categories: female alienors acting independently of male relatives (Hajdu) and female alienors acting independently of men (Wemple). Since many female alienors appear with men as consenters, their figures probably underrepresent the frequency of transactions with female alienors, perhaps by as much as a third to a half.[16]

13. Grouping the charters into fifty-year periods, there was a range from 10.5% to 21.2%, but this change over time is not statistically significant (significance level .05). The figures are as follows:

1000–1049, 21.2% (11 acts out of 52, with 6 of these being donations of countess Hildegarde of Anjou to Le Ronceray, a monastery she was instrumental in founding)
1050–1099, 11.7% (22 acts out of 188)
1100–1149, 10.5% (44 acts out of 420)
1150–1199, 14.8% (13 acts out of 88)
1200–1249, 10.7% (9 acts out of 84)

14. Jean Verdon, "Notes sur la femme en Limousin vers 1300," *Annales du Midi* 90 (1978): 319–20. Verdon includes acts of homage, and other types of acts, in addition to donations and sales. Since Verdon may have coded a female alienor accompanied by someone other than her children in a separate category (*groupes non-conjugaux*), it is possible that his figures are slightly low.

15. Herlihy, "Land, Family and Women," pp. 106–8, and the tables on pp. 116–20, from which I have derived the figure of 8.6%. (Herlihy also used documents from Italy, Spain, southern France, and Germany. The percentage of female alienors in the period 1001–1200 in all these areas, including northern France, is 11.0%.)

16. For example, out of 188 Angevin donations and sales in the period 1050–1099, 22 (11.7%) had a female alienor, but only 13 (6.9%) had a female alienor acting independently of male relatives.

Utilizing documents from Poitou and Picardy in the period 1101–1300, Hajdu found a relatively stable participation by female alienors (without male relatives) at a level of about 6%.[17] Wemple, studying a much earlier period, found an independent participation by women ranging from 5.3% (Brittany, first half of the ninth century) to 14.4% (E. Francia, 800–814).[18] These figures for northern and central France are somewhat lower than what has been found for Catalonia and Spain, where closer to 20% of transactions were accomplished by female alienors.[19]

Women participated much more frequently as consenters than they did as alienors: nearly half of all transactions (44.5%) had at least one woman in a consenting role. (This includes 16.9% of all transactions having at least one female co-alienor and 32.2% having at least one female concessor, with 4.6% having both a female co-alienor and a female concessor.) These figures are similar to findings from other regions, but there are greater fluctuations over time and across regions in women's participation as consenter than as alienor.[20] The basic pattern of women's participation is thus a combination of marginality and high frequency, with only about one in nine transactions being made by a woman as the principal alienor, but with over half the transactions (52.9%) having a female participant as either alienor, co-alienor, or concessor.

17. Robert Hajdu, "The Position of Noblewomen in the *pays des coutumes*, 1100–1300," *Journal of Family History* 5 (1980): 126, 128. Hajdu's study concerns noble-women only.

18. Suzanne Fonay Wemple, *Women in Frankish Society: Marriage and the Cloister, 500 to 900* (Philadelphia: University of Pennsylvania Press, 1981), table 3, p. 110 (E. Francia); table 5, p. 117 (Brittany). The figures for Brittany are derived from the cartulary of the monastery at Redon; the figures for E. Francia come from Lorsch. Wemple also gives figures for another category of participation by women: "women appearing as coactors with their husbands, sons, brothers, or fathers, either as equals of the males in the transaction or in a secondary role by approving with their signatures the alienation of property by male relatives" (p. 109). This category would seem to include a charter with a female alienor and a consenting son as well as one with a male alienor and a consenting wife. See her table 3, p. 110.

19. In tenth-century Catalonia, 19.2% of sales were made by women alone or women accompanied by their children: Pierre Bonnassie, *La Catalogne du milieu de Xe à la fin du XIe siècle: Croissance et mutations d'une société*, 2 vols. (Publications de l'Université de Toulouse-le Mirail, série A, vol. 23, 29) (Toulouse, 1975–76), 1: 266. In eleventh- and twelfth-century Spain, 18% of the principal alienors were women: Herlihy, "Land, Family and Women," p. 108.

20. See below, pp. 134–36.

The pattern of participation is further complicated by the changing participation of a woman over the course of her life cycle. As a daughter, a girl played a consenting role similar to that of her brother, though she was less frequently called upon than he to give explicit consent. Once married, however, the female's role diverged sharply from the male's, to converge again only in widowhood. Thus, when comparing male and female control of property, we need to look at the stages of the life cycle. We then see that women had rights to property throughout their lives but that their active control of that property was limited to the period of their widowhood.

The role of children in the charters reflects the basic structure of medieval French inheritance rules, rules that embodied a basic ambivalence toward women's relationship to property: both male and female children have rights to inheritance, but usually with a definite preference toward male children; this pattern is found widely in preindustrial societies.[21] While a child's appearance in a charter of property transfer did not necessarily derive strictly from inheritance rights, the ways in which sons and daughters participated in the charters as consenters to their parents' donations is certainly compatible with a principle of joint but unequal inheritance. In the Angevin charters, both sons and daughters appear with some regularity, but two-and-a-half times as many transfers include sons as include daughters (29.1% as compared to 11.6%). While close to a third of the transfers that include children include both sons and daughters, two-thirds of such transfers include only sons, and only a small proportion (9.0%) include only daughters. The preponderance of sons points to a preference given to male children beyond their actual number in the family. On the other hand, the steady participation of daughters is as significant as the preponderance of sons. For example, in the sixty-five acts including both sons and daughters (and in which the exact number of each sex is clear), the actual number of sons is greater than that of daughters, but only by 1.5 to 1.

This pattern of males and females participating in similar roles but with differing frequency can also be seen in the participation of the brothers and sisters of the alienor. Neither brothers nor sisters are

21. Of the 93 preindustrial societies surveyed by Martin King Whyte, 38% displayed such a pattern; 31% had roughly equal inheritance rights, 25% gave inheritance only to males, and 6% gave preference to females in inheritance rights (Whyte, p. 65). For a summary of inheritance practices in northern France, see Hajdu, pp. 132–34.

prominent among the consenters, but brothers appear about two-and-a-half times more frequently than sisters (in 8.9% as opposed to 3.4% of the charters).[22] Nephews and nieces appear even more rarely than brothers and sisters, although here the divergence in male/female experience is large enough to suggest a qualitative difference in the participation of nephews and nieces. Nephews appear in forty-five acts (5.4%), while nieces appear in only nine (1.1%).

The most significant difference in participation occurs, however, in the roles of married men and women.[23] Here there is not simply a quantitative difference in the frequency of participation, but, rather, the whole structure of male and female participation is different. Both married men and women appear with great frequency in the charters, but whereas a married woman appears most regularly as a consenter to a transfer made by her husband, a married man only very rarely appears as a consenter to a transfer by his wife. Nearly a third of all transfers (30.8%) include a wife's consent, while fewer than 1% include a husband's consent (0.7%).[24] The charter evidence thus clearly supports the legal evidence existing from the latter part of the period under study, evidence that has conveniently been summarized by Hajdu:

> Once married, the woman was under the guardianship and control of her husband according to the codes of customary law. She could not make contracts, testate, or offer legal testimony without his authorization; he controlled "her" property, demanded obedience from her, and punished her when he found it necessary. But the husband's freedom of action was in turn restrained by the need for his wife's consent to transactions dealing with her *propres*, i.e., property devolving on her from her family of birth. In short, the wife was placed in a subordinate position, but was not excluded from all participation.[25]

22. Hajdu mentions that sisters appear in 4.5% of the Picard documents (p. 131, n. 25); he does not mention the frequency of the appearance of brothers.

23. It is impossible to discuss the participation of unmarried adult men and women. They may well participate in transfers, but the charters never explicitly identify anyone as unmarried.

24. In Poitou, the percentage of noble transfers including wives was 26.3%, and in Picardy it was 35.4% (Hajdu, p. 126; these figures were derived by adding together Hajdu's figures for wives' participation as consenters [concessors] and co-actors). Few authors comment on the infrequency with which a husband consents to an alienation by his wife (but see Tabuteau, pp. 747–48).

25. Hajdu, p. 125. See also Pierre Petot and André Vandenbossche, "Le statut de la

For both men and women, marriage entailed an important shift away from the property transactions of their natal families. Yet for a man, marriage meant entrance into full control of his own property and limited control over his wife's, while for a woman marriage entailed little change; she continued to participate in transfers of property in a role identical to that of a child—as consenter. This continued limitation on active control was in spite of a woman's increased rights to property that accrued to her at marriage, since in addition to whatever inheritance would come to her as an heir of her parents, she would now also be a potential heir to her husband and would have certain property rights related to the assignment of dower and dowry.[26] The paradox of a married woman's situation with respect to property is that her rights to property are clearer and more extensive than when she was an unmarried daughter, but her control is just as limited as it was before.

Given the large percentage of acts in which wives participated (34.9% of acts by men), it seems likely that wives had certain rights in all property pertaining to the marriage: acquisitions, the patri-

---

femme dans les pays coutumiers français du XIIIe au XVIIe siècle," in *La femme, Recueils de la société Jean Bodin* 12 (1962): 245–46.

26. Dowry is the property that a woman brings with her into marriage; the Latin terms found in the charters are *maritagium* and *matrimonium*. Dower is that property settled on a woman by her husband at the time of their marriage for the purpose of providing for her after his death; the Latin terms are *dotalitium* and *dos*. (The term *dos*, however, meant "dowry" in Roman law, and the increasing familiarity with Roman law in the twelfth century caused an eventual shift in the medieval usage of the term. See Jean Hilaire, "Les régimes matrimoniaux aux XIe et XIIe siècles dans la région de Montpellier," *Recueil de mémoires et travaux publié par la société d'histoire du droit et des institutions des anciens pays de droit écrit* [Toulouse], fasc. 3, 1955, pp. 18–19; G. d'Espinay, *Les cartulaires angevins; étude sur le droit de l'Anjou au moyen-âge* [Angers, 1864], pp. 181–82, 287.) A convenient summary of Angevin evidence on inheritance, dower, and dowry may be found in G. d'Espinay, "Le droit de l'Anjou avant les coutumes, d'après les notes de M. Beautemps-Beaupré," *Mémoires de la société nationale d'agriculture, sciences et arts d'Angers*, 5th ser., 4 (1901): 35–43. In his eagerness to show that the wife had a dignified status in medieval law, one "perfectly equal to that accorded her in modern law" (p. 38), d'Espinay sometimes exaggerates the role of the wife, asserting, for example, that "the wife intervenes in all the acts of her husband; she sanctions all the donations that he makes to monasteries, all the transactions into which he enters either with them or with other lords; the wife is the associate of her husband for all the acts of his life" (ibid.). This is clearly an overstatement of the Angevin evidence, as there are numerous occasions on which one sees a man make a donation with his wife in one charter but without her in another.

mony of either spouse, dower, dowry. The charters only infrequently specify the provenance of the property being alienated, but we can examine the few charters that make explicit mention of a wife's inheritance, dower, or dowry, to ascertain the wife's control of this property assigned to her by her family or husband.

Eight of the Angevin charters describe a transfer of property pertaining to a wife by inheritance. In two of these cases the woman herself made the transfer, with no participation by a husband. Whether the husbands of these women were alive or dead cannot be ascertained.[27] In six other cases both husband and wife participated in the alienation of the wife's inheritance, but in five of these six cases it was the husband who acted as alienor and the wife as consenter.[28] The same pattern is also found in other regions.[29] The relative roles of husband and wife are similar in transactions involving dower property. Of the thirteen such transfers among the Angevin documents, eight show the husband as alienor and his wife as consenter.[30] In two cases, a son alienated the dower of his mother, with her consent.[31] One *calumpnia* tells of a gift of her dower by a woman, with the consent of her children; no husband is mentioned.[32] Finally, two cases show a woman as donor of her dower, with her husband as consenter or witness. Special circumstances clarify why the usual roles were reversed in these two instances. In one case, the husband was a monk at Saint-Aubin. He urged his wife to give her dower to the monastery, and when she did, he served as one of the witnesses to the act.[33] In the second case, a woman in her second marriage gave

27. F599, fol. 12r; A320.

28. A87; A91; A292; A304; F880, fol. 120r (which involves land originally belonging to the wife's father, possibly dowry rather than inheritance). The one donation of her inheritance by the woman herself is F629quattuor, fol. 21r). These transfers, and the following ones involving dower and dowry, are described in more detail in Gold, "Image and Reality," pp. 243–61.

29. See Verdon, "Notes sur la femme," pp. 327–28; François [Pontenay] de Fontette, *Recherches sur la pratique de la vente immobilière dans la région parisienne au moyen âge (fin Xe-début XIVe siècle)* (Paris: R. Pichon et R. Durand-Auzias, 1957), p. 43.

30. A143; A247; A324; A354; F692, fol. 41v; F853, fol. 107r; BN5480, p. 206; BN5480, p. 505.

31. F629, fol. 20v; F632, fol. 22r.

32. A213. We know of the donation from a later *calumpnia* by the son-in-law of the donor.

33. A171: "Rostha de Calvone donavit Deo et Sancti Albini, rogatu Orrici viri sui, qui tunc monachus erat ejusdem Sancti, unam terram . . . quamque predictus Orricus eidem Rosche uxori sue in dotem donaverat."

property from the dower of her first marriage; her second husband, among other relatives, consented to this gift. The gift of this dower property had been pledged by the donor's first husband, but the transfer had not been accomplished before his death. His widow is carrying out the promised gift, to which she had earlier given her consent.[34]

Although she was not usually the alienor of her dower, the woman's consent to such alienation was probably necessary, as evidenced by the ten transfers by husband or son that included the woman's consent. The concern for the protection of a woman's right to her dower is illustrated by a charter that recounts a wife's challenge to a sale of land to Saint-Aubin on the grounds that part of her dower had been included in the sale.[35] A similar concern can be seen in a case where three sons were excommunicated by the bishop of Poitiers because of their usurpation of their mother's dower.[36] Furthermore, it was common for an exchange to be made when some part of a woman's dower was to be alienated, in order that her dower not be diminished, since the dower property would be her primary economic security should her husband predecease her.[37]

34. A287.

35. A364, with relevant background in A362 and A363. Unfortunately, the issue of the wife's right to this dower property was not decided in the judgment, as the judges concluded that none of the claimants had any rights to the property, which had been purchased improperly from a serf of Saint-Aubin. For evidence from the abbey of Marmoutier of the necessity of the wife's consent to the alienation of her dower or dowry, see Stephen D. White, "Pactum . . . Legum Vincit et Amor Judicium: The Settlement of Dispute by Compromise in Eleventh-Century Western France," American Journal of Legal History 22 (1978): 290–91.

36. M&L 101H217. For a description of this dispute, see below, p. 133.

37. For example, A354; A364; BN5480, p. 505. (For a similar exchange for property alienated from dowry, see A350.) Such reassignment of dowers became very common in the thirteenth century; for Anjou, see d'Espinay, "Droit," p. 36; for the Paris region, see de Fontette, p. 66; for Picardy, see Robert Fossier, La terre et les hommes en Picardie jusqu'à la fin du XIIIe siècle (Paris: Beatrice-Nauwelaerts, 1968), 1: 272–73.

This pattern of limited control by a woman over her dower is often seen to be a "decline" from earlier practice (as known through various Germanic codes and formularies) according to which the dower was given to the bride to do with as she pleased (for example, André Lemaire, "Les origines de la communauté de biens entre époux dans le droit coutumier français," Revue historique de droit français et étranger (ser. 4) 7 [1928]: 588–90; d'Espinay, "Droit," pp. 36–37). However, the situation, at least in Anjou, seems to be more complex. Some of the evidence most commonly cited to show the full control that early medieval women had over their dowers is from a set of Angevin formulae dating from the sixth and seventh centuries. Two of the formulae

The nature of a woman's rights over her dowry is less clear than
those over inheritance and dower, which were both property assigned to the woman, even though she may not have had full control
over its disposition. The dowry, on the other hand, is sometimes
referred to as being given to the daughter, and sometimes to the

---

that deal with dower show us the husband giving his bride her dower "to have, to
hold, to possess, and to do with what she wishes" ("abiat, teniat, possediat, faciat
quod voluerit" and "abias, tenias, possedias, et ab hac die facias quod volueris": *Formulae Andegavenses*, in Charles Giraud, *Essai sur l'histoire du droit français au moyen-
âge*, 2 vols. [Paris, 1846], 2: 447, *formulae* 34. 1 and 34. 2). But other *formulae* prescribe
different conditions: one puts the dower in the woman's control, but seems to limit
her power if there are children (1. 3, p. 434); another gives the woman the usufruct of
the property while she lives (39, pp. 449–50); another states that while both spouses
live, they will hold the dower equally together; if there are children the dower will be
passed on to them, but if there are no children, the woman, when widowed, will get
the dower (53, p. 456). Thus, we see in the Angevin *formulae* the prescription of a wide
range of powers, from full power, to full power if there are no children, to shared
power, to usufruct only. André Vandenbossche concludes that there was a development from full to restricted power, but he admits that the chronology is impossible to
specify, and that all forms of assignment of dower coexisted before the tenth century
(*Contribution à l'histoire des régimes matrimoniaux: La "dos ex marito" dans la Gaule
franque* [Paris: Editions Domat, 1953], pp. 202–10.) He also observes that the explicit
mention of the husband's right to control his wife's dower in only one of the *formulae*
(53) is an indication that the husband's authority would have been assumed in this
period, and so would not need to be spelled out explicitly (ibid., p. 222). Is not the
lesson of these early *formulae* that there were no hard and fast rules and that practice
could vary significantly from case to case? This probably holds true until at least the
thirteenth century, at which time people began to seek out uniformity, as evidenced by
the numbers of customaries then compiled.

Another common assertion regarding a decline of female control of property is that
from about the mid-twelfth century dower payments became less important and
dowry more important, with, in some places, a complete shift from dower to dowry.
(The case is clearest for Italy; see for example, David Herlihy, "The Medieval Marriage
Market," *Medieval and Renaissance Studies. Proceedings of the Southeastern Institute of
Medieval and Renaissance Studies, Summer, 1974*, ed. Dale B. J. Randall [Medieval and
Renaissance Series, no. 6] [Durham, North Carolina: Duke University Press, 1976],
pp. 5–7; Diane Owen Hughes, "From Brideprice to Dowry in Mediterranean Europe," *Journal of Family History* 3 [1978]: 262–96). If this were the case, it would be of
some significance to women's lives, since a requirement of a substantial dowry when a
comparable dower would not be assigned in exchange would mean that daughters
would be viewed as more burdensome than their brothers. Few wills or marriage contracts survive from northern France for this period, leaving us only with monastic
charters as evidence of actual practice with regard to dower and dowry. From what
little information we can glean from the charters, a shift from dower to dowry does
not seem to have occurred in Anjou. Mentions of dowry are found before the twelfth
century (A287, 1066–1087; A276, ca. 1080; A132, 1060–1087; A364, ca. 1090; A231,

daughter's husband.[38] Only five charters deal explicitly with the transfer of dowry property. In three of these five, the woman was the donor of her own dowry, but in one case the husband is not mentioned as present and so might be dead,[39] and in the other two the woman was in her second marriage, donating from the dowry of her first

---

1055–1093; A327, mid-eleventh century), and mentions of dower continue after the mid-twelfth century (BN5480, p. 254, 1185; BN5480, p. 505, 1218; BN5480, p. 206, 1227). The most useful studies on this question have been done with documents from southern France, where marriage contracts have survived. Jean Hilaire, in his study of Montpellier, does not find a shift from dower to dowry. Pierre Bonnassie's study of tenth- and eleventh-century Catalonian documents similarly finds coexistence of dowry and dower (1: 256–60). Pierre Toubert also disputes the idea of a sudden shift in systems (*Les structures du Latium médiévale: Le Latium méridional et la Sabine du IXe siècle à la fin du XIIe siècle*, 2 vols. [Rome: Ecole française de Rome, 1973], 1: 749–50). R.-J. Aubenas presumes a shift rather than proving it: "Quelques réflexions sur le problème de la pénétration du droit romain dans le Midi de la France au Moyen Age," *Annales du Midi* 76 (1964): 371–77.

The following studies are among those most useful for an understanding of the complicated and fluctuating practice with regard to dower and dowry in the Middle Ages: G. Comet, "Quelques remarques sur la dot et les droits de l'épouse dans la région d'Arles aux XIIe et XIIIe ss.," in *Mélanges offerts à René Crozet* (Poitiers: Société d'études médiévales, 1966) 2: 1031–34; Abel Ridard, *Essai sur le douaire dans l'ancienne Bourgogne* (Dijon: Imprimerie Jobard, 1906); Lemaire, "Origines"; Lemaire, "La 'dotatio' de l'épouse de l'époque mérovingienne au XIIIe s.," *Revue historique de droit français et étranger* (ser. 4) 8 (1929): 569–80; L.-M.-A. Cornuey, *La régime de la "dos" aux époques mérovingienne et carolingienne* (Alger: Impr. "La Typo-Litho," 1929); Vandenbossche, "Contribution"; Wemple; Florence Griswold Buckstaff, "Married Women's Property in Anglo-Saxon and Anglo-Norman Law and the Origin of the Common-Law Dower," *Annals of the American Academy of Political and Social Science* 4 (1894): 233–64; Georges Duby, *The Knight, the Lady and the Priest: The Making of Modern Marriage in Medieval France*, trans. Barbara Bray (New York: Pantheon, 1983; originally published in French in 1981), pp. 95–106; S. F. C. Milsom, "Inheritance by Women in the Twelfth and Thirteenth Centuries," in *On the Laws and Customs of England: Essays in Honor of Samuel E. Thorne* (Chapel Hill: University of North Carolina Press, 1981), pp. 60–89. The following anthropological studies are also helpful: Ernestine Friedl, "Some Aspects of Dowry and Inheritance in Boetia," in *Mediterranean Countrymen: Essays in the Social Anthropology of the Mediterranean*, ed. J. Pitt-Rivers (Paris: Mouton, 1963), pp. 113–35; Lucy Mair, *Marriage* (London: Penguin Books, 1971).

38. Charters referring to dowry as given to the daughter: A132; F845, fol. 98r; A392. Charters referring to dowry as given to the daughter's husband: A276; A327; M&L 101H55. A thirteenth-century Angevin customary also speaks of the dowry as going to the husband (C.-J. Beautemps-Beaupré, *Coutumes et institutions de l'Anjou et du Maine antérieures au XVIe s., textes et documents, avec notes et dissertations*, 8 vols. [Paris, 1877–97] 1: 71, 74, 140). The same customary refers to the dower as the wife's (1: 74).

39. A392.

marriage, with the consent or the witness of her second husband.[40] In two cases the dowry came from the current marriage and both spouses were alive; in these cases the husband was the alienor and the wife the consenter, along with members of her natal family.[41]

These charters involving women's inheritance, dower, and dowry show that even for that property most closely associated with a married woman, the wife's control was usually secondary to that of her husband. Only infrequently were women the principal alienors of this property, and when they were, they were widows, or women in a second marriage alienating property from the first. More frequently the husband, or sometimes the son, played the primary role of alienor. Yet the woman's consent to the alienation of this property was probably necessary, and women may thus have had considerable say in the disposition of "their" property.

It is only at the last stage of their life cycle, that of widowhood—a stage that only those women who survived their husbands would reach—that women's participation in the transfer of property again became similar to men's.[42] As widows, it was normal for women to be the alienors of property, just as it was for widowers, although for men this represents a continuity of role rather than a change. The use of the special term *vidua* (widow) symbolizes the importance of the break that widowhood made in a woman's life, and the special legal capacity reserved for widowhood is suggested in one Angevin charter, in which the female donor is described as being "constituted in widowhood and in unrestricted power."[43]

It is impossible to know exactly how many alienors were widows. Of the ninety-nine female alienors, twenty-four are clearly identified as widowed, either by use of the term *vidua*, or by a direct reference to a dead husband. Another thirty-eight were accompanied by one or more children, though not by a husband; these women were also probably widows. In twelve cases, the woman clearly was currently married, but in four of these cases she was in her second marriage,

40. A132; A287 (this charter also included a gift of dower property).
41. A276; A350.
42. Based on a limited body of genealogical data, Hajdu estimates that 62.4% of married women survived their husbands and that the average length of widowhood was 19.5 years (p. 130).
43. "Ego Aeliz humilis comitissa Augi in viduitate et in libera potestate constituta . . ." (M&L 101H85).

and it was the second husband who accompanied her.[44] Finally, for twenty-five cases, there are no clues as to the marital status of the alienor. Thus a maximum of ninety-one transfers were made by a widow or by a woman in her second marriage (91.9% of acts by women; 10.9% of the total number of acts). The evidence of other studies suggests that widows made up a large proportion of female alienors in other regions as well.[45] Widows may, in fact, appear with a frequency in accord with their numbers among the land-holding population, which has been estimated at 10%-15%.[46] The stability of women's participation as alienors is probably related to the dominance of widows in the role of primary alienor. Given a steady proportion of widows in society, and given the acceptance of widows' control of property, we can expect the number of transfers made by women (mostly widows) to remain relatively stable, as it does in Anjou (at an average level of 11.9%).[47]

Was a widow's control of property more restricted than a man's? The evidence is conflicting. On the one hand, male and female alienors appear independent of any consenting parties with equal fre-

44. Another four of the twelve donations by a married woman present special circumstances. Two are donations made to Le Ronceray by Hildegarde, countess of Anjou, who was the founder of that nunnery (R1, which records a series of gifts by Fulk and Hildegarde and then gifts by Hildegarde alone; R32). Another donation was made by a woman who was the consort of a cleric (R394), and the fourth was by a woman whose husband had become a monk (A171).

45. Verdon, "Limousin," p. 324; Paolo Cammarosano, "Les structures familiales dans les villes de l'Italie communale (XIIe-XIVe ss.)," in *Famille et parenté dans l'Occident médiéval*, Actes du Colloque de Paris, (6–8 juin 1974): organisé par l'Ecole Pratique des Hautes Etudes (VIe section) en collaboration avec le Collège de France et l'Ecole française de Rome: Communications et débats, ed. G. Duby and J. Le Goff (Rome: Ecole française de Rome, 1977), pp. 193–94. Hajdu found that thirty-six of his forty-seven independent female alienors (in Picardy) were widows (p. 130).

46. Hajdu, p. 130. This estimate is based on a census of the nobility of the Ile-de-France carried out in the early thirteenth century by officials of Philip Augustus. Difficult as it is to identify with certainty all widows in the charters, widowers are even more elusive because their identification was not usually linked to a spouse, as was a woman's. (See Marie-Thérèse Lorcin, *Vivre et mourir en Lyonnais à la fin du moyen âge* [Paris: CNRS, 1981], pp. 58–65.)

47. Herlihy, who has presented the largest set of data on female alienors, found statistically significant change over time. Yet it may be questioned whether the small variation found, even though statistically significant, is representative of historically significant change. Herlihy found for northern France the following percentage of acts with female alienors (by century, from the eighth to the twelfth): 15%, 7%, 11%, 8%, 9% ("Land, Family and Women," p. 108).

quency (36.4% of female alienors, 34.1% of male alienors). On the other hand, when looking specifically at consent by children, we find women accompanied by one or more children more frequently than men (44.4% of female alienors, 30.3% of male alienors).[48] The disparity in the participation of mothers and fathers in transfers by their children also indicates a possible restriction on the widow's full control of property. Of the twenty-nine Angevin charters which show a parent consenting to a transfer by a child, twenty-seven are transfers by a son, with his mother consenting. Only two charters include a father: one transfer by a daughter, with the consent of her father, and another by a son, with the consent of both father and mother.[49] The near total absence of fathers as consenters indicates that children would not come into control of their property while their father was alive. The continued presence of the widowed mother, however, was not always an inhibition to the child's control of his property. In addition, a son might have control not only over his own property but his mother's as well: in two of the charters by a son with a mother consenting the property being transferred was from the mother's dower.[50]

Thus, while a widow's control of property was much closer to the pattern of male control than was a married woman's, there were still certain limitations on her exercise of control. A few stories from the charters highlight the somewhat ambiguous position of a widow with respect to property. In one case, a widow's control of property was ambiguous enough that while she gave some land to a certain priest in order that he say a mass every week for the soul of her husband, her son, not knowing the land had been given away, gave the land to another man. When the son found out about his mother's gift, he gave the land to Saint-Aubin on the same condition of a weekly mass for his father.[51] In the end, it was the son who controlled the disposition of the land, yet his mother presumably thought the

48. The differential was much larger in tenth-century Catalonia, where 27.8% of the female alienors were accompanied by children, but only 0.8% of the male alienors (Bonnassie, 1: 266).

49. A287 (with the daughter in her second marriage, giving from the dowry and dower of her first marriage); BN5480, p. 455 (a gift to Fontevrault in 1185 by Richard, count of Poitou, with the consent of his father and mother, Henry II and Eleanor of Aquitaine).

50. F629, fol. 20v; F632, fol. 22r.

51. A312.

right was hers. Another case shows that even a widow's dower might not be secure if her children were sufficiently impatient. Willelmus, viscount of Thouars, and his brothers Guido and Gaufridus usurped their mother's dower and were excommunicated on that account by Willelmus Adelelmi, bishop of Poitiers (1124–1140). The ban of excommunication was lifted by his successor, Grimoardus, who negotiated a truce between mother and sons, according to which Agnes, the mother, relinquished to her sons from her dower a castle and various fiefs, in order that there would be no further dissension between mother and sons.[52]

Another case, while showing us a generous son, also highlights the almost pathetic situation in which a widow could find herself. A woman named Aimburgis wanted to become a nun at Le Ronceray d'Angers. She asked her son Hugo de Cantosciaco to give to the nunnery "for her a little something from his patrimony, since she herself had neither gold nor silver nor garments, except worthless ones."[53] Her son agreed to make the gift "with great joy," and he gave to the nunnery land, tithes, and other rights. It is difficult to imagine a widower similarly dependent on the help of his son to join a monastery.

Looking back over the male and female life cycles, we see that men and women participated in similar ways when acting as sons and daughters, brothers and sisters, and widows and widowers, but that as adult married persons their participation diverged, with the married woman continuing to participate in a role similar to a child's at a time when a man's participation changed to one of primary alienor. This change occurs for a woman only at widowhood, or under certain special circumstances (for example, in a second marriage and giving property from the first). It is ironic that although women only came into independent control of property as widows, it was as married women, consenting to the transfers made by their husbands, that women were most frequently visible in the charters.[54]

52. M&L 101H217; Agnes was the daughter of the duke of Aquitaine.
53. "Aimburgis, mater Hugonis de Cantosciaco, volens se tradere sancti religioni, consilio et assensu filii, elegit cenobium sancte ecclesie Caritatis: ibi quod reliquum [sic] erat etatis, post mortem viri sui, Goscelini agere decrevit, petivitque filium suum ut aliquantulum de patrimonio suo S. Marie concederet pro ea; quia ipsa neque aurum neque argentum neque vestimenta, nisi vilia, habebat" (R344).
54. Hajdu, p. 131. For a discussion of the intersection between life cycle and gender roles as evidenced in court records from late medieval England, see Judith M. Bennett,

A female's experience of her relationship to property must have been one of uncertainty. No one's capacity to control property was clear-cut and fixed in this period, yet sons could be more certain than daughters that their consent would be requested, as could brothers as compared to sisters, and nephews as compared to nieces. As a wife, a woman's consent was much more regularly sought, and certain rights with regard to dower and dowry, and perhaps inheritance, would have been settled, yet the large number of charters that show a male alienor without a wife (65.1% of transfers by men) indicates that even as a wife a woman could not be certain of inclusion in transfers. Only in widowhood could a woman probably feel a sense of certainty about the nature and extent of her control of her property.

This uncertainty in a female's relationship to property is further highlighted by the continuities and fluctuations in women's participation as consenters over the 250-year period from 1000 to 1249. Although the participation of women as alienors was steady over both time and space, with several regions showing roughly comparable levels of participation, the participation of women as consenters varied greatly, not only over time but from region to region, and even from one monastery to another within one region. In Anjou, the percentage of donations and sales with at least one female consenter ranged as follows in fifty-year periods from 1000 to 1249: 30.8%, 41.5%, 49.5%, 36.4%, 42.9%. Exactly comparable figures are not available from other regions, but comparison of other measures indicates that the Angevin figures are fairly typical in the level of participation of women and in the fact of significant fluctuation over time. We can compare, for example, the participation of *wives* as consenters in Poitou, Picardy, and Anjou (table 1).[55] For Picardy and Anjou, we can also compare the participation of women in any capacity (table 2).[56] Not only do all regions show fluctuation over time for these cat-

---

"'Whether She Be Maid, or Widow, or Else Wife': Being Female in a Medieval English Village" (paper presented at the Sixth Berkshire Conference on the History of Women, 1984).

55. For the figures for Poitou and Picardy, I have added together Hajdu's figures for wives as consenters and wives as coactors (Hajdu, p. 126). Hajdu's "consenter" and "coactor" are the equivalent of my terms "concessor" and "co-alienor."

56. Fossier counted acts that included women as "either donors or witnesses" (Fossier, 1: 278). I assume that by "donor" Fossier means women who were either alienors or consenters. My figures from Anjou do not include the women who participated as witnesses to charters, but their numbers were so low that their inclusion would not

Table 1
Percentage of Acts with Wives as Consenters

Poitou [a]		Picardy [a]		Anjou	
Years	%	Years	%	Years	%
				1000–1049	19.2
				1050–1099	28.7
1101–1150	27.4			1100–1149	33.3
1151–1200	29.4	1141–1200	37.2	1150–1199	25.0
1201–1250	26.5	1201–1250	36.1	1200–1249	32.1
1251–1300	21.9	1251–1300	32.3		

[a] Figures for Poitou and Picardy are drawn from Robert Hajdu, "The Position of Noblewomen in the *pays de coutumes*, 1100–1300," *Journal of Family History* 5 (1980): 126.

Table 2
Percentage of Acts with Women Participating in Any Capacity

Picardy [a]		Anjou	
Years	%	Years	%
		1000–1049	50.0
1075–1100	50	1050–1099	50.8
1100–1125	21		
1125–1150	21	1100–1149	55.1
1150–1175	30		
1175–1200	32	1150–1199	48.9
1200–1225	37		
1225–1250	42	1200–1249	51.2
1250–1275	46		
1275–1300	52		
1300–1325	68		

[a] Figures for Picardy are drawn from Robert Fossier, *La terre et les hommes en Picardie jusqu'à la fin du XIIIe siècle* (Paris: Beatrice Nauwelaerts, 1968), 1: 278.

egories of participation, but within one region there can also be variation from monastery to monastery. Although all investigators have presumed some kind of unity of custom and experience within a region (with Fossier, however, calculating also for subregions within Picardy), there can in fact be more variation from one monastery to another within a region than there is for the aggregate figures over time. For example, in Anjou the percentage of acts with women as

change my figures greatly. (On female witnesses, see Gold, "Image and Reality," appendix 3).

consenters ranged from 30.8% to 49.5% over the 250-year period. But
the peak figure of 49.5% for the period 1100–1149 is the aggregate of
the following figures from the three monasteries:

Le Ronceray d'Angers	29.2% of 137 acts
Saint-Aubin d'Angers	48.8% of 41 acts
Fontevrault	61.2% of 242 acts

The substantial difference between Saint-Aubin and Le Ronceray is
particularly interesting, since the two communities were in the same
city. Yet in the previous fifty-year period, the participation of women
as consenters was very comparable (41.2% for Saint-Aubin, 42.1% for
Le Ronceray; table 3).[57]

The interpretation and explanation of these kinds of fluctuations—
from century to century, region to region, and monastery to monastery—present a serious challenge. The numbers by themselves, of
course, tell us nothing, and historians have disagreed on the interpretation of even the most basic figures. Herlihy, for example, who
found that 11.0% of the alienors of property were female,[58] speaks of
the "extraordinary role in the management of family property" that
women played in the period studied. He also refers to the effects of
this "prominence" of women on social customs and economic life.[59]
Yet Jean Verdon, who found approximately 10% of alienors to be female, comments that "the place of the woman in the Limousin . . .
was not as important as one might have thought."[60] If the aggregate
levels of female participation provoke such differing assessments, the
changes over time in the levels of women's participation are even
more difficult to interpret. How much of a change in percentage of
transfers by women or with female consenters may be interpreted as
indicating a significant change in women's experience? Herlihy, for
example, considers significant, and explains at some length, changes
in levels of participation of women as alienors that range between
about 8% and 12%.[61] Most other authors have followed Herlihy in
taking any change in level that passes a test of statistical significance

---

57. Tabuteau comments on the diversity of practice from one monastery to another
in Normandy (pp. 619–20). This degree of variation should make one cautious in
using the results of studies in which data is drawn from only one institution (for example, Verdon, "Notes sur la femme").
58. See above, n. 15.
59. Herlihy, "Land, Family and Women," p. 89.
60. Verdon, "Notes sur la femme," p. 329.
61. Herlihy, "Land, Family and Women," p. 109, graph 3.

Table 3
Percentage of Acts with Women Participating,
by Institution (Anjou)

	1	2	3	Total Number of Acts
		Saint-Aubin		
1000–1049	6.2%	31.2%	31.2%	16
1050–1099	9.2	41.2	49.6	131
1100–1149	19.5	48.8	61.0	41
1150–1199	10.0	40.0	50.0	10
1200–1249				...
				198
		Fontevrault		
1000–1049				...
1050–1099				...
1100–1149	9.9	61.2	65.3	242
1150–1199	14.5	38.7	50.0	62
1200–1249	10.7	42.9	51.2	84
				388
		Le Ronceray		
1000–1049	25.0	30.6	58.3	36
1050–1099	17.5	42.1	54.4	57
1100–1149	8.0	29.2	35.0	137
1150–1199	18.8	25.0	43.8	16
1200–1249				...
				246

Note: 1 = acts with a woman as principal alienor, 2 = acts with a woman as consenter (co-alienor or concessor), 3 = acts with a woman participating in any capacity.

to be a change of historical significance, demanding an explanation.[62]
    While scholars have agreed that these types of changes demand explanation, the types of explanations offered have varied greatly, drawing on diverse aspects of the female experience. Herlihy offers a vari-

62. For a recent example using Carolingian documents, see Wemple, pp. 106–23. Special caution might have been used in interpreting this data, since much of it is drawn from individual institutions (for example, data on E. Francia is from Lorsch, table 3, p. 119), and where more than one institution was used, the variation between monasteries, though unremarked by the author, is sometimes greater than the changes over time elsewhere noted (for example, the variations among the three institutions compared in table 4, p. 114).

ety of possible causes of regional difference and change over time, from the differing provisions of Germanic legal codes to the periods of extensive male mobilization because of military or geographic expansion.[63] Suzanne Wemple emphasizes the effect of Carolingian marriage legislation on women's property control, although other factors are also discussed.[64] Hajdu relates changes in female participation to changes in the nature and extent of family solidarity, an interpretation in keeping with the work of Duby and Fossier, who in turn relate changes in family solidarity to fluctuations in the extent of centralized political authority.[65]

No author has hesitated to interpret an increased level of female participation as indicating an improvement in women's socioeconomic situation, yet changes in the participation of female family members in property transactions may have had nothing to do with their sex. In Anjou, for example, the pattern of change over time in consent by female relatives of the alienor is closely parallel to the changes over time in consent by male relatives (table 4).[66] The change in women's participation is thus not a change relative to men's participation, but is, rather, part of a fluctuation in group as opposed to individual action.

There are many reasons for caution, both in deciding that a change in level of participation is worthy of explanatory effort, and in determining the most appropriate explanation of that change. The collection of data from monastic charters is problematic in ways that, if more widely acknowledged, might give readers pause when presented with firm interpretations.[67] Imprecisions in the charters are, when coded, turned into certainties: for example, the date of a

63. Herlihy, "Land, Family and Women," pp. 110, 112. Hajdu, however, states convincingly that women do not seem to have assumed control of conjugal property in the absence of their husbands (p. 129).

64. Wemple, pp. 108, 111, 122–23.

65. Fossier, 1: 267–69. Georges Duby, *La société aux XIe et XIIe siècles dans la région mâconnaise* (Paris: S.E.V.P.E.N., 1971, p. 122); idem, "Lignage, noblesse et chevalerie au XIIe siècle dans la région mâconnaise. Une révision," *Annales: Economies, sociétés, civilisations* 27 (1972): 813–16 (essay also in Georges Duby, *The Chivalrous Society*, trans. Cynthia Postan [Berkeley and Los Angeles: University of California Press, 1980], pp. 59–80).

66. Because of the asymmetry of the participation of wives and husbands as consenters (see above, p. 124), they have been excluded from table 4. The table includes all other consenters identified as relatives of the alienor.

67. For a similar concern and a list of many of the problems, see White, "*Laudatio Parentum*," p. 2, n. 8.

Table 4
Percentage of Acts with Relatives of Alienors as Consenters (Anjou)

Years	Total Number of Acts	Percentage of Acts with Female Relatives	Percentage of Acts with Male Relatives
1000–1049	52	5.8	11.5
1050–1099	188	11.2	35.1
1100–1149	420	23.8	50.0
1150–1199	88	15.9	34.1
1200–1249	84	21.4	36.9

charter, or the relationship between participants, which is sometimes unclear or unstated. Similarly, the social status of a person is not always indicated, making it difficult to sort out with certainty those transfers made by nobles.[68]

Another type of problem rests in the difficulty of defining clear categories to accommodate the information contained in the charters, and the difficulty of then comparing studies that have utilized differing categories. For example, with regard to categorization of participatory roles, some have distinguished simply between alienors and consenters, while some have divided the role of consenter further into co-alienor (co-actor) and consenter (concessor), and some count a witness as a consenter as well. Investigators have also differed with regard to the types of transactions utilized (donations, sales, calumpniae, separate concessions to transfers already made). In addition to the type of transaction, the geographical provenance of the alienor and of the property being transferred must be taken into account, and a decision made as to whether property or individuals from outside the region being studied should be counted when a gift is made to an institution within the region. Another way in which the investigator shapes the data is by deciding how to categorize the relationships between participants in a transfer, and here the prior questions posed by the investigator play a determining role. Fossier, for example, who was more concerned with changing types of familial participation than participation by sex, distinguished between acts by an individual (male or female), by a couple, and by a group of relatives.[69] Duby, more interested in lineage than in family, cate-

---

68. Too few alienors in the Angevin charters are identified as nobles to allow for separate consideration. See Gold, "Image and Reality," appendix 2.

69. Fossier considered an act including the eldest son of an alienor to be an act by

gorized consenters as brothers, sons, father or mother, and *proximi* to the alienor, excluding information on wives, sisters, daughters, and other female relatives.[70] Even investigators who include "female" as a category have rarely discriminated among female participants in their roles as wives, daughters, sisters, or nieces.

All the above problems with the collecting, counting, and categorization of data should encourage caution in concluding that statistically significant changes, arrived at through the manipulation of such data, are historically significant changes, worthy of interpretive effort. But once the decision has been made that a change is of sufficient magnitude to be considered historically significant, the further problem remains of assigning a cause for that change, and many historians have fallen into the interpretive pitfall of asserting univocal causes for changes in women's participation. Suzanne Wemple, for example, has asserted a relationship between Carolingian marriage legislation and women's changing participation in property transfers, even though she herself lists various other hidden factors that might influence action.[71] Some of the factors that would alter women's participation have to do directly with changes in women's lives: changes in property arrangements at marriage, changes in inheritance patterns, or more generally, changes in the acceptability of female control of property. Demographic factors are also a possible influence (for example, change in male/female population ratios). Yet other factors that might impinge on women's participation have little to do with women as women but rather affect men and women alike, for example, the desirability or necessity of the participation of relatives in a transfer of property. And what could be the cause of such a change? Could it be changes in the political situation, thus putting the root of changes in female participation further back, into an area also not directly related to attitudes toward women or to changes in women's own experience? Or, remembering that there was a wide variation from one Angevin monastery to another, was there some

---

an individual, but it is unclear how he distinguished a participating son as the eldest. Did he assume that if only one son was mentioned that he was the eldest?

70. Duby, "Lignage, noblesse et chevalerie," pp. 803–23. This consequence of Duby's stress on lineage is noted by Susan Mosher Stuard, who puts it within the context of the influence of structuralism on the *Annales* school: "The Annales School and Feminist History: Opening Dialogue with the American Stepchild," *Signs: Journal of Women in Culture and Society* 7 (1981): 141–42.

71. Wemple, pp. 108, 111.

historical force that operated not at a regional level but on an institutional level, so that patterns of family consent should be seen in the context of the history of a particular monastery?

It is thus difficult, if not impossible, to isolate those factors that most influenced the relative participation of men and women in property transfers.[72] The search for causal factors has, in fact, blinded us to the observation of an important aspect of the charter activity: the uncertainty and changeability of women's participation in the transfer of property at all stages of life, except perhaps widowhood. Rather than engage in an interpretive struggle against the apparent fluidity, lack of clear chronological development, and lack of regularity of practice (particularly with regard to patterns of consent), we can instead take this fluidity and irregularity as our subject. When looking at women's participation in the charters, whether over time or space, between institutions or over the life cycle, it is the phenomenon of fluctuation and lack of predictability that is significant. We have seen that women's participation is frequent but not continuous in the same role. This has been discussed most fully with respect to the changing participation of a woman over the course of her life cycle, with the significant transition in woman's relationship to her property coming at widowhood, as opposed to the more continuous control exercised by a man throughout his adult life. An adult woman (if she survived into widowhood) had a fractured experience of property control, with her secondary role as consenter while a wife changed into the primary role of alienor when a widow. As discussed above, there seems to be for a married woman a bifurcation between property rights and property control. The rights a wife had to property—whether by inheritance, dower, dowry, acquisition—were an integral part of the property system, but she did not exercise effective control over that property until, as a widow, she stepped into the vacated seat of authority.[73] Yet even at this stage of life, a second husband or selfish children could hamper that control. Even more im-

72. Even if appropriate factors could be isolated, it would be difficult to test their strength statistically, given the type of data we have. On the misuse of tests of significance in this regard, see Robert F. Winch and Donald T. Campbell, "Proof? No. Evidence? Yes. The Significance of Tests of Significance," *American Sociologist* 4 (1969): 140; D. Gold, "Statistical Tests and Substantive Significance," *American Sociologist* 4 (1969): 46.

73. For a similar pattern in urban Italy (twelfth to fourteenth centuries), see Cammarosano, pp. 193–94.

portant is that while married, the wife's consent to an alienation by her husband was often obtained, but not always. There were, in fact, no fixed rules with regard either to the establishment or to the control of marital property until the end of the twelfth century and the beginning of the thirteenth century, when, in the general movement toward the regularization of customary practice, written rules began to appear.[74] Women were clearly important in the system according to which property was given, sold, and exchanged, but it could not have been clear to medieval people, nor can it be to modern observers, exactly when, or in what circumstances, a woman's participation in the alienation of property would have been demanded. A woman, unless a widow, could not count on being taken into account when it came to the transfer of property. This uncertainty of expectation needs to be considered as itself a shaping influence on women's experience.

Also defining women's experience with respect to property control was the contrast between women's possible roles and their usual roles. Women could, in certain circumstances, carry out all the same roles as men, including that of alienor, but women were much more usually found in the relatively dependent role of consenter.[75] This pattern of similar but secondary is found in many other aspects of the charter evidence. Perhaps most striking is the pattern of anonymity in the charters. While most of the participants in transactions are named, some individuals are identified only by their relationship to another party (usually the alienor or another participant), that is, as "son of N.," rather than as "N., son of N." Women make up approximately two-thirds of such unnamed participants in the Angevin documents. The most frequently appearing anonymous female is the wife of the alienor or another participant. But other relatives are also frequently unnamed, and one regularly finds cases in which comparable male and female relatives appear, with the male named and the female unnamed. For example, several transfers, in which both daughters and sons participate, indicate the names of the son(s) but leave the daughter(s) anonymous; there are no cases of the opposite

74. Lemaire, "Origines," pp. 584–85, 633.

75. For a discussion of a similar pattern in an African setting, see Donald Crummey, "Women, Property, and Litigation among the Bagemder Amhara, 1750s to 1850s," in *African Women and the Law: Historical Perspectives*, ed. Margaret Jean Hay and Marcia Wright, Boston University (Papers on Africa, 7) (Boston: African Studies Center of Boston University, 1982), p. 21.

pattern.[76] Another imbalance is when a female blood relative of the alienor or claimant is left anonymous, but a male related by marriage to that female is named. In the following case, for example, sisters are anonymous, but brothers-in-law are named: a certain Marbodus brought a claim against a gift his father had made to Saint-Aubin. When peace was made and Marbodus came to the monastery to accept the *beneficium* of the monastery, he came "with his brother, by the name of Paganellus, and with his sisters and his sisters' husbands, namely Gaufridus, Rotundus, and Haimardus."[77]

Another example of the woman present but secondary can be seen in the pattern of the *quid pro quo* payments made to participants. Two cases show a husband receiving a larger payment than his wife, even though the property transferred or under dispute came from her inheritance.[78] In many other cases, a larger payment was given to a male relative than to the comparable female relative (son/daughter, brother/sister, nephew/niece). For example, in the settlement of one claim, the son of the claimant received twelve *denarii*, the daughter six.[79]

Another sign of secondary participation is the exclusion of female participants from some portion of the ceremony. A woman was sometimes excluded from the signing of a charter, even though she was an important participant in the action.[80] In other cases a woman is mentioned as a donor or consenter but is not included in subsequent ceremonial action that confirms the action.[81] There are also cases in which a male, because of a relationship either through blood or marriage, participated more centrally in a transfer than did the woman through whom the property had passed. For example, a certain Hermenbertus brought a claim against Saint-Aubin with his son-in-law Radulfus Toaredi, although the charter later lists "Hivoreia, daughter of Hermenbertus, wife of Radulfus" as one of the people

76. For example, A323; R165; R197; F769, fol. 71v; F629quinque, fol. 21r; BN5480, p. 127. One charter includes two named daughters, one named son, with a blank space left for the name of a second son (F601, fol. 12v).

77. A127. Other examples: A119, A70.

78. A91, A148.

79. F660, fol. 30v. I have noticed only one case in which a woman was paid more than the comparable male relative: in one donation by a man and his sister, the man was paid 63 *solidi*, but his sister was given 100 (A336).

80. A35; A36. Females were not legally excluded from signing documents, as other charters include the signs of women (for example, A39, A237).

81. A251; F723, fol. 53v.

relinquishing the claim.[82] In another case, a man and his son-in-law gave a mill to Saint-Aubin, with the consent of the man's daughter.[83] A gift to Fontevrault was made by a man and his sister, with the man in the role of principal alienor even though the property is identified as the sister's.[84]

In summary, the role of women in the transfer of property is reminiscent of their described role in the *chanson de geste*: land-holding is organized on the basis of the family, and women, as members of families, both natal and marital, are integrated into the system of property rights and land-holding, but their participation is different from that of men. The tendency to define women relationally to men rather than independently (with the exception of widowhood) keeps women in the system but on the periphery, connected to the center, but not at the center. It is this ambivalence of inclusion, but inclusion usually in secondary roles, that is deeply characteristic of female imagery and of female experience, in both the secular and religious spheres.

82. A378.
83. A117.
84. F862, fol. 112v. I suspect that A336 (cited above, n. 79) may represent a similar situation.

·5·

Conclusion

I set out in this book to make sense of the new images of women that were created in twelfth-century France, images powerful enough to have endured into the modern era: the image of the *dame* of romance and the image of Notre Dame, the Virgin Mary. The method used to explore the meaning of these images has been twofold: (1) to untangle the multiple meanings of each image by seeing it within the context of its own artistic setting; and (2) to compare the images with the contemporary experience of women, in order to explore the possible connections between images of women and the lives of actual women. When I first began this study, I expected to find similar patterns of chronological development in image and experience that would enable me to make judgments about the final meaning of the images: for example, that the romance image of the lady developed at the same time that property rights were becoming more restricted, thus demonstrating that romance was a "negative" development. Yet, as explained in the preface, the data could not be fit into such a tidy linear scheme, and I slowly came to understand that a value judgment on the moral quality of the images was inappropriate as well as impossible. There is a unity between image and experience; it lies, however, not in simultaneous chronological change but in the attitude of ambivalence toward women that is expressed both in images of women and in the institutional structures of religious life and property control.

Throughout this study I have used the word "ambivalent" to denote the particular type of complexity of attitudes toward women:

not just that there was more than one attitude toward women but that *conflicting* attitudes existed simultaneously, sometimes within a particular phenomenon, whether image or experience, and sometimes between contemporary phenomena. A review of the findings presented in each chapter will help clarify the pervasiveness of this structural pattern.

Secular literature displays perhaps the most intricate web of conflicting, yet connected, ideas about the nature of women's roles within male/female interactions. Both *chanson de geste* and romance contain conflicting attitudes toward women, and the two genres, co-existing from the mid-twelfth century into the thirteenth, themselves present conflicting views. The *chansons de geste* portray women acting together with men, sharing the same goals, pursuing the social values they share, often the honor of the family. But as women, characters like Guiburc and Aalais must participate from the periphery, from their separate sphere of the home; the encouragement and advice they give to their men comes from a position as "outsider," and sometimes is received with resentment or sometimes ignored by the men engaged in the central activity of warfare. Epic men and women have similar concerns, but they do not engage closely enough in the same activities to be either friends (like Roland and Oliver) or enemies (like Raoul and Bernier).

In romances the ambivalence toward women is even more striking. At the center of the romance is the individual quest of the male hero to integrate the two spheres of women and men, love and prowess, within his own life. The woman, rather than co-actor, is an object to be attained by the man—a good, beautiful, and very desirable object. But the pursuit of the love of a woman invariably interferes with the hero's pursuit of honor and valor in the sphere of men, and this conflict in turn causes anxiety, tension, and sometimes death for the hero.

The difference between the epic and romance images, contemporary as they are, is also significant. Characters like Aalais and Guiburc are forceful women, making themselves felt on men either for good or ill. Characters like Laudine and Lavine are women in distress or under siege, in need of help from the heroic knight. Even Guinevere—not the most passive of women—must rely on Lancelot to defend her against Mador de la Porte. Yet the opposition between the images of epic and romance may be understood if we see them as alternative solutions to a dilemma of male identity: to what extent and in what ways does male success and selfhood depend upon a relationship with women? Both epic and romance show that some male/female interaction is necessary for a man's success, but epics show a man in an established relationship with a woman who advises, nurtures, and prods him toward success, while romances show a man on his own, pursuing the two competing goals of prowess/honor/adventure and a love relationship with a woman.

The complex ways in which a man's success might depend on interaction with women can be seen in a concrete form if we turn from secular literature to secular life and review our findings on male/female interaction in the transfer of property. Possession of property was essential to material success and identity, and since the donation of property to monastic communities was frequently done in exchange for or in expectation of prayers for the sake of the soul of the donors, the ability to dispose of property was also linked to spiritual success. Although the activities of property exchange, like the action in *chanson de geste* and romance, were dominated by men, who appear in the charters both more frequently and more centrally than women, a man's control of property regularly intersected with, or was bounded by, the property rights of his female relatives, whether daughter, mother, or wife. Just as the comparative importance of individual and family were an issue in contemporary literature (with the family central in *chanson de geste* and the individual central in romance), so too the balance between individual control and family participation was at issue in the possession and transfer of property. Except for the small percentage of transfers made by women (mostly widows), property was most directly handled by men. As in *chansons de geste*, the common ground of the family was the basis for, and made necessary, male/female interaction. But the rules of such interaction were not rigidly established, and practice varied widely. The uncertainties and fluctuations in this situation would affect men and women differently. For the typical male participant (a married man), whose central role was clear, the participation of others may have been an encumbrance. However, for the typical female participant (a married woman), whose participation was in the peripheral role of consenter, the collective nature of property transfers was the major vehicle for exercise of property rights. She might encourage her husband to make a donation,[1] or she might insist on her inclusion in a

---

1. Several charters explicitly mention that the donor was urged by his wife and/or mother to make the gift: for example, from the cartulary of Le Ronceray d'Angers, numbers 5, 26, 126, 170, 397.

transfer of property, or she might try to withhold consent when her husband wanted to alienate property from her dower. What might such a woman feel while listening to *Raoul de Cambrai* and *Yvain*? It would seem that her own experience, although not central to the epic, is at least depicted with some accuracy. The romance vision of male/female interaction is not only further removed from experience but also centers on questions of identity and selfhood in a way pertinent only to men.

Turning to the religious sphere, we find patterns similar to those found in secular literature and life. Religious imagery of women, in particular of the Virgin Mary, expresses conflicting attitudes, and the experience of women in religious life exhibits a complex interplay of power and restraint. The virgins of real life elicited conflicting feelings in religious men, whose symbolic world had as an increasingly prominent figure a Virgin of special qualities.

As seen in Chapter 2, the qualities of the Virgin Mary that were stressed varied from image to image. Four major images of the Virgin developed over the course of the twelfth and thirteenth centuries. Thus, in addition to noting the proliferation of images, we must deal with the variety produced. The Romanesque image of the seated Virgin and Child is less concerned with mothers and children than with an iconic, theological statement of the Incarnation of Christ in which his humanity is stressed by an emphasis on his birth through a human mother. The Gothic trumeau figure of the Virgin and Child, however, shares with other Gothic imagery a narrative and humanized quality that invites identification by the human viewer. A man seeing such a figure might have a more simple process of identification than would a woman. A man could identify with the male child, and experience vicariously the maternal tenderness of the Virgin. But a female viewer had to go through a more ambiguous process: Was she to identify with the male child and think of herself as being mothered, or was she to identify with the Virgin, and think of herself as mothering others? Just as epic and romance expressed more directly the concerns of their predominantly male authors, so too these images of the Virgin express male needs and concerns more directly and intentionally than female ones.

The development of the images of the Triumph and Coronation of the Virgin show further experimentation with the images of male/female relationships. These images stress the marital relationship rather than the maternal, but they focus on different aspects of that relationship. The short-lived Triumph of the Virgin emphasized a near equality between the adult male and female, seated side by side in a common reign. The Coronation of the Virgin, while retaining the glorification of the Virgin within a cycle devoted to her death, assumption, and reign in heaven, incorporates the additional theme of humble submission of the bride to Christ. The Coronation image thus brilliantly encompassed two opposing attitudes, a resolution that embodied the ambivalence toward women and that enjoyed enormous popularity throughout the rest of the Middle Ages.

In looking at monastic movements, we have the chance to see how religious men actually related to more ordinary virgins—their monastic sisters. Again in this sphere we see ambivalence toward women, and a diversity of individual and institutional expressions of that ambivalence. The availability of a monastic vocation for women essentially similar to that for men was an affirmation of the spiritual worth of women. Yet the exclusion of women from the priesthood emphasized their spiritual difference from, and inferiority to, men. The frequent economic reliance of nuns on monks further emphasized their dependence on men. Male resentment of the *cura monialium* was sometimes enhanced by the fear of women as a source of sexual temptation. These competing attitudes yielded a variety of responses to the needs and concerns of religious women. Some men, while confirming the validity of a monastic life for women, also acknowledged the special need for support that religious women had, and went about providing that support. Examples of such men include Robert of Arbrissel and his male followers, Norbert of Xanten, the many abbots, monks, priests, and bishops who encouraged and supported local communities of women, and popes like Innocent III who prevailed upon recalcitrant orders to provide for the women in their ranks. But, as we have seen, other men, thinking more of their own overburdened and imperfect communities, tried to minimize all contact with women, religious as well as secular. This response was common among the leadership of most monastic orders, particularly toward the end of the twelfth and early thirteenth centuries. Furthermore, with the exception of Fontevrault, the governance of medieval religious orders remained in the hands of men, and women, even if accommodated on the local level, remained at the periphery of formal institutional structures.

Given the conflicting attitudes toward women that permeated image and experience, both secular and religious, one cannot help but wonder what women's response was to this ambivalence. What is at first puzzling is that there seems to be no response, or no response other than acceptance. Partly this is a historiographical problem: writing by medieval women has been overlooked because of scholarly bias against women as a legitimate object of historical study; this problem is now beginning to be remedied by studies of particular authors, although much more work needs to be done.[2] Partly it is a problem of sources: given the limitations on women's participation in the dominant structures of intellectual life, relatively few medieval women were authors—certainly very few in comparison to the flood of female writers found in the seventeenth, eighteenth, and nineteenth centuries. Yet neither the small number of sources nor the neglect of those that exist can alter the fact that there was nothing resembling a feminist movement in the twelfth and thirteenth centuries, no self-conscious criticism by significant numbers of women or men of society's ordering of the sexes, or of the contradictory attitudes and structures that shaped women's lives.

Medieval women's acceptance of these structures must be seen in the context of a value system that held hierarchy to be the dominant principle of social order.[3] It was not only women who accepted and lived within the framework of their prescribed roles but also serfs and lords, children and parents, laity and priest, bishops and pope, subjects and king. Hierarchy is a vision of order created through the ranking of elements, one superior to another. Inasmuch as one element is in a different rank from another, the two elements are separate, with different functions and perhaps different natures. Yet the different ranks are established in relation to some whole; no one rank can exist without the others. Thus a relationship between ranks is as essential to hierarchy as the separation of ranks.[4] This contradictory

2. For analysis of a variety of authors, see Peter Dronke, *Women Writers of the Middle Ages: A Critical Study of Texts from Perpetua (†203) to Marguerite Porete (†1310)* (Cambridge: Cambridge University Press, 1984).

3. For a general, anthropological perspective on hierarchy, see the introduction and postface in Louis Dumont, *Homo Hierarchicus: The Caste System and Its Implications*, trans. Mark Sainsbury et al., rev. ed. (Chicago: University of Chicago Press, 1980). For a detailed study of the medieval hierarchical vision, see Georges Duby, *The Three Orders: Feudal Society Imagined*, trans. Arthur Goldhammer (Chicago: University of Chicago Press, 1980; originally published in French in 1978).

4. See Dumont, who describes hierarchy as a relation of "the encompassing of the

dynamic within hierarchy helps explain the ambivalent and contradictory attitudes we have seen expressed in images of women and in the experience of women. For although men and women are in separate ranks in a hieratic system, they are also drawn together by a strong contradictory force of interrelationship, as men and women have biological as well as social drives toward unity. Male/female ranking is also complicated by the coexistence of men and women within a rank, for example, noble men and noble women as opposed to peasant men and women. This helps explain the occasional flexibility in medieval male/female hierarchies. The family and the church were hierarchical organizations that included women, usually in a subordinate position, but also occasionally allowed, under particular circumstances, a more extensive exercise of power by women (as abbess, as widow). In this regard the medieval hierarchy was more flexible than those of other cultures that prescribe a more absolute separation of men and women, or of one caste from another (ancient Greece, Middle Eastern cultures, India). Yet in the medieval hierarchy there was still little room for any notion of equality. Hierarchy was maintained through respect for authority, the assumption that some had legitimate authority and others did not. Bolstered by such regard for authority, the hierarchical vision was a mental habit deeply ingrained in medieval minds.

Equality, with its concomitant challenge to authority, was a notion first successfully expressed in the Early Modern period, with the Protestant Reformation and the English Revolution marking off early stages of the challenge in the religious and political spheres.[5] But it has been only in the modern period that equality can be seen to have replaced hierarchy as the predominant social principle, with the French Revolution and its critique of the social as well as the political and religious orders serving as the watershed. Racial and sexual hierarchies have been the last to be challenged. Given that we in the West have now been long accustomed to equality as a value, and

---

contrary" (pp. 238–45). See also Duby, who discusses the importance of reciprocity between ranks, for example, pp. 34, 59; Sherry B. Ortner, "Gender and Sexuality in Hierarchical Societies: The Case of Polynesia and Some Comparative Implications," in *Sexual Meanings: The Cultural Construction of Gender and Sexuality*, ed. Sherry B. Ortner and Harriet Whitehead (Cambridge: Cambridge University Press, 1981), p. 397.

    5. Earlier expressions of equality, such as the peasant revolts of the fourteenth century, were largely unsuccessful. For a discussion of the contrast between the modern notion of equality and the traditional notion of hierarchy, see Dumont, pp. 1–20.

that we are currently in the midst of an active application of this value to the structures of male/female interaction, it is difficult for us to look back on the medieval situation without imposing a judgment based on our own experience and values. We have become caught up in applying our own values as the standard, seeking cultures in the past or in remote areas of the world that may have been based on the equality between men and women that we ourselves seek. Many have found in the Middle Ages a dark period of oppression, while others see it as a high point from which the Early Modern period was a decline. We should abandon the measuring rod and try instead to understand medieval people within their own terms. Only then will we be able to appreciate more fully how modern images, attitudes, and experience differ from the medieval, and how much of a fundamental ambivalence, and acceptance of difference and hierarchy we still share with the Middle Ages.

Selected Bibliography

Note: This bibliography consists primarily of a list of works cited, although some works of limited pertinence have been dropped, and other useful works not specifically cited have been included.

Primary Sources

Manuscript Sources

Archives nationales, Paris
  J. 178.
  K. 177, 222.
  L. 1018, 1019.
  LL. 1599 ᴬ.
Bibliothèque nationale, Paris
  Cartulary of Fontevrault, ms. nouv. acq. lat. 2414.
  Collection Gaignières, *Extraict des titres originaux de l'abbaye de Fontevraud au diocèse de Poitiers*, 1699; ms. lat. 5480.
  sources for the iconography of the Virgin: ms. lat. 8, 10, 116, 238, 792, 796, 946, 1077, 9436, 9448, 11508, 12054, 12056, 14813, 15616, 17325, 18005; ms. nouv. acq. lat. 2246.
Archives départementales de Maine-et-Loire
  101 H 1, 3, 4, 8, 9, 25, 29, 53, 55, 56, 57, 69, 70, 80, 85, 95, 153, 154, 155, 156, 157, 158, 159, 160, 161, 163, 166, 167, 168, 203, 206, 207, 209, 214, 216, 217, 218, 225, 225bis, 375.
  Collection Célestin Port, carton 27.
Bibliothèque municipale d'Angers
  ms. 1025 (895).
  ms. 829 (745).

Printed Sources

Aelred of Rievaulx. *A Letter to His Sister.* Edited by Geoffrey Webb and Andrian Walker. London: A. R. Mowbray, 1957.

Archives d'Anjou: Recueil de documents et mémoires inédits sur cette province. Edited by Paul Marchegay. 3 vols. Angers, 1843–53.

Beautemps-Beaupré, C.-J. *Coutumes et institutions de l'Anjou et du Maine antérieures au XVIe siècle; textes et documents, avec notes et dissertations.* 8 vols. Paris, 1877–97.

Cartulaire de l'abbaye de Saint-Aubin d'Angers. Edited by Bertrand de Broussillon. 3 vols. Documents historiques sur l'Anjou, vols. 1–3. Angers, 1896–1903.

Cartulaire de l'abbaye du Ronceray d'Angers (1028–1184). Edited by Paul Marchegay. Paris: A. Picard, 1900.

La chanson de Guillaume. Edited by Duncan McMillan. 2 vols. Paris: Picard, 1949–50. *The Song of William.* Translated by Lynette Muir. In *William, Count of Orange: Four Old French Epics.* Edited by Glanville Price. Totowa, N.J.: Rowman and Littlefield, 1975.

Chrétien de Troyes. *Les romans de Chrétien de Troyes.* Vol. 1: *Erec et Enide.* Edited by Mario Roques. Les classiques français du moyen âge, 80. Paris: Champion, 1953. *Erec et Enide.* Translated by W. W. Comfort. In *Arthurian Romances.* London: Dent, 1914.

———. *Les romans de Chrétien de Troyes.* Vol. 4: *Le chevalier au lion (Yvain).* Edited by Mario Roques. Les classiques français du moyen âge, 89. Paris: H. Champion, 1960. *Yvain.* Translated by W. W. Comfort. In *Arthurian Romances.* London: Dent, 1914.

Chroniques des eglises d'Anjou. Edited by Paul Marchegay and Emile Mabille. Paris, 1869.

Eneas, roman du XIIe siècle. Edited by J. J. Salverda de Grave. Classiques français du moyen âge, vols. 44, 62. Paris: Champion, 1925–29. *Eneas: A Twelfth-Century French Romance.* Translated by John A. Yunck. New York: Columbia University Press, 1974.

de Fleury, Paul, ed. "Pancarte sous forme authentique contenant diverses donations faites à l'abbaye de Fontevraud au commencement du XIIe siècle." *Bulletin de la société des antiquaires de l'Ouest* 11 (1865–67): 189–99 (inventory, pp. 29–32).

Formulae Andegavenses. Edited by Eugène de Rozière. In Charles Giraud, *Essai sur l'histoire du droit français au moyen-âge,* 2: 425–59. Paris, 1846.

Hesbert, R. J., and E. Bertaud, eds., *L'Assomption de Notre-Dame.* Vol. 1: *Des origines au XVIe siècle.* Paris: Librairie Plon, 1952.

Idung of Prüfening. *Cistercians and Cluniacs: The Case for Cîteaux. A Dialogue between Two Monks; An Argument on Four Questions.* Kalamazoo, Mich.: Cistercian Publications, 1977.

Layettes du tresor des chartes. Edited by Alexandre Teulet. 2 vols. Paris, 1863–66.

The Letters of Abelard and Heloise. Translated by Betty Radice. Baltimore: Penguin Books, 1974.

The Life of Christina of Markyate, a Twelfth-Century Recluse. Edited and Translated by C. H. Talbot. Oxford: Clarendon, 1959.

McLaughlin, T. P. "Abelard's Rule for Religious Women." *Mediaeval Studies* 18 (1956): 241–92.

La mort le roi Artu. Edited by Jean Frappier. 3rd ed. Geneva: Droz, 1964. *The Death of King Arthur.* Translated by James Cable. Baltimore: Penguin Books, 1971.

Partonopeu de Blois: A French Romance of the Twelfth Century. Edited by Joseph Gildea, O.S.A. 2 vols. Villanova, Pa.: Villanova University Press, 1967–70.

Patrologiae cursus completus: Series latina. Edited by J.-P. Migne. 221 vols. Paris, 1844–64.

Petigny, J. de. "Lettre inédite de Robert d'Arbrissel à la comtesse Ermengarde." *Bibliothèque de l'Ecole des Chartes* (ser. 3) 5 (1854): 209–35.

Raoul de Cambrai. Edited by P. Meyer and A. Longnon. 1882. Reprint. Paris: Johnson Reprint Corporation, 1965. *Raoul de Cambrai: An Old French Feudal Epic.* Translated by Jessie Crosland. New York: Cooper Square Publishers, 1966.

Recueil d'annales angevines et vendômoises. Edited by Louis Halphen. Paris: A. Picard, 1903.

Regula ordinis Fontis-Ebraldi. La reigle de l'ordre de Font-Evrauld. Paris, 1642.

Sacrorum conciliorum nova et amplissima collectio. Edited by J. D. Mansi. 31 vols. Venice, 1759–98.

Statuta capitulorum generalium ordinis cisterciensis ab anno 1116 ad annum 1786. Edited by J. Canivez. Louvain: Bureaux de la Revue d'Histoire Ecclésiastique, 1933–41.

Stenton, F. M. *Transcripts of Charters Relating to the Gilbertine Houses of Sixle, Ormsby, Catley, Bullington, and Alvingham.* Horncastle: W. K. Morton and Sons for the Lincoln Record Society, 1922.

Secondary Works

Abels, Richard, and Ellen Harrison. "The Participation of Women in Languedocian Catharism." *Mediaeval Studies* 41 (1979): 215–51.

Adams, Henry. *Mont-Saint-Michel and Chartres.* Boston: Houghton Mifflin, 1904.

Adler, Alfred. "Militia et Amor in the Roman de Troie." *Romanische Forschungen* 72 (1960): 14–29.

Ahsmann, Hubertus. *La culte de la sainte Vierge et la littérature française pro-*

fane du moyen âge. Dissertation, University of Amsterdam, 1930.

d'Alverny, Marie-Thérèse. "Comment les théologiens et les philosophes voient la femme." *Cahiers de civilisation médiévale* 20 (1977): 105–29.

Aubenas, R. "La famille dans l'ancienne Provence." *Annales d'histoire économique et sociale* 8 (1936): 523–41.

———. "Quelques réflexions sur le problème de la pénétration du droit romain dans le Midi de la France au moyen âge." *Annales du Midi* 76 (1964): 371–77.

Aubert, Marcel. *Monographie de la cathédrale de Senlis.* Senlis: E. Dufresne, 1910.

———. "Le portail occidental de la cathédrale de Senlis." *Revue de l'art chrétien* (1910): 157–72.

Auerbach, Erich. *Mimesis: The Representation of Reality in Western Literature.* Translated by Willard Trask. Garden City, N.Y.: Doubleday, Anchor Books, 1957. First published in German in 1946.

Baker, Derek, ed. *Medieval Women.* Oxford: Basil Blackwell, 1978.

Barber, M. C. "Women and Catharism." *Reading Medieval Studies* 3 (1977): 45–62.

Barré, Henri. "La croyance à l'Assomption corporelle en Occident de 750 à 1150." *Bulletin de la société française d'études mariales* 2 (1949): 63–123.

———. "Marie et l'Eglise du vénérable Bède à saint Albert le Grand." *Bulletin de la société française d'études mariales* 9 (1951): 59–143.

———. *Prières anciennes de l'occident à la mère du Sauveur: Des origines à saint Anselme.* Paris: P. Lethielleux, 1963.

Bateson, Mary. "The Origin and Early History of Double Monasteries." *Transactions of the Royal Historical Society,* n.s. 13 (1899): 137–98.

Beech, George T. *A Rural Society in Medieval France: The Gâtine of Poitou in the Eleventh and Twelfth Centuries.* Baltimore: Johns Hopkins University Press, 1964.

Beissel, Stephan. *Geschichte der Verehrung Marias in Deutschland während des Mittelalters. Ein Beitrag zur Religionwissenschaft und Kunstgeschichte.* Freiburg im Breisgau: Herder, 1909.

Bender, Karl-Heinz. "Des chansons de geste à la première épopée de croisade. La présence de l'histoire contemporaine dans la littérature française du XIIe siècle." *Société Rencesvals. VIe Congrès International. Actes.* (1974): 485–500.

Benton, John F. "Clio and Venus. An Historical View of Medieval Love." In *The Meaning of Courtly Love.* Edited by F. X. Newman, pp. 19–42. Albany: State University of New York Press, 1968.

———. "Consciousness of Self and Perceptions of Individuality." In *Renaissance and Renewal in the Twelfth Century.* Edited by Robert L. Benson and Giles Constable, pp. 263–95. Cambridge: Harvard University Press, 1982.

———. "The Court of Champagne as a Literary Center." *Speculum* 36 (1961): 551–91.

———. "The Evidence for Andreas Capellanus Reexamined Again." *Studies in Philology* 59 (1962): 471–78.

———. "Men at Le Paraclet." Paper presented to the Fourth Annual Sewanee Medieval Colloquium, 16 April 1977.

———. "A Reconsideration of the Authenticity of the Correspondence of Abelard and Heloise." In *Petrus Abaelardus, 1079–1142: Person, Werk und Wirkung.* Edited by Rudolf Thomas. *Trierer theologische Studien*, 38, pp. 41–52. Trier, 1980.

Berlière, Ursmer. "Les monastères doubles aux XIIe et XIIIe siècles." Académie royale de Belgique, Classe des lettres et des sciences morales et politiques, *Mémoires* (ser. 2) 18, fasc. 3 (1923).

Bernards, Matthäus. *Speculum virginum. Geistigeit und Seelenleben der Frau im Hochmittelalter.* Cologne-Graz: Böhlau-Verlag, 1955.

Beumer, Johannes. "Die marianische Deutung des Hohen Liedes in der Frühscholastik." *Zeitschrift für katholische Theologie* 76 (1954): 411–39.

Bezzola, Reto R. *Les origines et la formation de la littérature courtoise en Occident (500–1200).* 3 vols. in 5. Paris: H. Champion, 1944–63.

———. *Le sens de l'aventure et de l'amour (Chrétien de Troyes).* Paris: La Jeune Parque, 1947.

Bienvenu, Jean-Marc. "Le conflit entre Ulger, évêque d'Angers, et Pétronille de Chemillé, abbesse de Fontevrault (vers 1140–1149)." *Revue Mabillon* 58 (1972): 113–32.

———. "Les deux *Vitae* de Robert d'Arbrissel. In *La littérature angevine médiévale. Actes du colloque du samedi 22 mars 1980*, pp. 63–76. (Maulévrier: Hérault, 1981).

———. *L'éttonnant fondateur de Fontevraud; Robert d'Arbrissel* (Paris: Nouvelles Editions Latines, 1981).

———. "Aux origines d'un ordre religieux: Robert d'Arbrissel et la fondation de Fontevrauld (1101)." *Cahiers d'histoire publiés par les Universités de Lyon, Grenoble, Clermont-Ferrand, St. Etienne, Chamberry (Lyon)* 20 (1975): 227–51.

———. "Pauvreté, misères et charité en Anjou aux XIe et XIIe siècles." *Moyen âge* 72 (1966): 389–424; 73 (1967): 189–216.

———. "Recherches sur le diocèse d'Angers au temps de la réforme gregorienne (XIème siècle et première moitié du XIIème)." Thèse pour le doctorat du troisième cycle, Université de Paris, Faculté des lettres et des sciences humaines, 1968.

Bloch, Marc. *Feudal Society.* Translated by L. A. Manyon. Chicago: University of Chicago Press, Phoenix Books, 1964.

Bloch, R. Howard. *Etymologies and Genealogies: A Literary Anthropology of the French Middle Ages.* Chicago: University of Chicago Press, 1983.

———. *Medieval French Literature and Law.* Berkeley and Los Angeles: University of California Press, 1977.

Bolton, Brenda. "Mulieres Sanctae." In *Women in Medieval Society.* Edited by

Susan Mosher Stuard, pp. 141–58. Philadelphia: University of Pennsylvania Press, 1976.

Bonnassie, Pierre. *La Catalogne du milieu de Xe à la fin du XIe siècle: Croissance et mutations d'une société.* 2 vols. Publications de l'Université de Toulouse-le Mirail, série A, vols. 23, 29. Toulouse, 1975–76.

————. "Une famille de la campagne barcelonaise et ses activités économiques aux alentours de l'An Mil." *Annales du Midi* 76 (1964): 261–303.

Borodine, Myrrha. *La femme et l'amour au XIIe siècle d'après les poèmes de Chrétien de Troyes.* Paris: A. Picard, 1909.

Boussard, Jacques. *Le comté d'Anjou sous Henri Plantagenet et ses fils (1151–1204).* Bibliothèque de l'Ecole des Hautes Etudes, fasc. 271. Paris, 1938.

————. "La vie en Anjou aux XIe et XIIe siècles." *Moyen âge* 56 (1950): 29–68.

Boutet, Dominique, and Strubel, Armand. *Littérature, politique et société dans la France du moyen âge.* Paris: Presses Universitaires de France, 1979.

Bouton, Jean de la Croix. "L'établissement des moniales cisterciennes." *Mémoires de la société pour l'histoire du droit et des institutions des anciens pays bourguignons, comtois et romands.* Fasc. 15 (1953): 83–116.

————. "Saint Bernard et les moniales." In *Mélanges Saint Bernard.* XXIVe Congrès de l'association bourguignonne des sociétés savantes, pp. 225–47. Dijon, 1953.

Brooke, Rosalind, and Brooke, Christopher. "St Clare." In *Medieval Women.* Edited by Derek Baker, pp. 275–87. Oxford: Basil Blackwell, 1978.

Brouillette, Diane Cynthia. "The Early Gothic Sculpture of Senlis Cathedral." Ph.D. dissertation, University of California, Berkeley, 1981.

Brown, Elizabeth A. R. "Eleanor of Aquitaine: Parent, Queen, and Duchess." In *Eleanor of Aquitaine: Patron and Politician.* Edited by William W. Kibler. Austin: University of Texas Press, 1976.

Buckstaff, Florence Griswold. "Married Women's Property in Anglo-Saxon and Anglo-Norman Law and the Origin of the Common-Law Dower." *Annals of the American Academy of Political and Social Science* 4 (1894): 233–64.

Buhot, Jacqueline. "L'abbaye normande de Savigny, chef d'ordre et fille de Cîteaux." *Moyen âge* (ser. 3) 7 (1936): 1–19, 104–21, 178–90, 249–72.

Bynum, Caroline Walker. "Did the Twelfth Century Discover the Individual?" In *Jesus as Mother: Studies in the Spirituality of the High Middle Ages,* pp. 82–109. Berkeley and Los Angeles: University of California Press, 1982.

————. "Jesus as Mother and Abbot as Mother: Some Themes in Twelfth-Century Cistercian Writing." In *Jesus as Mother: Studies in the Spirituality of the High Middle Ages,* pp. 110–69. Berkeley and Los Angeles: University of California Press, 1982.

Calin, William C. *The Epic Quest: Studies in Four Old French Chansons de Geste.* Baltimore: Johns Hopkins University Press, 1960.

————. *A Muse for Heroes: Nine Centuries of Epic in France*. Toronto: University of Toronto Press, 1983.

————. *The Old French Epic of Revolt: "Raoul de Cambrai," "Renaud de Montauban," "Gormond et Isembard."* Geneva: Droz, 1962.

Cammarosano, Paolo. "Les structures familiales dans les villes de l'Italie communale (XIIe–XIVe ss.)." In *Famille et parenté dans l'Occident médiéval*. Actes du Colloque de Paris (6–8 juin 1974): organisé par l'Ecole Pratique des Hautes Etudes (VIe section) en collaboration avec le Collège de France et l'Ecole française de Rome: Communications et débats. Edited by G. Duby and J. Le Goff, pp. 181–94. Rome: Ecole française de Rome, 1977.

Capelle, D. B. "Le témoinage de la liturgie." *Bulletin de la société française d'études mariales* 2 (1949): 35–62.

Casey, Kathleen L. "The Cheshire Cat: Reconstructing the Experience of Medieval Women." In *Liberating Women's History: Theoretical and Critical Essays*. Edited by Bernice A. Carroll, pp. 224–49. Urbana: University of Illinois Press, 1976.

Castaing-Sicard, Mireille. "Les donations toulousaines, Xe–XIIIe siècles." *Annales du Midi* 70 (1958): 27–64.

Chanson de Geste und höfischer Roman. Heidelberger Kolloquium, 30. Januar 1961. Heidelberg: Carl Winter, 1963.

Chartrou, Josephe. *L'Anjou de 1109 à 1151: Foulque de Jerusalem et Geoffroi Plantagenet*. Paris: Presses Universitaires de France, 1928.

Chatel, Marie Louise. "Le culte de la Vierge en France du Vc au XIIe siècle." Thèse Lettres, Paris, 1945.

Chenu, M.-D. "La croyance à l'Assomption en Occident de 1150 à 1250." *Bulletin de la société française d'études mariales* 3 (1950): 13–32.

Chettle, H. F. "The English Houses of the Order of Fontevrault." *Downside Review* 60 (1942): 33–55.

Coathalem, Hervé. *Le parallelisme entre la sainte Vierge et l'Eglise dans la tradition latine jusqu'à la fin du XIIe siècle. Analecta Gregoriana*, vol. 74, sectio B, no. 27. Rome, 1954.

Combarieu du Gres, Micheline de. *L'idéal humain et l'expérience morale chez les héros des chansons de geste, des origines à 1250*. 2 vols. Aix-en-Provence: Université de Provence, 1979.

Comet, G. "Quelques remarques sur la dot et les droits de l'épouse dans la région d'Arles aux XIIe et XIIIe ss." In *Mélanges offerts à René Crozet*, 2: 1031–34. Poitiers: Société d'études médiévales, 1966.

Comfort, W. W. "The Character Types in the Old French Chansons de Geste." *PMLA* 21 (1906): 279–434.

————. "The Essential Difference between a *Chanson de Geste* and a *Roman d'Aventure*." *PMLA* 19 (1904): 64–74.

Conan, Anne Marie. "Essai sur l'iconographie du Couronnement de la Vierge en France pendant le moyen âge dans la sculpture, la peinture, et les miniatures." Thèse Ecole du Louvre, Paris, 1948.

Connor, Sister Michael [Elizabeth]. "The First Cistercian Nuns and Renewal Today." *Cistercian Studies* 5 (1970): 131–68.

Coppin, Joseph. *Amour et mariage dans la littérature française du Nord au moyen âge.* Paris: Librairie d'Argences, 1961.

Cormier, Raymond J. *One Heart One Mind: The Rebirth of Virgil's Hero in Medieval French Romance.* University, Miss.: Romance Monographs, 1973.

Cornuey, L.-M.-A. *La régime de la "dos" aux époques mérovingienne et carolingienne.* Alger: Impr. "La Typo-Litho," 1929.

Crist, Larry. "Deep Structures in the *chansons de geste*: Hypotheses for a Taxonomy." *Olifant* 3 (1975): 3–35.

Crozet, René. "Fontevrault." *Congrès archéologique de France* 122 (1964): 426–77.

Crummey, Donald. "Women, Property, and Litigation among the Bagemder Amhara, 1750s to 1850s." In *African Women and the Law: Historical Perspectives.* Edited by Margaret Jean Hay and Marcia Wright, pp. 20–32. Boston University Papers on Africa, no. 7. Boston: African Studies Center of Boston University, 1982.

Davis, Natalie Z. "City Women and Religious Change in Sixteenth Century France." In *Society and Culture in Early Modern France*, pp. 65–95. Stanford, Calif.: Stanford University Press, 1975.

Diefendorf, Barbara B. "Widowhood and Remarriage in Sixteenth Century Paris." *Journal of Family History* 7 (1982): 379–95.

Diverres, A. H. "Chivalry and *fin'amor* in *Le Chevalier au lion.*" In *Studies in Medieval Literature and Languages in Memory of Frederick Whitehead.* Edited by W. Rothwell et al., pp. 91–116. Manchester: Manchester University Press; New York: Barnes and Noble, 1973.

Dronke, Peter. *Abelard and Heloise in Medieval Testimonies.* Glasgow: University of Glasgow Press, 1976.

———. *Women Writers of the Middle Ages: A Critical Study of Texts from Perpetua (†203) to Marguerite Porete (†1310).* Cambridge: Cambridge University Press, 1984.

Duby, Georges. *The Chivalrous Society.* Translated by Cynthia Postan. Berkeley and Los Angeles: University of California Press, 1980.

———. "Dans la France du Nord-Ouest. Au XIIe siècle: Les 'jeunes' dans la société aristocratique." *Annales: Economies, sociétés, civilisations* 19 (1964): 835–46. Essay translated in Duby, *The Chivalrous Society*, pp. 112–22.

———. *The Knight, the Lady and the Priest: The Making of Modern Marriage in Medieval France.* Translated by Barbara Bray. New York: Pantheon, 1983. Originally published in French in 1981.

———. "Lignage, noblesse et chevalerie au XIIe siècle dans la région mâconnaise. Une révision." *Annales: Economies, Sociétés, Civilisations* 27 (1972): 803–23. Essay translated in Duby, *The Chivalrous Society*, pp. 59–80.

———. *Medieval Marriage: Two Models from Twelfth-Century France.* Translated by Elborg Forster. Baltimore: Johns Hopkins University Press, 1978.

————. "Problèmes d'économie seigneuriale dans la France du XIIe siècle." In *Probleme des 12. Jahrhunderts, Reichenau-Vorträge, 1965–67*, pp. 161–67. Stuttgart, 1968.

————. "Situation de la noblesse en France au début du XIIIe siècle." In *Hommes et structures du moyen âge*, pp. 343–52. Paris: Mouton, 1973. Essay translated in Duby, *The Chivalrous Society*, pp. 178–85.

————. *La société aux XIe et XIIe siècles dans la région mâconnaise.* Paris: S.E.V.P.E.N., 1971.

————. *The Three Orders: Feudal Society Imagined.* Translated by Arthur Goldhammer. Chicago: University of Chicago Press, 1980. Originally published in French in 1978.

Duby, Georges, and Le Goff, Jacques. *Famille et parenté dans l'occident médiéval.* Actes du Colloque de Paris (6–8 juin 1974) organisée par l'Ecole Pratique des Hautes Etudes (VIe section) en collaboration avec le Collège de France et l'Ecole française de Rome: Communications et débats. Rome: Ecole française de Rome, 1977.

Dumont, Louis. *Homo Hierarchicus: The Caste System and Its Implications.* Rev. ed. Translated by Mark Sainsbury et al. Chicago: University of Chicago Press, 1980. Originally published in French in 1966.

Eckenstein, Lina. *Woman under Monasticism.* Cambridge: Cambridge University Press, 1896.

Edouard, l'Abbé. *Fontevrault et ses monuments, ou histoire de cette royale abbaye depuis sa fondation jusqu'à sa suppression (1100–1793).* 2 vols. Paris, 1873–74.

Elkins, Sharon. "Double Monasteries of Twelfth Century England." Paper delivered at the Seventeenth International Congress on Medieval Studies, Kalamazoo, May 1982.

————. "Female Religious in Twelfth Century England." Ph.D. dissertation, Harvard University, 1977.

Erens, A. "Les soeurs dans l'ordre de Prémontré." *Analecta Praemonstratensia* 5 (1929): 5–26.

Erickson, C., and Casey, K. "Women in the Middle Ages: A Working Bibliography." *Mediaeval Studies* 37 (1975): 340–59.

d'Espinay, Gustave Marie. *Les cartulaires angevins; étude sur le droit de l'Anjou au moyen âge.* Angers, 1864.

————. "Le droit de l'Anjou avant les coutumes, d'après les notes de M. Beautemps-Beaupré." *Mémoires de la société nationale d'agriculture, sciences et arts d'Angers* (ser. 5) 4 (1901): 5–69.

————. "Les formules angevines." Extract from the *Mémoires de la Société impériale d'agriculture, sciences et arts d'Angers,* 1858.

Evergates, Theodore. "The Aristocracy of Champagne in the Mid-thirteenth Century: A Quantitative Description." *Journal of Interdisciplinary History* 5 (1974/75): 1–18.

Ferrante, Joan M. *The Conflict of Love and Honor: The Medieval Tristan Legend in France, Germany and Italy.* The Hague: Mouton, 1973.

————. "The Conflict of Lyric Conventions and Romance Forms." In *In Pursuit of Perfection: Courtly Love in Medieval Literature*. Edited by Joan M. Ferrante and George D. Economou, pp. 135–78. Port Washington, N.Y.: Kennikat Press, 1975.

————. "Male Fantasy and Female Reality in Courtly Literature." *Women's Studies* 11 (1984): 67–97.

————. *Woman as Image in Medieval Literature from the Twelfth Century to Dante*. New York: Columbia University Press, 1975.

Fontette, Micheline de. *Les religieuses à l'âge classique du droit canon: Recherches sur les structures juridiques des branches féminines des ordres*. Paris: J. Vrin, 1967.

"Fontevrault." *Congrès archéologique de France* 77 (1911): 48–64.

Forsyth, Ilene H. *The Throne of Wisdom: Wood Sculptures of the Madonna in Romanesque France*. Princeton: Princeton University Press, 1972.

Fossier, Robert. *La terre et les hommes en Picardie jusqu'à la fin du XIIIe siècle*. 2 vols. Paris: Beatrice-Nauwelaerts, 1968.

Fournée, Jean. "Les orientations doctrinales de l'iconographie marial à la fin de l'époque romane." *Centre international d'études romanes* (1971) 1: 23–56.

Fourrier, Anthime. *Le courant réaliste dans le roman courtois en France au moyen âge*. Vol. 1: *Les débuts (XIIe siècle)*. Paris: A. G. Nizet, 1960.

Frappier, Jean. *Les chansons de geste du cycle de Guillaume d'Orange*. 2 vols. Paris: Société d'Edition d'Enseignement Supérieur, 1955.

————. *Etude sur "Yvain" ou le "Chevalier au lion" de Chrétien de Troyes*. Paris: Société d'édition d'enseignement supérieur, 1969. First published in 1952.

————. "Reflexions sur les rapports des *chansons de geste* et de l'histoire." *Zeitschrift für romanische Philologie* 63 (1957): 1–19.

Freed, John B. "Urban Development and the *cura monialium* in Thirteenth-Century Germany." *Viator* 3 (1972): 311–27.

Friedl, Ernestine. "The Position of Women: Appearance and Reality." *Anthropological Quarterly* 40 (1967): 97–108.

————. "Some aspects of dowry and inheritance in Boetia." In *Mediterranean Countrymen: Essays in the Social Anthropology of the Mediterranean*. Edited by J. Pitt-Rivers, pp. 113–35. Paris: Mouton, 1963.

Galais, Pierre. "Littérature et mediatisation. Réflexions sur la genèse du genre romanesque." *Etudes littéraires* 4 (1971): 39–72.

Ganshof, François-L. "Le statut de la femme dans la monarchie franque." In *La femme. Recueils de la société Jean Bodin* 12 (1962): 5–57.

Gazeau, Roger. "La clôture des moniales au XIIe siècle en France." *Revue Mabillon* 58 (1974): 289–308.

Giraudot, Francis, and Bouton, Jean de la Croix. "Bernard et les Gilbertins." In *Bernard de Clairvaux*. Commission d'histoire de l'ordre de Cîteaux, 3, pp. 327–38. Paris: Editions Alsatia, 1953.

Gist, Margaret Adlum. *Love and War in the Middle English Romances*. Philadelphia: University of Pennsylvania Press, 1947.

Godfrey, John. "The Double Monastery in Early English History." *Ampleforth Journal* 79 (1974): 19–32.

Gold, Penny S. "Image and Reality: Women in Twelfth-Century France." Ph.D. dissertation, Stanford University, 1977.

———. "The Marriage of Mary and Joseph in the Medieval Ideology of Marriage." In *Sexual Practices and the Medieval Church*. Edited by James Brundage and Vern Bullough, pp. 102–17. Buffalo: Prometheus Books, 1982.

Golding, Brian. "St. Bernard and St. Gilbert." In *The Influence of St. Bernard: Anglican Essays with an Introduction by Jean Leclercq*. Edited by Benedicta Ward, pp. 41–52. Oxford: SLG Press, 1976.

Goode, William J. "The Theoretical Importance of Love." *American Sociological Review* 24 (1959): 38–47.

Goody, Jack. "Strategies of Heirship." *Comparative Studies in Society and History* 15 (1973): 3–20.

Goody, Jack; Thirsk, Joan; and Thompson, E. P., eds. *Family and Inheritance: Rural Society in Western Europe, 1200–1800*. Cambridge: Cambridge University Press, 1976.

Gougaud, L. "*Mulierum consortia*: Etude sur le syneisaktisme chez les ascètes celtiques." *Eriu, the Journal of the School of Irish Learning* 9 (1921/23): 147–56.

Graef, Hilda. *Mary: A History of Doctrine and Devotion*. Vol. 1: *From the Beginnings to the Eve of the Reformation*. New York: Sheed and Ward, 1963.

Graham, Rose. S. *Gilbert of Sempringham and the Gilbertines: A History of the Only English Monastic Order*. London: E. Stock, 1901.

Graves, Coburn V. "English Cistercian Nuns in Lincolnshire." *Speculum* 54 (1979): 492–99.

Grélier (now Perelman), Françoise. "Le temporel de l'abbaye de Fontevrault dans le haut-Poitou, des origines à la réforme du XVe siècle." Thèse, Ecole des Chartes, 1960.

Gripkey, Mary Vincentine. "The Blessed Virgin Mary as Mediatrix in the Latin and Old French Legend Prior to the Fourteenth Century." Ph.D. dissertation, Catholic University of American, 1938.

Grundmann, Herbert. *Religiöse Bewegungen im Mittelalter: Untersuchungen über die geschichtlichen Zusammenhänge zwischen der Ketzerei, den Bettelorden und der religiösen Frauenbewegung im 12 und 13. Jahrhundert und über die geschichtlichen Grundlagen der deutschen Mystik*. Hildesheim: Georg Olms, 1961. First published in 1935.

Guillot, Olivier. *Le comte d'Anjou et son entourage au XIe siècle*. 2 vols. Paris: Editions A. & J. Picard, 1972.

Guldan, Ernst. *Eva und Maria. Eine Antithese als Bildmotiv*. Graz-Köln: Böhlau, 1966.

Hajdu, Robert. "The Position of Noblewomen in the pays des coutumes, 1100–1300." *Journal of Family History* 5 (1980): 122–44.

Halphen, Louis. *Le comté d'Anjou au XIe siècle*. Paris: A. Picard et Fils, 1906.
———. "Les institutions judiciaires en France au XIe siècle—région an-
gevine." *Revue historique* 77 (1901): 279–307.
Hanning, Robert W. *The Individual in Twelfth-Century Romance*. New
Haven: Yale University Press, 1977.
———. "The Social Significance of Twelfth-Century Chivalric Romance."
Medievalia et Humanistica 3 (1972): 3–29.
Henderson, Margaret W. "Woman in the Medieval French Epic." Ph.D. dis-
sertation, New York University, 1965.
Hentsch, Alice A. *De la littérature didactique du moyen âge s'addressant spé-
cialement aux femmes*. Geneva: Slatkine Reprints, 1975. First published as
author's inaugural dissertation, 1903.
Herlihy, David. "Computer-assisted Analysis of the Statistical Documents of
Medieval Society." In *Medieval Studies: An Introduction*. Edited by James M.
Powell, pp. 185–211. Syracuse: Syracuse University Press, 1976.
———. "Land, Family and Women in Continental Europe, 701–1200." *Tra-
ditio* 18 (1962): 89–121.
———. "Life Expectancies for Women in Medieval Society." In *The Role of
Woman in the Middle Ages*. Papers of the Sixth Annual Conference of the
Center for Medieval and Early Renaissance Studies, State University of
New York at Binghamton, 6–7 May 1972. Edited by Rosmarie Thee More-
wedge, pp. 1–22. Albany: State University of New York Press, 1975.
———. "The Medieval Marriage Market." *Medieval and Renaissance Studies*.
Proceedings of the Southeastern Institute of Medieval and Renaissance
Studies, Summer 1974. Edited by Dale B. J. Randall. Medieval and Renais-
sance Series, no. 6, pp. 3–21. Durham, N.C.: Duke University Press, 1976.
———. "Women in Medieval Society." Smith History Lecture, 1971.
Houston: University of St. Thomas, 1971. Reprinted in David Herlihy.
The Social History of Italy and Western Europe, 700-1500: Collected Studies.
London: Variorum Reprints, 1978.
Hilaire, Jean. "Les régimes matrimoniaux aux XIe et XIIe siècles dans la ré-
gion de Montpellier." *Recueil de mémoires et travaux publié par la société
d'histoire du droit et des institutions des anciens pays de droit écrit* (Toulouse),
fasc. 3 (1955): 15–37.
Hilpisch, Stephanus. *Die Doppelklöster: Entstehung und Organization*. In
Beiträge zur Geschichte des alten Mönchtums und des Benediktiner Ordens,
fasc. 15. Münster i. W., 1928.
———. *History of Benedictine Nuns*. Translated by Sister M. Joanne Muggli.
Edited by Leonard J. Doyle. Collegeville, Minn.: St. John's Abbey Press,
1958.
Histoire de l'ordre de Fontevrault, 1100-1908, by the Religieuses de Sainte-
Marie de Fontevrault de Boulaur (Gers). 3 vols. Auch: Cocharaux, 1911–15.
Hughes, Diane Owen. "From Brideprice to Dowry in Mediterranean Eu-
rope." *Journal of Family History* 3 (1978): 262–96.

Hunt, Noreen. "Notes on the History of Benedictine and Cistercian Nuns in Britain." *Cistercian Studies* 8 (1973): 157–77.

Huyghebaert, N. "Examen des plus anciennes chartes de l'abbaye de Messines." *Bulletin de la commission royale d'histoire* 121 (1956): 175–222.

———. "Les femmes laïques dans la vie religieuse des XIe et XIIe siècles dans la province ecclésiastique de Reims." *I laici nella "societas christiana" dei secoli XI e XII.* Atti della terza settimana internazionale di studio, Mendola, 21–27 agosto 1965, pp. 346–89. Milan, 1968.

Iogna-Prat, Dominique. "La femme dans la perspective pénitentielle des ermites du Bas-Maine (fin XIème début XIIème siècle)." *Revue d'histoire de la spiritualité* 53 (1977): 47–64.

Jackson, W. T. H. "The Nature of Romance." *Yale French Studies* 51 (1974): 12–25.

Jameson, Frederic. "Magical Narratives: Romance as Genre." *New Literary History* 7 (1975/76): 135–63.

Jones, Rosemarie. *The Theme of Love in the "Romans d'Antiquité."* London: Modern Humanities Research Association, 1972.

Jonin, Pierre. *Les personnages féminins dans les romans français de Tristan au XIIe siècle: Etude des influences contemporaines.* Publication des Annales de la Faculté des Lettres Aix-en-Provence, n.s., no. 22, 1958.

Jullian, R. "Evolution des thèmes iconographiques: Le Couronnement de la Vierge." In Paul Guth et al., *Le siècle de Saint Louis,* pp. 153–60. Paris: Librairie Hachette, 1970.

Kahn Blumstein, Andrée. *Misogyny and Idealization in the Courtly Romance.* Bonn: Bouvier, 1977.

Katzenellenbogen, Adolf. *The Sculptural Programs of Chartres Cathedral: Christ-Mary-Ecclesia.* New York: Norton, 1964. First published 1959.

Kelly-Gadol, Joan. "Did Women Have a Renaissance?" In *Becoming Visible: Women in European History.* Edited by Renate Bridenthal and Claudia Koonz, pp. 137–64. Boston: Houghton Mifflin, 1977.

———. "The Social Relations of the Sexes: Methodological Implications of Women's History." *Signs: Journal of Women in Culture and Society* 1 (1976): 809–23.

Ker, W. P. *Epic and Romance: Essays on Medieval Literature.* 2nd ed. 1908. Reprint. New York: Dover Publications, 1957.

Kittel, Margaret Ruth. "Married Women in Thirteenth-Century England: A Study in Common Law." Ph.D. dissertation, University of California, Berkeley, 1973.

Kitzinger, Ernst. "Byzantium and the West in the Second Half of the Twelfth Century: Problems of Stylistic Relationships." *Gesta* 9, no. 2 (1970): 49–56.

Knowles, David. *The Monastic Order in England: A History of Its Development from the Times of St. Dunstan to the Fourth Lateran Council, 940-1216.* 2nd ed. Cambridge: Cambridge University Press, 1966.

———. "The Revolt of the Lay Brothers of Sempringham." *English Historical Review* 50 (1935): 465–87.

Koch, Gottfried. "Die Frau im mittelalterlichen Katharismus und Waldensertum." *Studi medievali* (ser. 3) 5 (1964): 741–74.

———. *Frauenfrage und Ketzertum im Mittelalter: Die Frauenbewegung im Rahmen des Katharismus und des Waldensertums und ihre sozialen Wurzeln (12.-14. Jahrhundert)*. Berlin: Akademie-Verlag, 1962.

Köhler, Erich. *L'aventure chevaleresque: Idéal et réalité dans le roman courtois. Etudes sur la forme des plus anciens poèmes d'Arthur et du Graal*. Translated by E. Kaufholz. Paris: Gallimard, 1974. First published in German in 1956, *Ideal und Wirklichkeit in der höfischen Epik*.

———. "Quelques observations d'ordre historico-sociologique sur les rapports entre la chanson de geste et le roman courtois." In *Chanson de geste und höfischer Roman*. Heidelberger Kolloquium, 30. Januar 1961, pp. 21–30. Heidelberg: C. Winter, 1963.

Kok, Bertha L. de. *Guibourc et quelques autres figures de femmes dans les plus anciennes chansons de geste*. Paris: Presses Universitaires de France, 1926.

Kostoroski, Emilie. "Quest in Query and the Chastelaine de Vergi." *Medievalia et Humanistica* 3 (1972): 179–98.

Krenig, Ernst G. "Mittelalterliche Frauenklöster nach den Konstitutionen von Cîteaux, unter besonderer Berücksichtigung fränkischer Nonnenkonvente." *Analecta sacri ordinis cisterciensis* 10 (1954): 1–105.

Lamy, Hugues. *L'abbaye de Tongerloo, depuis sa fondation jusqu'en 1263*. In *Recueil de travaux publiés par les membres des conférences d'histoire et de philologie de l'Université de Louvain*, fasc. 44. Louvain, 1914.

de Laplanche, J. *La réserve coutumière dans l'ancien droit français*. Paris, 1925.

Leclercq, Jean. *Monks and Love in Twelfth-Century France: Psycho-Historical Essays*. New York: Oxford University Press, 1979.

———. "Saint Bernard et la dévotion médiévale envers Marie." *Revue d'ascétique et de mystique* 30 (1954): 361–71.

———. "S. Pierre Damien et les femmes." *Studia Monastica* 15 (1973): 43–55.

Lécuyer, J. "Marie et l'Eglise comme mère et épouse du Christ." *Bulletin de la société française d'études mariales* 10 (1952): 23–41.

Lefay-Toury, Marie-Noëlle. "Roman breton et mythes courtois. L'évolution du personnage féminin dans les romans de Chrétien de Troyes." *Cahiers de civilisation médiévale* 15 (1972): 193–204, 283–93.

Lehmann, Andrée. *Le rôle de la femme dans l'histoire de France au moyen âge*. Paris: Berger-Levrault, 1952.

Lejeune, Rita. "La femme dans les littératures française et occitane du XIe au XIIIe siècle." *Cahiers de civilisation médiévale* 20 (1977): 201–17.

Lekai, Louis J. *The Cistercians: Ideals and Reality*. Kent, Ohio: Kent State University Press, 1977.

Lemaire, André. "La 'dotatio de l'épouse' de l'époque mérovingienne au

XIIIe s." *Revue historique de droit français et étranger* (ser. 4) 8 (1929): 569–80.

———. "Les origines de la communauté de biens entre époux dans le droit coutumier français." *Revue historique de droit français et étranger* (ser. 4) 7 (1928): 584–643.

Lepointe, Gariel. *Droit romain et ancien droit français. Régimes matrimoniaux, libéralités, successions.* Paris: Editions Montchrestien, 1958.

Levy, Raphael. "Chronologie approximative de la littérature française du moyen âge." *Beihefte zur Zeitschrift für romanische Philologie* 98 (1957).

Lewis, Archibald R. *The Development of Southern French and Catalan Society, 718-1050.* Austin: University of Texas Press, 1965.

Leyser, K. J. *Rule and Conflict in an Early Medieval Society: Ottonian Saxony.* Bloomington: Indiana University Press, 1979.

Lorcin, Marie-Thérèse. *Vivre et mourir en Lyonnais à la fin du moyen âge.* Paris: CNRS, 1981.

Ludden, Franklin Monroe. "The Early Gothic Portals of Senlis and Mantes." Ph.D. dissertation, Harvard University, 1955.

Luscombe, D. E. "The *Letters* of Heloise and Abelard since 'Cluny 1972.'" In *Petrus Abaelardus, 1079-1142: Person, Werk und Wirkung.* Edited by Rudolf Thomas. *Trierer theologische Studien,* 38, pp. 19–39. Trier, 1980.

McDonnell, Ernest W. *The Beguines and Beghards in Medieval Culture, with Special Emphasis on the Belgian Scene.* New Brunswick, N.J.: Rutgers University Press, 1954.

McGuire, Brian Patrick. "The Cistercians and the Transformation of Monastic Friendships." *Analecta Cisterciensia* 37 (1981): 1–63.

McLaughlin, Barry, ed. *Studies in Social Movements: A Social Psychological Perspective.* New York: Free Press, 1969.

McLaughlin, Eleanor C. "Equality of Souls, Inequality of Sexes: Women in Medieval Theology." In *Religion and Sexism: Images of Woman in the Jewish and Christian Traditions.* Edited by Rosemary Radford Ruether, pp. 213–66. New York: Simon and Schuster, 1974.

———. "Women, Power, and the Pursuit of Holiness in Medieval Christianity." In *Women of Spirit: Female Leadership in the Jewish and Christian Traditions.* Edited by Rosemary Ruether and Eleanor McLaughlin, pp. 99–130. New York: Simon & Schuster, 1979.

McLaughlin, Mary Martin. "Peter Abelard and the Dignity of Women: Twelfth Century 'Feminism' in Theory and Practice." In *Pierre Abelard, Pierre le Vénérable: Les courants philosophiques, littéraires et artistiques en occident au milieu du XIIe siècle.* Colloques Internationaux du Centre de la Recherche Scientifique, Abbaye de Cluny 2 au 9 juillet 1972, pp. 287–334. Paris: C.N.R.S., 1975.

———. "Women and the Monastic Life in the Twelfth Century: The Case of the Paraclete." Paper delivered at the Second Berkshire Conference in Women's History, 1974.

Maclean, Ian. *The Renaissance Notion of Woman: A Study in the Fortunes of Scholasticism and Medical Science in European Intellectual Life.* Cambridge: Cambridge University Press, 1980.

McNamara, Jo Ann, and Wemple, Suzanne. "The Power of Women through the Family in Medieval Europe: 500-1100." *Feminist Studies* 1 (1973): 126–41.

————. "Sanctity and Power: The Dual Pursuit of Medieval Women." In *Becoming Visible: Women in European History.* Edited by Renate Bridenthal and Claudia Koonz, pp. 90–118. Boston: Houghton Mifflin, 1977.

Mahuet, J. de. "Essai sur la part de l'Orient dans l'iconographie mariale de l'Occident." *Bulletin de la société française d'études mariales* 19 (1962): 145–83.

Mâle, Emile. *The Gothic Image: Religious Art in France of the Thirteenth Century.* Translated by Dora Nussey. New York: Harper Torchbooks, 1958. First published in English in 1913.

————. "Le portail de Senlis et son influence." *La revue de l'art ancien et moderne* 29 (1911): 161–76.

————. *Rome et ses vieilles églises.* Paris: Flammarion, 1942.

Maltz, Daniel P. "The Bride of Christ Is Filled with His Spirit." In *Women in Ritual and Symbolic Roles.* Edited by Judith Hoch-Smith and Anita Spring, pp. 27–44. New York: Plenum Press, 1978.

Marchalonis, Shirley. "Above Rubies: Popular Views of Medieval Women." *Journal of Popular Culture* 14 (1980): 87–93.

Marchegay, Paul. *Recherches sur les cartulaires d'Anjou.* Angers, 1843.

Marchello-Nizia, Christiane. "Amour courtois, société masculine et figures du pouvoir." *Annales: Economies, sociétés, civilisations* 36 (1981): 969–82.

Maria. Etudes sur la sainte Vierge. Edited by Hubert Du Manoir. 6 vols. Paris: Beauchesne, 1949–61.

Matarasso, P. *Recherches historiques et littéraires sur "Raoul de Cambrai."* Paris: Nizet, 1962.

Meyer, Marc A. "Land Charters and the Legal Position of Anglo-Saxon Women." In *The Women of England from Anglo-Saxon Times to the Present: Interpretive Bibliographic Essays.* Edited by Barbara Kanner, pp. 57–82. Hamden, Conn.: Archon Books, 1979.

————. "Women in the Tenth Century English Monastic Reform." *Revue Benedictine* 87 (1977): 34–61.

Milis, Ludo. *L'ordre des chanoines reguliers d'Arrouaise: Son histoire et son organisation, de la fondation de l'abbaye-mère (vers 1090) à la fin des chapitres annuels (1471).* 2 vols. Bruges: De Tempel, 1969.

Milsom, S. F. C. "Inheritance by Women in the Twelfth and Thirteenth Centuries." In *On the Laws and Customs of England: Essays in Honor of Samuel E. Thorne,* pp. 60–89. Studies in Legal History. Chapel Hill: University of North Carolina Press, 1981.

Moller, Herbert. "The Social Causation of the Courtly Love Complex." *Comparative Studies in Society and History* 1 (1958/59): 137–63.

Moore, John C. *Love in Twelfth-Century France.* Philadelphia: University of Pennsylvania Press, 1972.

Moore, R. I. "The Reconstruction of the Cartulary of Fontevrault." *Bulletin of the Institute of Historical Research* (London University) 41 (1968): 86–95.

de Moreau, E. "Les monastères doubles, leur histoire, surtout en Belgique." *Nouvelle revue théologique* 66 (1939): 787–92.

Morewedge, Rosmarie Thee, ed. *The Role of Woman in the Middle Ages.* Papers of the Sixth Annual Conference of the Center for Medieval and Early Renaissance Studies, State University of New York at Binghamton, 6–7 May 1972. Albany: State University of New York Press, 1975.

Morris, Colin. *The Discovery of the Individual, 1050–1200.* New York: Harper Torchbooks, 1972.

Morris, Joan. *The Lady Was a Bishop: The Hidden History of Women with Clerical Ordination and the Jurisdiction of Bishops.* New York: Macmillan, 1973.

Mussetter, Sally. "The Education of Chretien's Enide." *Romanic Review* 73 (1982): 147–66.

Neff, Theodore Lee. *La satire des femmes dans la poésie lyrique française au moyen âge.* (Ph.D. dissertation, University of Chicago.) Paris: V. Giard and E. Brière, 1900.

Newman, F. X., ed. *The Meaning of Courtly Love.* Albany: State University of New York Press, 1968.

Nichols, John A. "The Internal Organization of English Cistercian Nunneries." *Cîteaux. Commentarii Cistercienses* 30 (1979): 23–40.

Nicquet, Honorat. *Histoire de l'ordre de Font-Evraud.* Paris, 1642.

Niderst, René. *Robert d'Arbrissel et les origines de l'ordre de Fontevrault.* Rodez: G. Subervie, 1952.

Nitze, William Albert. "Erec's Treatment of Enide." *Romanic Review* 10 (1919): 26–37.

―――. "The Romance of Erec, Son of Lac." *Modern Philology* 11 (1914): 445–89.

Nübel, Otto. *Mittelalterliche Beginen- und Sozialsiedlungen in den Niederlanden: Ein Beitrag zur Vorgeschichte der Fuggerei.* Tübingen: J. C. B. Mohr, 1970.

Ong, Walter J. "The Writer's Audience Is Always a Fiction." *PMLA* 90 (1975): 9–21.

Ortner, Sherry B., and Whitehead, Harriet, eds. *Sexual Meanings: The Cultural Construction of Gender and Sexuality.* Cambridge: Cambridge University Press, 1981.

Painter, Sidney. "The Family and the Feudal System in Twelfth Century England." *Speculum* 35 (1960): 1–16.

Paquette, Jean-Marcel. "Epopée et roman: continuité ou discontinuité?" *Etudes littéraires* 4 (1971): 9–38.

Parisse, Michel. "Les chanoinesses dans l'Empire germanique (IXe-XIe ss.)." *Francia* 6 (1978): 107–26.

Payen, Jean-Charles. "Destruction des mythes courtois dans le roman arthurien. La femme dans le roman en vers après Chrétien de Troyes." *Revue des langues romanes* 78 (1969): 213–28.

———. "Figures féminines dans le roman médiéval français." In *Entretiens sur la renaissance du douzième siècle, le 21 au 30 juillet 1965*, pp. 407–28. Paris: Mouton, 1968.

de Petigny, J. "Robert d'Arbrissel et Geoffroi de Vendôme." *Bibliothèque de l'Ecole des Chartes* (ser. 3) 5 (1854): 1–30.

Petot, Pierre and André Vandenbossche. "Le statut de la femme dans les pays coutumiers français du XIIIe au XVIIe siècle." In *La femme. Recueils de la société Jean Bodin* 12 (1962): 244–54.

Piolanti, Antonio. "'Sicut Sponsa ornata monilibus suis': Maria come 'Sponsa Christi' nella teologia fino all'inizio del sec. XIII." *Euntes docete* 7 (1954): 299–311.

Piolin, P. "Le moine Raoul et le bienheureux Raoul de la Fustaye." *Revue des questions historiques* 42 (1887): 497–509.

Poirion, Daniel. "Chanson de geste ou épopée? Remarques sur la définition d'un genre." Centre de philologie et de littératures romanes de l'Université de Strasbourg. *Travaux de linguistique et de littérature, Etudes littéraires* 10, no. 2 (1972): 7–20.

[Pontenay] de Fontette, François. *Recherches sur la pratique de la vente immobilière dans la région parisienne au moyen âge (fin Xe-début XIVe siècle)*. Paris: R. Pichon et R. Durand-Auzias, 1957.

Port, Celestin. *Dictionnaire historique, géographique et biographique de Maine-et-Loire et de l'ancienne province d'Anjou*. 3 vols. Paris, 1876–78. Vol. 1 revised by Jacques Levron. Angers, 1965.

Porter, Arthur Kingsley. *Romanesque Sculpture of the Pilgrimage Roads*. 10 vols. Boston: Marshall Jones, 1923.

Power, Eileen. "The Position of Women." In *The Legacy of the Middle Ages*. Edited by C. G. Crump and E. F. Jacob, pp. 401–33. Oxford: Clarendon, 1926.

Prell-Foldes, Riv-Ellen. "Coming of Age in Kelton: The Constraints of Gender Symbolism in Jewish Ritual." In *Women in Ritual and Symbolic Roles*. Edited by J. Hoch-Smith and A. Spring, pp. 75–99. New York: Plenum Press, 1978.

Quinn, Naomi. "Anthropological Studies on Women's Status." *Annual Review of Anthropology* 6 (1977): 181–225.

Raison, L., and R. Niderst. "Le mouvement érémitique dans l'Ouest de la France à la fin du XIe siècle et au début du XIIe siècle." *Annales de Bretagne* 55 (1948): 1–46.

Rambaud-Buhot, Jacqueline. "Le statut des moniales chez les pères de l'église, dans les règles monastiques et les collections canoniques, jusqu'au XIIe siècle." *Sainte Fare et Faremoutiers* (1957), pp. 149–74.

Reiter, Rayna R. "Men and Women in the South of France: Public and Private Domains." In *Toward an Anthropology of Women*. Edited by Rayna Reiter, pp. 252–82. New York: Monthly Review Press, 1975.

Renouard, Y. "Essai sur le rôle de l'empire angevin dans la formation de la France et de la civilisation française aux XIIe et XIIIe siècles." *Revue historique du droit français et étranger* (1945): 289–304.

Reynolds, Roger E. "*Virgines subintroductae* in Celtic Christianity." *Harvard Theological Review* 61 (1968): 547–66.

Richardson, H. G. "The Letters and Charters of Eleanor of Aquitaine." *English Historical Review* 74 (1959): 193–213.

Ridard, Abel. *Essai sur le douaire dans l'ancienne Bourgogne*. Dijon: Imprimerie Jobard, 1906.

Riemer, Eleanor Sabina. "Women in the Medieval City: Sources and Uses of Wealth by Sienese Women in the Thirteenth Century." Ph.D. dissertation, New York University, 1975.

Roberts, Nanette McNiff. "Making the Mold: The Roles of Women in the Middle English Metrical Romance, 1225–1500." Ph.D. dissertation, New York University, 1976.

Robertson, Howard. "*La Chanson de Willame*": *A Critical Study*. University of North Carolina Studies in the Romance Languages and Literatures, no. 65. Chapel Hill: University of North Carolina Press, 1966.

Rockwell, Joan. *Fact in Fiction: The Use of Literature in the Systematic Study of Society*. London: Routledge & Kegan Paul, 1974.

Rogers, Katharine M. *The Troublesome Helpmate: A History of Misogyny in Literature*. Seattle: University of Washington Press, 1966.

Rohault de Fleury, Charles. *La Sainte Vierge: Etudes archéologiques et iconographiques*. 2 vols. Paris, 1878.

Roisin, Simone. "L'efflorescence cistercienne et le courant féminin de piété au XIIIe siècle." *Revue d'histoire ecclésiastique* 39 (1943): 342–78.

Rosaldo, Michelle Zimbalist. "The Use and Abuse of Anthropology: Reflections on Feminism and Cross-cultural Understanding." *Signs: Journal of Women in Culture and Society* 5 (1980): 389–417.

Rosaldo, Michelle Zimbalist, and Lamphere, Louise, eds. *Woman, Culture, and Society*. Stanford: Stanford University Press, 1974.

de Rougemont, Denis. *Love in the Western World*. Translated by Montgomery Belgion. Greenwich, Conn.: Fawcett Publications, 1966.

Roussier, Jules. "La donation de biens communs par le mari en droit coutumier parisien." *Revue historique de droit français et étranger* (ser. 4) 31 (1953): 498–520.

Ruether, Rosemary. *Mary—the Feminine Face of the Church*. Philadelphia: Westminster Press, 1977.

Ruether, Rosemary, and McLaughlin, Eleanor, eds. *Women of Spirit: Female Leadership in the Jewish and Christian Traditions*. New York: Simon and Schuster, 1979.

Russel, Edith. "Bernard et les dames de son temps." In *Bernard de Clairvaux*, pp. 411–25. Commission d'histoire de l'ordre de Cîteaux, 3. Paris, 1953.

Sabbé, E. "Le culte marial et la genèse de la sculpture médiévale." *Revue belge d'archéologie et d'histoire de l'art* 20 (1951): 101–25.

Sauerländer, Willibald. *Gothic Sculpture in France 1140–1270*. Translated by Janet Sondheimer. New York: Harry Abrams, 1972.

———. "Die Marienkrönungsportale von Senlis und Mantes." *Wallraf-Richartz Jahrbuch* 20 (1958): 115–62.

———. "Sculpture on Early Gothic Churches: The State of Research and Open Questions." *Gesta* 9, no. 2 (1970): 32–48.

Schmitz, Philibert. *Histoire de l'ordre de Saint-Benoît*. 7 vols. Liege: Maredsous, 1942–56.

Schulenburg, Jane Tibbetts. "Strict Active Enclosure and Its Effects on the Female Monastic Experience (500–1100)." In *Distant Echoes: Medieval Religious Women*. Vol. 1. Edited by John A. Nichols and Lillian Thomas Shank, pp. 51–86. Kalamazoo, Mich.: Cistercian Publications, 1984.

Sheehan, Michael M. "The Influence of Canon Law on the Property Rights of Married Women in England." *Mediaeval Studies* 25 (1963): 109–24.

Sinding, Olav. *Mariae Tod und Himmelfahrt: Ein Beitrag zur Kenntnis der frühmittelalterlichen Denkmäler*. Christiania, 1903.

Smith, H. A. "La femme dans les chansons de geste." *Colorado College Studies* 9 (1901): 6–24; 10 (1903): 24–40.

Smith, Jacqueline. "Robert of Arbrissel: *Procurator Mulierum*." In *Medieval Women*. Edited by Derek Baker, pp. 175–84. Oxford: Basil Blackwell, 1978.

Southern, R. W. *The Making of the Middle Ages*. New Haven: Yale University Press, 1953.

———. *Western Society and the Church in the Middle Ages*. Harmondsworth, England: Penguin Books, 1970.

Southworth, Marie-José. *Etude comparée de quatre romans médiévaux: "Jaufre," "Fergus," "Durmart," "Blancandin."* Paris: Nizet, 1973.

Sponslor, Lucy A. *Women in the Medieval Spanish Epic and Lyric Traditions*. Lexington: University Press of Kentucky, 1975.

Stein, Frederick Mark. "The Religious Women of Cologne: 1120–1320." Ph.D. dissertation, Yale University, 1977.

Stenton, Doris. *The English Woman in History*. London, 1957.

Stevens, John. *Medieval Romance: Themes and Approaches*. London: Hutchinson, 1973.

Stuard, Susan Mosher. "The Annales School and Feminist History: Opening Dialogue with the American Stepchild." *Signs: Journal of Women in Culture and Society* 7 (1981): 135–43.

————, ed. *Women in Medieval Society*. Philadelphia: University of Pennsylvanis Press, 1976.

Suckale Robert. *Studien zu Stilbildung und Stilwandel der Madonnenstatuen der Ile-de-France zwischen 1230 und 1300*. Dissertation, Ludwig-Maximillians-Universität, Munich, 1971.

Suter-Raeber, Regula. "Die Marienkrönung im 12. und frühen 13. Jahrhundert." *Zeitschrift für schweizerische Archäologie und Kunstgeschichte* 23 (1963/64): 197–211.

Tabuteau, Emily Zack. "The Legal Capacity of Women in Eleventh-Century Normandy." Paper delivered at the Third Berkshire Conference in Women's History, 1976.

————. "Transfers of Property in Eleventh-Century Norman Law." Ph.D. dissertation, Harvard University, 1975.

Taviani, Huguette. "Le mariage dans l'hérésie de l'An Mil." *Annales: Economies, sociétés, civilisations* 32 (1977): 1074–89.

Thérel, Marie-Louise. "Les portails de la Charité-sur-Loire. Etude iconographique." *Congrès archéologique de France, Nivernais*. CXXVe session, pp. 86–103. Paris, 1967.

————. "Sources et évolution du thème symbolique Marie-Eglise des origines à la mosaïque de Sainte-Marie du Transtevère." Ecole Pratique des Hautes Etudes, Ve section (Sciences religieuses). *Annuaire* 73 (1965–66): 192–94.

Thompson, Alexander Hamilton. "Double Monasteries and the Male Element in Nunneries." In *The Ministry of Women: A Report by a Committee Appointed by His Grace the Lord Archbishop of Canterbury*. London: Society for Promoting Christian Knowledge, 1919.

Thompson, Sally. "The Problem of the Cistercian Nuns in the Twelfth and Early Thirteenth Centuries." In *Medieval Women*. Edited by Derek Baker, pp. 227–52. Oxford: Basil Blackwell, 1978.

Topsfield, L. T. *Chrétien de Troyes: A Study of the Arthurian Romances*. Cambridge: Cambridge University Press, 1981.

Toubert, Pierre. *Les structures du Latium médiévale: Le Latium méridional et la Sabine du IXe siècle à la fin du XIIe siècle*. 2 vols. Rome: Ecole française de Rome, 1973.

Ulrich, Laurel Thatcher. *Good Wives: Image and Reality in the Lives of Women in Northern New England, 1650–1750*. New York: Knopf, 1982.

Utley, Francis Lee. *The Crooked Rib: An Analytical Index to the Argument about Women in English and Scots Literature to the End of the Year 1568*. Columbus: Graduate School of Ohio State University, 1944.

Uzureau, F. "La réforme de l'ordre de Fontevrault." *Revue Mabillon* 9 (1923): 141–46.

Valette, Francis Claude. "La tradition antiféministe dans la littérature française du moyen âge et sa continuation dans les contes du seizième siècle." Ph.D. dissertation, University of Illinois, 1966.

Vance, Eugene. "Signs of the City: Medieval Poetry as Detour." *New Literary History* 4 (1973): 557–74.

Vandenbossche, André. *Contribution à l'histoire des régimes matrimoniaux: La "dos ex marito" dans la Gaule franque.* Paris: Editions Domat, 1953.

Van Den Eynde, Damien. "En marge des écrits d'Abélard: Les 'Excerpta ex regulis Paracletensis monasterii.'" *Analecta Praemonstratensia* 38 (1962): 70–84.

van der Meulen, Jan, with Price, Nancy Waterman. *The West Portals of Chartres Cathedral.* Vol. 1: *The Iconology of the Creation.* Washington, D.C.: University Press of America, 1981.

Verdier, Philippe. *Le couronnement de la Vierge: Les origines et les premiers développements d'un thème iconographique.* Conférence Albert-le-Grand, 1972. Montreal: Institut d'études médiévales; Paris: J. Vrin, 1980.

———. "Suger a-t-il été en France le créateur du thème iconographique du couronnement de la Vierge?" *Gesta* 15 (1976): 227–36.

Verdon, Jean. "Le monachisme en Poitou au Xe siècle." *Revue Mabillon* 59: 272 (1978): 235–53.

———. "Les moniales dans la France de l'Ouest aux XIe et XIIe siècles. Etude d'histoire sociale." *Cahiers de civilisation médiévale* 19 (1976): 247–64.

———. "Notes sur la femme en Limousin vers 1300." *Annales du Midi* 90 (1978): 319–29.

———. "Notes sur le rôle économique des monastères féminins en France dans la seconde moitié du IXe et au début du Xe siècle." *Revue Mabillon* 58 (1975): 329–43.

———. "Recherches sur les monastères féminins dans la France du Nord aux IXe-XIe siècles." *Revue Mabillon* 59 (1976): 49–96.

———. "Recherches sur les monastères féminins dans la France du Sud au IXe-XIe siècles." *Annales du Midi* 88 (1976): 117–38.

———. "Les sources de l'histoire de la femme en occident aux Xe-XIIIe siècles." *Cahiers de civilisation médiévale* 20 (1977): 219–51.

Vinaver, Eugène. *The Rise of Romance.* Oxford: Clarendon, 1971.

Viollet, Paul Marie. *Le droit du XIIIe siècle dans les coutumes de Touraine-Anjou et d'Orléanais; étude historique.* Paris, 1881.

Walker, D. "The Organization of Material in Medieval Cartularies." In *The Study of Medieval Records: Essays in Honour of Kathleen Major.* Edited by D. A. Bullough and R. L. Storey, pp. 132–50. Oxford: Clarendon, 1971.

von Walter, Johannes. *Die ersten Wanderprediger Frankreichs: Studien zur Geschichte des Mönchtums.* Vol. 1: *Robert von Arbrissel.* Studien zur Geschichte der Theologie und der Kirche, vol. 9, no. 3. Leipzig: Dieterich, 1903. Vol. 2: *Bernhard von Tiron, Vital von Savigny, Girald von Sales.* Leipzig, 1906. The life of Robert is partially translated by J. Cahour in *Bulletin de la commission historique et archéologique de la Mayenne* 23 (1907): 257–92, 385–406. The life of Bernard de Thiron is translated in the *Bulletin* 24 (1908): 385–410; 25 (1909): 17–44.

Warner, Marina. *Alone of All Her Sex: The Myth and the Cult of the Virgin Mary*. New York: Knopf, 1976.

Warner, W. Lloyd. *The Living and the Dead: A Study of the Symbolic Life of Americans*. New Haven: Yale University Press, 1959.

Watson, Arthur. *The Early Iconography of the Tree of Jesse*. Oxford and London, 1934.

Weber, Max. *The Sociology of Religion*. Translated by Ephraim Fischoff. Boston: Beacon Press, 1963. First published 1922.

Wemple, Suzanne Fonay. *Women in Frankish Society: Marriage and the Cloister, 500-900*. Philadelphia: University of Pennsylvania Press, 1981.

Werner, Ernst. *Pauperes Christi: Studien zu sozial-religiösen Bewegungen im Zeitalter des Reformpapsttums*. Leipzig: Koehler & Amelang, 1956.

White, Stephen D. "The Laudatio Parentum in Northern France in the Eleventh and Twelfth Centuries: Some Unanswered Questions." Paper delivered at the Ninety-second annual meeting of the American Historical Association, Dallas, 28 December 1977.

———. "*Pactum . . . Legum Vincit et Amor Judicium*: The Settlement of Dispute by Compromise in Eleventh-Century Western France." *American Journal of Legal History* 22 (1978): 281-308.

Whyte, Martin King. *The Status of Women in Preindustrial Societies*. Princeton: Princeton University Press, 1978.

Wilhelm, Pia. "Die Marienkrönung am Westportal der Kathedrale von Senlis." Dissertation, Hamburg, 1941.

Wilmart, André. "Eve et Goscelin." *Revue Bénédictine* 46 (1934): 414-38; 50 (1938): 42-83.

Woods, Ellen Rose. *Aye d'Avignon: A Study of Genre and Society*. Geneva: Droz, 1978.

Woodward, Mary Skinner. "Women, the Family, and Ecclesiastical Reform in Early Medieval France." Paper delivered at the Social Science History Association, 1978.

Wulff, August. *Die frauenfeindlichen Dichtungen in den romanischen Literaturen des Mittelalters bis zum Ende des XIII Jahrhunderts*. Romanistische Arbeiten, vol. 4. Halle, 1914.

Yver, Jean. "Les caractères originaux du groupe de coutumes de l'Ouest de la France." *Revue historique de droit français et étranger* (ser. 4) 30 (1952): 18-79.

———. *Egalité entre héritiers et exclusion des enfants dotés. Essai de géographie coutumière*. Paris: Editions Sirey, 1966.

Zaddy, Z. P. *Chrétien Studies: Problems of Form and Meaning in "Erec," "Yvain," "Cliges," and the "Charrete."* Glasgow: University of Glasgow Press, 1973.

———. "Pourquoi Erec se décide-t-il à partir en voyage avec Enide?" *Cahiers de civilisation médiévale* 7 (1964): 179-85.

Zarnecki, George. "The Coronation of the Virgin on a Capital from Reading Abbey." *Journal of the Warburg Institute* 13 (1950): 1–12.

Zumthor, Paul. *Essai de poétique médiévale.* Paris: Editions du Seuil, 1972.

————. *Histoire littéraire de la France médiévale (VIe-XIVe siècles).* Paris: Presses Universitaires de France, 1954.

Index